Also available at all good book stores

9781785316470

9781785313929

9781785315466

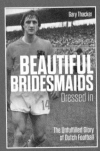

9781785318467

9781785318399

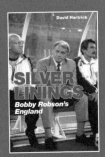

9781785317811

9781785317835

9781785315381

9781785316838

The fix

JAMES DIXON

The fix

How the First Champions League
Was Won and Why We All Lost

First published by Pitch Publishing, 2021

Pitch Publishing
A2 Yeoman Gate
Yeoman Way
Worthing
Sussex
BN13 3QZ
www.pitchpublishing.co.uk
info@pitchpublishing.co.uk

A CIP catalogue record is available for this book
from the British Library.

ISBN 978 1 78531 778 1

Typesetting and origination by Pitch Publishing
Printed and bound in India by Replika Press Pvt. Ltd.

Contents

For my wife, Jennie.

Thank you for all your support and patience.

I love you as much as you hate football.

Preface

IN MARCH 1991, there was a European Cup quarter-final between Yugoslavia's Red Star Belgrade and East Germany's Dynamo Dresden. The referee was Alexey Spirin from the USSR. Less than 18 months later two of the countries no longer existed, Yugoslavia was in the process of violently dissolving itself, and the very competition they were taking part in had metamorphosed into the Champions League.

The pace of political, economic and social change right across Europe during the late 1980s and early '90s was swifter than at any time since the Second World War, and football was by no means immune from being shaped and remodelled by these forces. The impact wasn't just felt behind the old Iron Curtain as our friends to the east of Stettin and Trieste undoubtedly experienced the most immediate turbulence through perestroika (economic and political reform), glasnost (openness and transparency) and lustration (purges of communist officials in their successor states).

The new post-communist world order meant the break-up of club and international teams, and domestic leagues, and it turbocharged a liberalisation of the market for human footballing capital. Athletic achievements were currency in the propaganda of the Cold War and the ruling parties would refuse players the opportunity to play abroad until they were past their prime.

No sooner had Nicolae Ceaușescu and Todor Zhivkov been toppled as the communist rulers of Romania and Bulgaria respectively did Gheorghe Hagi leave Steaua Bucharest for Real Madrid and Hristo Stoichkov depart CSKA Sofia for Barcelona. Money was talking. The eastern European players wanted it, their clubs needed it and the big-name western European clubs had it.

But it wasn't just the big-name players that wanted to go west, and with UEFA's three-foreigner rule making the hoarding of talented non-nationals at your club a luxury that few could afford, a wave of talented Czechs, Romanians, Yugoslavs and Ukrainians could soon be found at middling clubs in western Europe's domestic leagues where the wages would still dwarf what could be made back home.

Take Steaua Bucharest's 1989 European Cup Final team as an example. Virtually the entire line-up was scattered over the continent less than 12 months after going toe to toe with AC Milan for the biggest prize in continental club football. With the notable exception of Hagi, none were at what could be called fashionable clubs; Dan Petrescu was at Foggia and Marius Lăcătuş at Real Oviedo, while others could be found in Turkey, Belgium, the French Second Division and perhaps saddest of all, Ştefan Iovan, the owner of 34 international caps and the captain of Steaua's victorious 1986 European Cup Final side against Barcelona, was powerless to prevent Brighton and Hove Albion's relegation to the third tier of English football.

In the 1980s it was normal for two or three of the European Cup quarter-finalists to be from behind the Iron Curtain each season. In 1981/82 the east even had parity with the west when Universitatea Craiova (Romania), CSKA Sofia (Bulgaria), Red Star Belgrade (Yugoslavia) and Dynamo Kiev (Soviet Union) made the last eight alongside Aston Villa (England), Anderlecht (Belgium), Bayern Munich (West Germany) and holders Liverpool (England). Yet in a stunning contrast, there have only been two Champions League quarter-finalists from eastern Europe in the entire 21st century – CSKA Moscow in 2009/10 and Shakhtar Donetsk in 2010/11.[1]

---

1   Red Bull Leipzig reached the Champions League semi-finals in 2020. While Leipzig geographically was part of East Germany the club wasn't founded until 2009, making this success one of a unified Germany in this author's eyes.

While the tumult was most apparent on the eastern portion of the continent, the end of the post-war economic consensus and the importation of Americanised capitalism with its tenets of deregulation, monetarism and greed would impact European football more.

The 1992/93 season, which this book focuses on, was part of a three-year format innovation which helped pivot the old European Cup from a romantic lottery, pursuing the egalitarian ideal of champion versus champion, to what we recognise today as a de facto European Super League with virtually guaranteed participation, and crucially, income for the biggest club sides.

Of course, it was the openness of the European Cup and the quirks it spat out that the bigger clubs railed against. They might play more than 40 games to win their domestic league then draw one of the competition favourites or be caught cold by a plucky underdog and their European dreams and revenue streams would be over by September.

What's the point of having power and influence if you're not going to use it to stack the deck in your favour?

The high-rollers wanted bigger stakes and fewer risks. The more games they could play against each other the more revenue they would pocket – not just from the matchday fan coming through the turnstile but from selling television rights. Soon, not content with a loaded deck, the bigger clubs and leagues started to want to control who was let into the casino altogether.

Football and commercial television were crashing together and nowhere could this be seen more apparently than in Milan. Silvio Berlusconi, a TV magnate who was aggressively expanding his commercial TV holdings and providing a direct challenge to the Italian state broadcaster, Rai, bought AC Milan in 1986. Berlusconi was not in football for the municipal prestige that many traditional, largely benign owners were, although that would come in useful later in his political career. Television needed football and, in Berlusconi's eyes at least, football needed television. He may have been right, and to a large extent the European Cup only existed because of television.

Bizarrely, despite the first floodlit football match taking place at Bramall Lane, Sheffield, in 1878, the Football Association had outlawed the use of such lighting. Adding floodlights to an inauspicious list of 'things the FA has banned' that at one time or another has included players being able to earn money from football, England competing in the World Cup and women.

Only in 1950 did the FA somewhat relent, sanctioning the use of floodlights but only for non-competitive fixtures. Seventy-two years previously the Sheffield fixture had proved the popularity of night-time football by attracting 12,000 paying supporters, nearly three times the gate of that year's FA Cup Final.

Arsenal hosted 'floodlight friendlies' in 1951 against Hapoel Tel Aviv and Glasgow Rangers but Wolverhampton Wanderers popularised the practice. In 1953/54, while winning the First Division, they hosted South Africa, Celtic and Argentinian side Racing at Molineux. The following season the Charity Shield was played under lights between Wolves and FA Cup winners West Bromwich Albion. The two local rivals played out an entertaining 4-4 draw in front of 45,000 fans.

Later that season, Spartak Moscow played Wolves as part of their goodwill tour. This time the BBC cameras were in attendance, beaming coverage of the second half live to the nation. The enormity of the moment can only be summed up by its rarity. The BBC only showed ten minutes of highlights of England's 1954 World Cup victory over Switzerland – three days after the match was played – and the quarter-final defeat to Uruguay didn't trouble the schedulers at all.

Kenneth Wolstenholme was commentating for the BBC and later recalled, 'It was quite a foggy night at Molineux, which only added to the atmosphere and meant you could hardly see the other end of the pitch with the naked eye. Our cameras were at the wrong end when Wolves were attacking in the first half.' Fortunately for Kenneth, the BBC had decided to broadcast a student debate from the

University of London Union in lieu of the football during the first half. Wolves won 4-0 thanks to a thrilling final ten-minute spell in which all the goals were scored.

However, the visit of Honvéd of Budapest in December 1954 really captured the public imagination. The 'Magnificent Magyars' had become the first foreign team to beat England at Wembley in 1953, demolishing Walter Winterbottom's men 6-3 and skewering notions of English exceptionalism. Hungary had finished as runners-up to West Germany in the 1954 World Cup but were still considered by many as the best side in the world. The stars of that team – including Ferenc Puskás, Sándor Kocsis and Zoltán Czibor, who scored 18 goals between them at the World Cup in just five matches – were all in the Honvéd line-up to face Wolves.

The match was in many ways a mirror of the 1954 World Cup Final. The Hungarians raced into a two-goal lead but playing in bog-like conditions did not suit their passing style and as the game wore on their legs grew heavy. In what Germans to this day call Fritz-Walter-Wetter (Fritz Walter weather) after their inspirational captain in the 1954 final, Wolves also pulled off an improbable comeback to win 3-2.

Somewhat jingoistically the *Birmingham Gazette* declared Wolves 'Club Champions of the World'. It was a quip that made its way to the sports desk of *L'Équipe* and caught the attention of Gabriel Hanot.

Hanot played for France before the First World War and took up journalism afterwards. He is credited with helping start Ligue 1, he coached the national side after the Second World War and just so happened to work for the paper that had set up the Tour de France.

Reading the proclamation of Wolves as the best club side in the world had clearly raised Hanot's hackles: 'Before we declare that Wolverhampton are invincible, let them go to Moscow and Budapest. And there are other internationally renowned clubs: Milan and Real Madrid to name but two. A club world championship, or at least a European one – should be launched.'

Hanot's plan was to invite the continent's 16 leading clubs to play a knockout tournament under floodlights with the winner being declared the European champion club. There were a few bumps in the road during that initial season. *L'Équipe* had wanted Chelsea as league champions to represent England but in its never-ending folly the Football Association pressured the London side to decline. Holland Sport also declined to represent the Netherlands, as did Aberdeen in Scotland, wary of the cost of installing the requisite floodlights. Fortunately for Hanot, PSV Eindhoven, the club set up by light bulb manufacturers Philips, and Hibernian were happy to oblige him.

Berlusconi's plan for European football was equally simple and unconcerned with the sensibilities of governing bodies. Europe's top sides from Italy, Spain, Germany,

France and England would break away from the auspices of UEFA and form their own midweek competition that would guarantee them regular games against high-level opposition that could be packaged for TV channels like his own Canale 5. It was the exact same threat that Greg Dyke, then of ITV, and the big five English clubs (Arsenal, Everton, Liverpool, Manchester United and Tottenham Hotspur) were using towards the Football League to get the Premier League off the ground.

Both Dyke and Berlusconi owed a spiritual debt to Australian TV pioneer Kerry Packer for borrowing directly from his World Series Cricket playbook. Packer, who had been stymied from acquiring the broadcast rights to the Australian cricket team in the mid 1970s by the forces of conservatism in the governing body, decided to set up his own competition, World Series Cricket, and with the promise of better remuneration and elite-level competition he signed up most of the world's best players, including the captains of Australia, England and West Indies. On the field, World Series Cricket was a huge success and within two years the Australian Cricket Board was suing for peace. Packer's Channel 9 would be awarded long-term broadcast and commercial rights deals.

While the modern temptation is to dismiss Berlusconi as a bungling, bunga-bunga enthusiast, the younger Silvio did somewhat have a point. The best teams and players on the continent did not play against each other enough. Gary Lineker, a World Cup Golden Boot winner and Ballon d'Or runner-up, never played a European Cup match and neither did Paul Gascoigne, while Guiseppe Bergomi played in four World Cups and made over 750 appearances for Inter Milan but between 1981 and 1998 he only played twice in the European Cup/Champions League.

Diego Maradona, a candidate in anyone's eyes for being the greatest player of all time, spent 11 seasons in the prime of his career with top European clubs – Barcelona, Napoli, Seville – but appeared in just three European Cup ties. By contrast, Maradona's Argentine compatriot Lionel Messi and Messi's great rival Cristiano Ronaldo have combined for approximately 250 Champions League goals. For all the good the European Cup, UEFA Cup and Cup Winners' Cup had done for fans and clubs up to that point, European club football in the 1980s was unarguably underdeveloped. There was more demand than supply and Berlusconi was going to try to do something about that.

But it wasn't just the man from Milan trying to drive change. Another key proponent were Glasgow Rangers, the Scottish champions who had risen again in prominence thanks to coinciding their latest period of domestic dominance with the ban on English teams from European club competitions. However, the Gers had somewhat of a penchant for falling at the first hurdle with Osasuna, Bayern Munich and both the Pragues – Sparta and Dukla (made famous in a song by Half Man Half Biscuit) all inflicting the pain of single-tie continental campaigns within the span of a decade.

While Berlusconi had hired Saatchi and Saatchi to lobby for an 18-team super league, Rangers had a more moderate plan of playing four-team group stages first and then going into the knockout rounds. Essentially, it was the World Cup format that would be first used at France 98 and was eventually adopted by the Champions League for the 2003/04 season.

In its wisdom, UEFA, led by a new president in Lennart Johansson and a new general secretary in Gerhard Aigner, realised that it couldn't stem the tide demanding reform. So instead of casting themselves as powerless King Cnut-like figures to demand the reformists back down, its leading figures instead sought to shape what that reform might look like to keep as many of UEFA's member associations as happy as possible.

League versus cup is a debate almost as old as organised football itself. After the establishment of the Cambridge rules in 1848 the gentlemen amateurs who codified the game mostly favoured cup football. It chimed better with their Corinthian sporting ideals and socio-economic status. League play, meanwhile, appealed more to the working men in industrial areas who wanted to escape the mills, looms and pits. Also, crucially to the new wealthy industrialists who saw a bob or two to be made in football, leagues would give them a more dependable supply of meaningful fixtures from which they could profit.

William McGregor, a Scotsman with a drapery business in Aston, Birmingham, had been invited to join the committee of the local football team Aston Villa. After a spate of fixture cancellations owing to other sides' cup exploits, McGregor wrote to a group of leading clubs: 'Every year it is becoming more and more difficult for football clubs of any standing to meet their friendly engagements and even arrange friendly matches. The consequence is that at the last moment, through cup-tie interference, clubs are compelled to take on teams who will not attract the public.

'I beg to tender the following suggestion as a means of getting over the difficulty: that ten or 12 of the most prominent clubs in England combine to arrange home-and-away fixtures each season … and could be managed by [a] representative from each club.'

In 1888, the Football League was formed. A hundred years later echoes of the same debate were repeating themselves in UEFA's headquarters in Bern, Switzerland. The traditionalists and administrator-class wanted the cup and the newly monied impatiently clamoured for a league.

Cups are easier to administer and can handle more entrants than leagues; a key factor for an organisation like UEFA representing more than 40 national associations by 1992.

The main problem with forming new leagues is political – deciding who can be in it and who can't. Between 1986 and 1991 the European Cup was won by Romanian, Portuguese, Dutch, Italian and Yugoslav sides and under Berlusconi's plan all but the Italian past winners would have been excluded from the new European Super League.

Even McGregor's moves a century prior had political motives; he got the Football League to initially adopt a one club per town rule to keep out Villa's Birmingham rivals Small Heath and Mitchell St George's.

The new European Cup format that UEFA and the clubs eventually settled on was neither fish nor fowl. It preserved the lottery of knockout football in the initial two-legged rounds until the teams were whittled down to eight, where it switched to league play before reverting to a one-off final at a neutral venue – like the Super Bowl of European club football. We should be glad that they didn't take inspiration from baseball and instigate a seven-game series to crown the champions.

The new format meant that if you were one of the final eight sides you would be guaranteed at least ten games and a healthy share of the collectively sold television rights for the group stages. But only if the balls bounced kindly for you in that initial drawing.

The Iron Curtain Raiser

THE IDEA of Steaua Bucharest beating Barcelona to win the Champions League Final is today so fanciful that you would more readily believe a former Coventry City goalkeeper was the reincarnated son of God and only he can save the Earth from the lizard people.

However, in 1986 Steaua Bucharest did beat Barcelona to win the European Cup – in Spain, no less – and it was largely down to the 'Hero of Seville', Helmuth Duckadam. Duckadam was a Romanian of ethnic German ancestry as indicated by his name 'Helmuth', and possessed the most perfect permed mullet and moustache combination seen anywhere outside of a 1980s WWF wrestling ring. It's perhaps his innate Germanness that lent itself to breaking the heart of Barcelona's English manager Terry Venables via what would become the all-too-familiar medium of penalty kicks.

Even in 1986 the idea of the European Cup being won by a side from the Eastern Bloc was considered far-fetched. Since its invention 30 years previously, the tournament had only been won by teams from the west, and only once before had a club on the eastern side of the Iron Curtain made the final.

Barcelona were strong favourites and were playing in front of what was essentially a home crowd in Seville, due to restrictions on travelling Romanian fans should they then choose to defect. Around 200 security-vetted Romanian supporters had been allowed to travel and still 40 did cross to the other side.

Despite Barcelona's advantages, the showpiece match of the European club footballing calendar finished 0-0 for the first time.

Extra time could not end Steaua's dream so the match headed to penalties. Even in that lottery, Barcelona's experience of winning their semi-final on penalties seemingly gave them the edge. Such a hypothesis failed to account for the heroics of Duckadam, who flung himself in the way of all four kicks he faced to allow Steaua, who missed two of their own, to win the shoot-out 2-0. This remains the only shoot-out where a goalkeeper has saved the first four penalties they have faced.

A 26-year-old, European Cup-winning goalkeeper should have had the world at his feet and for a time Duckadam did. Real Madrid bought him a brand-new luxury Mercedes, a gift for preventing their arch-rivals winning their first continental championship, and

Duckadam would have time to enjoy it as Romania had failed to qualify for that summer's World Cup in Mexico.

Tragically, Seville was the last time Duckadam ever played for Steaua or for any team in top-flight football. The official version of what happened next says that while on holiday in the summer of 1986 Duckadam complained to his wife of a pain in his arm. Doctors diagnosed a thrombosis and he flew back to Bucharest for an emergency operation. Informed of the risk of blood clots and haemorrhaging that could prove fatal if he continued to play, he retired on the spot.

However, his return to second division football after the fall of Nicolae Ceaușescu, Romania's communist dictator, has fuelled speculation of a more sinister explanation for his disappearance from public sporting life.

Some accounts have Ceaușescu's son Nicu shooting Duckadam in the arm in a heated argument over who exactly should own and use the Mercedes provided by Real Madrid; others simply allege his popularity and acclaim were threatening to a regime that was slowly losing control of the country.

Duckadam though insists, 'People hated Ceaușescu so much that they invented incredible stories about him and his family.'

Whatever the truth, it was a fantastic achievement for a Romanian side to win the European Cup. Unfortunately, some predominantly Anglophile detractors pointed to the absence of the English champions Everton and Steaua's favourable route through to the final (via Denmark, Hungary, Finland and Belgium) as reasons to asterisk the victory. As the old adage goes, you can only beat what's in front of you and Steaua underlined that it wasn't a fluke by making the semi-finals in 1988 and a second final in 1989. The latter achievements followed the acquisition of Gheorghe Hagi from Bucharest's student team. Not bad for a team that had never won a European Cup tie before 1985

Prior to 1985, Eastern Bloc success in European football was limited to the Cup Winners' Cup. In 1969 Slovan Bratislava were the first communist team to win a UEFA club trophy, coincidentally, with a victory over Barcelona. Magdeburg from East Germany beat Milan in 1974, while 1975 saw the first all-communist final with Dynamo Kiev (USSR) beating Ferencváros (Hungary). Similarly Dinamo Tbilisi (USSR) got the better of Carl Zeiss Jena (East Germany) in 1981.

The exception to that rule was the city of Belgrade, then the capital of Yugoslavia. It might seem like semantics now but Yugoslavia was a bit of a Cold War quirk. It was communist and in the Eastern Bloc but not part of the Warsaw Pact and the Soviet Union's orbit. Indeed, Yugoslavia – alongside India and Egypt – was one of the leading countries in the Non-Aligned

Movement which sought a middle way between the policies of the USA and USSR.

In the second European Cup, in the 1956/57 season, Red Star Belgrade (known as Crvena Zvezda locally) reached the semi-finals. The following year they played Manchester United in the quarter-finals, a tie that would become infamous for the Munich air disaster. In the 1970s and '80s, Red Star were regulars in the latter stages of the European Cup

In the 1960s that burden fell to their city rivals Partizan. In 1963/64 Partizan lost to eventual winners Inter Milan in the quarter-finals, but two years later they became the first eastern team to make the final, where they lost 2-1 to Real Madrid in Brussels after defeating the French, German, Czech and English champions en route.

Spurred on by Steaua's success and horrified by the 4-1 lead they squandered against Real Madrid in the 1986/87 European Cup quarter-finals, Red Star came up with a five-year plan with the only goal being to win the European Cup. There was no problem a communist couldn't attempt to solve without a five-year plan.

Two of the key foundations of Red Star's eventual success were already in place: Stevan Stojanović, a goalkeeper who had come through the youth system, and a 21-year-old Dragan Stojković, one of the finest Yugoslav/Serbian footballers of all time who had transferred to Red Star from his hometown club, Radnički Niš. Owner of a poetic yet devastating left foot, Stojković's class can be measured by his future nomination to the 1990 World Cup All-Star Team. The midfield was Diego Maradona, Lothar Matthäus, Paul Gascoigne and Stojković.

The next piece of the Red Star jigsaw fell into their lap. Đuro Prosinečki wanted Dinamo Zagreb to give his 18-year-old son Robert a professional contract but the Dinamo coach refused, claiming that he would eat his coaching diploma if Prosinečki ever became a real football player.

Dragan Džajić, third in the 1968 Ballon d'Or voting behind George Best and Bobby Charlton, then Red Star's technical director, remembers the scenario: '[In Zagreb] I got approached by a man who introduced himself as Robert Prosinečki's uncle. He told me his nephew wasn't happy at Dinamo and asked me if we could arrange a try-out. I told them to come to Belgrade in a couple of days and they did.

'At the try-out I saw this kid do wonders with the ball and I immediately asked our head coach to schedule an afternoon practice session at the main stadium so that I could see the kid one more time. It was obvious we had a classy player on our hands, and I initiated the contract proceedings right away. Our lawyer informed us that we wouldn't have to pay a transfer fee to Dinamo so Robert's father Đuro and I agreed everything in five minutes.'

Dinamo's error was immediately apparent when Prosinečki was voted the best player at the 1987 World Youth Championships in Chile, leading Yugoslavia to their first age-group title. It was a true golden Yugoslav generation that in addition to Prosinečki also featured Davor Šuker, Predrag Mijatović and Zvonimir Boban.

Bosnian defender Refik Šabanadžović was added to Red Star's squad in 1987 from Sarajevo-based side Željezničar. He was followed the next season by Dejan Savićević, a Montenegrin attacking midfielder from FK Budućnost, and Darko Pančev, a striker from Macedonia's best side, Vardar. Red Star had assembled a true multinational, multi-ethnic side living up to the highest ideals of the Yugoslav state.

Winning the 1988 Yugoslav First League qualified Red Star for the 1988/89 European Cup where they would meet Arrigo Sacchi's Milan in the last 16. Luck was on the side of Džajić.

Firstly, Milan failed to win their home leg, a calamity by the standards of the day. Stojković, living up to his nickname 'Piksi', jinked through the vaunted Milanese defence including Franco Baresi to get the crucial away goal. Pietro Virdis equalised a minute later but no further scoring meant that Red Star took an advantage to the Marakana.

In the second leg Savićević scored just after half-time to put Red Star in front on aggregate. It was remarkable that he was even playing because at the time he was a serving soldier.

The urban legend is that a jilted Partizan (Yugoslavia's army club), upset that Red Star had gazumped them to Savićević's signing, called in a favour from the military brass and Savićević was called up for national service. The army stationed him in Skopje, over 400km from Belgrade, but there was an agreement that he could participate in European and national team matches. So, prior to lining up against Milan, Savićević's only games for Red Star had been against League of Ireland champions Dundalk.

Sadly for Savićević his strike was to count for nought, literally, as the German referee was forced to abandon the second leg due a thick fog that descended on the ground. When the Milan players got back to the dressing room they were surprised to see Virdis had already showered and was in his suit. Virdis informed his team-mates that he had been sent off ten minutes prior. The fog was so thick that no one had noticed.

'Milan were on their knees,' says Stojković. 'But then everything happened very quickly. After ten minutes of the second half the fog came in and, in one moment, suddenly it was invisible. The referee wanted to let us play but he had no choice, it was impossible.

'First, I couldn't see the stand. Then I couldn't see the goal. Then I couldn't see the penalty area. Then I couldn't see the ball!'

Despite playing two-thirds of the match, the two managers agreed to play the next afternoon, a decision of which Stojković said, 'We knew it was a bad idea, we needed a rest.'

Both sides would have to name the same starting XIs, except Milan were forced to replace the suspended Virdis and Carlo Ancelotti, who picked up his second yellow card of the tournament in the abandonment. However, the fresher legs may have helped rather than hindered the Rossoneri. The postponement did allow Ruud Gullit enough time to recover sufficiently from an injury to be named among the substitutes.

Stojković felt 'the advantage was now with Milan', and he added, 'They were monsters physically, with many good players on the bench who could help them. They had Gullit [as a substitute] back for the second game! I felt like I was playing alone.'

Quite harsh of Stojković to claim he was playing alone as the through ball he received from Savićević was different class. For once the Milan offside line was a dog-leg, with Baresi being the guilty party. Sadly though for Red Star that goal was an equaliser as Marco Van Basten had headed in Donadoni's far-post cross four minutes earlier.

Kicking off at 3pm deprived the Marakana, so nicknamed for its similarity to Brazil's famous mega-stadium, of some of its febrile atmosphere. Almost 100,000 came through the turnstiles the previous evening but estimates say around only 60,000 fans were present when the rearranged second leg kicked off.

Just before half-time, Donadoni took a heavy challenge and wasn't moving. More worryingly he wasn't breathing. His airway was blocked and he was turning blue. A quick-thinking Red Star physio punched the prone playmaker to break his jaw and open his airway but it wasn't immediately clear that he would be okay.

Adriano Galliani, Milan's powerful executive, recalls, 'The lads played the second half convinced that Donadoni was dead or dying. We were all crying during half-time.'

Gullit entered the action in place of Donadoni but his Dutch physio, who was flown out to Belgrade on Berlusconi's private jet, estimated that his injury would only hold for 45 minutes. However, the sides couldn't be separated during normal or extra time, so penalties were required.

That season the Yugoslav League had abolished the draw. There were two points for a win, none for a defeat and teams only got one point for a drawn game if they won a subsequent penalty shoot-out. The only problem was that Red Star weren't good at them. Of the seven league shoot-outs they participated in that season, they only won two.

Stojković scored the first penalty; right-footed presumably because he could. Baresi responded in kind for Milan, drilling the ball high and central, a tactic he would attempt six years later against Cláudio Taffarel with less success.

Prosinečki and Van Basten likewise found the net. Savićević drilled his penalty low and central but it almost arrived too fast and Galli saved. Evani then scored, and Galli kept out the next Red Star attempt.

Now Milan had two kicks to win, but with Rijkaard's coolness they only need the one and they were celebrating wildly on the pitch as if they had just won the competition before sprinting to the tunnel behind one of the Marakana goals. Red Star were left shell-shocked on the pitch. The Milan dynasty was saved by the fog of Belgrade.

'That Milan team was not one of the best, it was the best from my point of view. The best ever,' says Stojković.

'After the game as captain I said to my team-mates be happy, don't cry. Rijkaard came to me and told me to be proud. He said, "You are a really big player." He told me Milan were very lucky.'

The games in Belgrade seemed to take a lot out of the Rossoneri and they lost four out of their next seven, including at home to Atalanta and away at Cesena. Milan slipped from second in Serie A to seventh and were not able to challenge Inter again for the Scudetto. Their only route back to the European Cup would be via winning it – and that's just what they did.

There would be no dream rematch the following season as Yugoslavia was instead represented by Vojvodina from Novi Sad. Vojvodina were better than Red Star at penalties and had claimed the Yugoslav First League title because they won five of their six penalty shoot-outs.

It would prove to be an important setback for Red Star as missing out on the European Cup berth and their embarrassing UEFA Cup exit against FC Köln the following season prompted a coaching overhaul. Dragoslav Šekularac is one of only five players to be honoured with the Star of Red Star, an award for the club's greatest players, but he was replaced by Ljupko Petrović.

Petrović was part of the coaching setup when Yugoslavia won the World Youth Championships and managed the Vojvodina team that pipped Red Star to the league.

His first task was to oversee a pre-season tour of England and Wales, which began in Torquay before moving on to non-league Hinckley United (a 9-1 victory), Crewe Alexandra (4-0), Merthyr Tydfil (1-

1), Scarborough (4-2) and finishing in Bradford (a 2-1 defeat).

The new coach added the final few pieces to the jigsaw. Vladimir Jugović was called up to the first team and cultured midfielder Siniša Mihajlović was signed from Petrović's old team.

Mihajlović joined for a transfer fee of 1m Deutsch-marks, commanded a four-year contract plus the club bought him a Mazda 323F and a three-bedroom apartment in Belgrade to sweeten the deal. Mihajlović was needed and Red Star had the funds to acquire him because their key playmaker Stojković was sold to Olympique Marseille for £5.5m.

His World Cup performances had made Stojković an irresistible target for Bernard Tapie. Marseille too were on a quest for the European Cup. In his bid for Marseille to become the first French team to win the tournament, Tapie added Stojković, Basile Boli and World Cup-winning coach Franz Beckenbauer to an already stellar cast featuring Jean-Pierre Papin, Eric Cantona, Chris Waddle, Carlos Mozer, Jean Tigana and Abedi Pele.

The departure of Stojković, though debilitating on paper, actually proved to be addition by subtraction. Not only did it provide the funds to sign Mihajlović but it allowed Prosinečki, by then 21, to take on more of the creative responsibility. When given the opportunity he wowed, and in March 1991 *World Soccer* said Prosinečki was 'the finest player in Yugoslavia and potentially one of the finest in Europe'.

When Rangers drew Red Star in the 1990/91 European Cup second round, Graeme Souness dispatched his then assistant Walter Smith to scout Red Star. Smith's scouting report was just two words: 'We're fucked.' The feedback was as curt as it was correct.

In the semi-final Red Star drew Bayern, a side peppered with recent World Cup winners who had also beaten Yugoslavia's golden generation 4-1 in the 1990 World Cup. They travelled to Munich for the first leg and went behind to a fabulous team goal.

Jürgen Kohler played a one-two with Brian Laudrup down the left flank before Kohler sprayed a cross-field pass the width of the vast old Olympiastadion pitch to Manfred Schwabl. Schwabl fed Stefan Effenberg, who returned it to Schwabl to beat Prosinečki, and slide a through ball in to Olaf Thon. Facing away from goal, Thon back-heeled the ball into Roland Wohlfarth's path to lift over the onrushing keeper from a sharp angle. It was a beautiful goal, yet arguably only the third-best scored in that stadium that evening.

Red Star's reply was a devastating length-of-the-field counter-attack that all disciples of *gegenpressing* should seek out. Slobodan Marović took a break from scything down Laudrup to intercept a Bayern through ball and feed Miodrag Belodedici, then another touch found Prosinečki, who pinged a 50-yard ball up the right to the pacy Dragiša Binić in stride. Binić crossed low to the far post and Pančev crashed the ball into the net. Devastating.

Stefan Effenberg hadn't learned his lesson. The shock of blond hair wearing an incongruous number six for a playmaker played a loose through ball on the edge of the Red Star penalty box. Five touches and ten seconds later the men in red-and-white-striped shirts had gone the length of the field again to take a lead back to Belgrade, Savićević finishing the move off.

In the second leg Bayern developed a tactic to deal with Red Star's speed on the break – hacking. Thomas Strunz sideswiped Savićević during his first promising break but the German keeper Raimond Aumann could do nothing with the resulting free kick from Mihajlović, a sweet left-footed curler from nearly 35 yards out.

To call Mihajlović a free-kick expert is inadequate praise. He may have been the greatest dead-ball striker of all time. His skills had been honed from a misspent youth kicking ball after ball at his neighbours' metal gates. In his later career he would score a hat-trick of free kicks for Lazio against Sampdoria. His options were varied too, having the ability to score with both power and guile. A recent Bleacher Report list ranked Mihajlović as the second-best free-kick taker in football history, ahead of dead-ball luminaries like Ronald Koeman, David Beckham and Zico.

Aumann kept out a Pančev header while Binić lashed a shot against the side-netting and Savićević tripped himself up when surging on the Bayern goal. Prior to the interval it was one-way traffic at autobahn speeds.

However, there was a certain fragility to the Yugoslav football psyche. As a national team they had lost in five finals (three Olympic and two European) and when Klaus Augenthaler's free kick squirmed underneath the body and through the legs of Stevan Stojanović, panic set in.

The goalkeeper's reaction to his own error could have been the original inspiration for the long-running *Soccer AM* 'Platoon' segment. Back arched with head in hands, Stojanović fell to the Marakana turf to contemplate life momentarily.

Four minutes later Bayern had an undeserved lead. Effenberg's heavy cross missed his intended target but hit an unsighted Red Star defender on the knee before ricocheting into Manfred Bender's path to score.

Jonathan Wilson, the acclaimed football journalist, described what happened next as the most extraordinary 20 minutes in the history of football as Red Star, having lost faith in their ability to defend, opted to attack.

Mihajlović tried to one-up himself in the free kick stakes but his 40-yard effort just whistled past the post. Then Prosinečki resorted to playing street football to evade the increasingly agricultural tackling, hurdling challenges and then utilising well-timed drag-backs to leave German defenders kicking at air. Bayern were so wary of getting hit on the break that their back four remained inside their own half even when they won a corner.

Eventually Bayern fashioned a chance and Thon fed the striker Wohlfarth, who – echoing the first leg – chipped Stojanović, only this time the ball hit the upright and the rebound evaded an unmarked Effenberg. A third away goal would have ended the tie as a contest.

As the clock hit 90 minutes, Jugović surged forward, riding three Bayern lunges as he carried the ball goalwards. It was worked to Mihajlović but the delivery of the cross was poor and Augenthaler as the first man shaped to clear. But instead of making a clean connection, World Cup-winner Augenthaler sliced across the leather and the ball took the most improbable about-turn, creeping under the bar while Aumann looked helplessly on. If Phil Mickelson took out his lofted wedge and wanted to flop a ball on to a firm green he would have been happy with the arc that Augenthaler got.

Pandemonium ensued at the final whistle barely a minute later. Crestfallen Bayern players slumped to the grass while a huge pitch invasion was going on around them. Such scenes were commonplace in the pre-sanitised days of football but in modern times would have UEFA killjoys throwing the rule book at the transgressors. Joyous fans were ripping up the turf to take home as souvenirs.

In many ways this was not only the last stand of Yugoslav football but of Yugoslavia itself as Serbs, Croats, Montenegrins, Macedonians and Bosnians all found common cause under the Red Star banner.

The fabric of the nation had been slowly fraying since the death of Marshal Tito in 1980. Tito was surprisingly well loved for someone who had declared himself president for life. Seen as a benevolent and unifying leader, as well as a war hero with dual Slavic heritage (Croat and Slovene), he bonded the country together.

Economic as well as political factors were at play. Double-digit growth and low borrowing were a feature of the Yugoslav economy in the early 1970s, until the OPEC Oil Crisis hit. Then the government heavily borrowed from both the United States and the Soviet Union to weather the shock. By the mid-1980s servicing this liability was becoming nigh-on impossible. National debt went above $20bn, unemployment north of 15 per cent and inflation at one point hit 1,000 per cent. The country defaulted, devalued its currency and agreed to sweeping economic reforms in order to secure foreign reserves. This austerity was the perfect environment for nationalism to ferment and in Serbia it rose behind the leadership of Slobodan Milošević.

Milošević offered simple populist solutions to deep, structural issues and blamed the country's ills on corruption and bureaucrats. The Serbian republic had just one of eight votes in the Yugoslav presidency council but Milošević's supporters organised protests and opposition to the governments in Kosovo, Montenegro and Vojvodina that brought Milošević sympathisers to power.

The rise of Serb nationalism made Slovenes, Croats, Bosnians and Kosovar Albanians nervous, especially with the commitment to a Greater Serbia that involved extending the protective arms of the Serbian state around ethnic locals regardless of their geographic location within Yugoslavia.

This tension boiled over on the football pitch and towards the end of the 1990 season Red Star travelled to Zagreb to play Dinamo. Red Star had the league sewn up by then but fanning the tension was the first multi-party elections in Croatia, won by parties favouring Croatian independence.

A riot ensued between the 3,000 travelling 'Delije' – Red Star's ultras – and Dinamo supporters. Predictably, both sides blamed the other for provocation. What wasn't disputed, however, was that the Delije were vandalising the Dinamo stadium and the home fans were upset at lacklustre police response.

Taking matters into their own hands, Dinamo supporters breached the security fencing around the pitch and attempted to charge their Serbian rivals. The police were overwhelmed.

Zvonimir Boban, now the deputy general secretary of UEFA but then captain of Dinamo, says, 'The hooligans from Belgrade were ruining our stadium. The police at the time, who were absolutely a regime police, the police did nothing to stop them.'

Boban says he remonstrated with the police and was given two sharp baton blows for his troubles. The red mist descended and Boban launched at the officer with a flying kick.

It's been called the kick that started a war but the reality was it was one of many skirmishes on the path to eventual conflict, including a September 1990 match between Hajduk Split and Partizan where Hajduk fans chased the Partizan players from the field before burning the stadium's Yugoslav flag in a match broadcast live on Yugoslav television.

Boban did align his actions with the cause of Croatian independence, in doing so becoming a folk hero from Dalmatia to the Danube. But he paid a footballing price as he was suspended for six months, including missing the 1990 World Cup finals.

The 1991 European Cup Final was played in Bari, in an attempt to provide a thin justification for building a 58,000-seat, white elephant stadium for the 1990 World Cup. The southern Italian city welcomed Red Star and

Olympique Marseille, meaning Red Star would be reunited with their old friend Stojković.

Realistically, given the worsening political situation, the Red Star players and management had to assume that this would be their last chance to capture the European Cup. The first casualties of the Yugoslav Wars had occurred at an armed stand-off at Plitvice Lakes National Park in Croatia and missile attacks were beginning. The five-year plan had suddenly become a four-year plan but fortunately they had one player in the side who knew what it took to win a European Cup.

Miodrag Belodedici was one of the last great liberos; an elegant Romanian defender who was completely comfortable on the ball. Even though he emerged in the back-pass era it was rare to see him resort to utilising his goalkeeper, and when in possession he was looking to create.

Belodedici's first European Cup triumph was as part of the Steaua team that beat Barcelona but after that victory he didn't feel the players were treated as they should have been.

'I didn't like the regime. Old players weren't treated as well as they had been before. They weren't allowed to go abroad. I decided to go,' he recalled.

But leaving Ceauşescu's Romania wasn't a straightforward process, especially when you were technically an army officer as Steaua's players were. Belodedici (pronounced without the 'i' and a soft 'ch') had family ties to Yugoslavia and Red Star was his favourite club.

'Something told me to go to Belgrade,' he told *The Guardian* years later. The only snag was he didn't have his passport. The passports Romanian players used to travel to international matches were confiscated upon their return.

Belodedici was born in small village on the Serbian-Romanian border but brought up in Romania. He continued, 'I asked Valentin Ceauşescu [the president's son] and the president of Steaua, Ion Alecsandrescu – he was the general who ran the club – for a passport. They asked why I wanted it and I told them that my mother had a permit to cross into Yugoslavia to visit her family and I wanted to go for a week to take her and then come back.'

In Yugoslavia, Belodedici was granted political asylum but back in his native Romania he became persona non grata. Belodedici was sentenced to ten years' imprisonment for desertion from the army.

After watching a Red Star match from the stands he went to find Dragan Džajić and offer his services: 'I explained who I was and where I'd come from. I had to explain six times. He looked at me and he couldn't understand. But then [Džajić] suddenly realised who I was.'

Once Džajić twigged who he was talking to, he signed Belodedici to a contract on the spot but UEFA were not happy. According to the organisation, Belodedici had broken his contract with Steaua. Subsequently he was handed a year-long ban from football, which actually lasted for longer than the Ceauşescu regime Belodedici was fleeing. On Christmas Day 1989 Nicolae Ceauşescu and his wife Elena were executed by firing squad after a brief show trial. Ion Iliescu, the leader of the National Salvation Front that toppled Ceauşescu and later served two terms as president of Romania subsequently called the trial 'shameful, but necessary'.

Relations immediately improved between Romania and Yugoslavia and when Belodedici's ban expired in January 1990 he made his Red Star debut in a friendly against Steaua, which was won 4-1.

Barry Davies, commentating on the 1991 European Cup Final for the BBC, introduced the showpiece event to viewers at home as 'two teams better equipped to attack than defend'.

'All round Europe there are expectations of fireworks,' added the silky-voiced commentator. 'In the past the Champions Cup Final has sometimes proved a damp squib but this surely is a night for the sparklers.'

What actually transpired was 'the most boring final in European Cup history' according to Mihajlović, who played in it. He said, 'A few hours before the match, seven of us were shown tapes of Marseille matches. I remember Ljupko Petrović telling us, "If we attack them, we'll leave ourselves open for counter-attacks," to which I asked, "So, what do we do then?" His answer was, "When you get the ball, give it back to them." So we spent 120 minutes on the pitch practically without touching the ball.'

Red Star showed virtually no attacking intent but the famed Marseille front three of Waddle, Pele and Papin could not break down the red-and-white wall. In the second half of extra time and with more than half an eye on penalties, Marseille coach Raymond Goethals turned to Stojković and introduced him in place Eric Di Meco.

The Serb had endured a frustrating first season at Marseille. He had made only seven league starts and had undergone knee surgery that kept him out for most of the campaign. The previous weekend in a game against Nice saw Stojković play a full 90 minutes for the first time since September.

'I think it was a mistake that I didn't play in Bari. The Zvezda [Red Star] players were scared of me,' insists Stojković. 'Of course I was the best player there. Definitely. I respected all the players, but I felt superior.'

In the lull following the end of extra time, Goethals and Petrović were sourcing their penalty takers. Marseille were already without the services of Waddle, who didn't want to repeat the anguish of his 1990 World Cup semi-final miss, when Stojković informed his manager that he too was not going to take one.

'I didn't want to take a penalty. I said to Raymond Goethals when he chose me to take one that I didn't want to take this responsibility against Zvezda. Other players have to take responsibility,' he recounted.

Pascal Olmeta, who hadn't had a save to make in 120 minutes, would now try to deny Red Star their first European Cup. Prosinečki gave Red Star the early advantage, which Stojanović solidified when he saved Manuel Amoros's kick. The next six efforts were all scored before Darko Pančev, the goal-a-game striker, stepped up. Pančev wasn't going to die wondering and off a long run-up he walloped the ball. Olmeta wisely stood his ground in the middle of the goal but the power of the shot made up for how central it was.

A Yugoslav team had finally become champions of Europe after 36 years of trying. Belodedici became the first player to play on the winning team for two different clubs in a European Cup Final (defender Saul Malatrasi played for Inter in their 1964/65 European Cup season but didn't make the XI for the final and later won the competition with AC Milan in 1969; Jimmy Rimmer was on the bench for Manchester United in the 1968 final and started the 1982 final for Aston Villa, before being injured and substituted after nine minutes).

Prosinečki credits Ljupko Petrović for the victory, '[Petrović] brought something new, some new spirit. He persuaded us we could achieve big things. One of the most important aspects of a coach is not only to get the tactics right, to choose 4-4-2 or 4-3-3, but to make the players believe they are capable of achieving something. Ljupko Petrović did that.'

That Red Star achieved what they did when their country was collapsing around them is all the more remarkable.

'We didn't know it, but a few months later the war would change everything – both in terms of our relationships and the future the team should have had,' yearned Prosinečki.

'We didn't have time to realise what we had just achieved and build on it. If that team could have gone on for a few more years with the same players, it could have dominated European football.'

Belodedici agrees, 'We could have gone on winning for years. Some players would have left but we had very good young players.'

Less than four months later, when the defence of their European crown began against Portadown of Northern Ireland, UEFA banned Red Star from playing home games in Yugoslavia due to the deteriorating security situation.

Red Star played their 'home' matches in Hungary and Bulgaria, and they qualified for the semi-final group stage. After four matches Red Star were top of Group A but two defeats, at 'home' to Sampdoria and away to Anderlecht meant they finished second, which wouldn't be enough to see them through to another final.

All of this was achieved without Prosinečki, who had been sold to Real Madrid in the summer of 1991, and in spite of the diplomatic incident caused by Pančev who declared his nationality as Macedonian on a landing card when Red Star travelled to Athens. Macedonia had declared independence in September 1991 but Greece, which also has a region named Macedonia, didn't recognise the country's sovereignty until 1995 (the dispute continued until 2018 when Macedonians voted in a referendum to rename themselves 'North Macedonia').

In total, half the players who played in Bari left Red Star the following season: the captain Stojanović, hard defender Slobodan Marović, his more cultured counterpart Refik Šabanadžović, the pacy Binić and substitute Vlada Stošić

In December 1991, Red Star represented Europe in the Intercontinental Cup against the South American champions Colo-Colo. The Chileans were managed by Mirko Jozić, the Croatian who had coached the Yugoslav youth team to their World Cup triumph in Chile four years earlier.

Many Red Star players had a point to prove to Jozić as many felt his selections had an anti-Serbian bias. Despite Savićević being sent off in the first half, Red Star cantered to a 3-0 victory with two goals from Jugović and one by Pančev.

Despite the uneven playing field they faced, Red Star Belgrade entered 1992 as the European and de facto world champions of club football but even they couldn't defeat the United Nations.

On 30 May 1992, the United Nations Security Council passed UN Security Council Resolution 757 by a 13-0 vote; only China and Zimbabwe abstained. It banned all international trade, scientific and technical cooperation, sports and cultural exchanges from the Federal Republic of Yugoslavia. French president François Mitterrand initially threatened to veto Resolution 757 and proposed that the sports ban be removed, but in the UN horse-trading that followed it was kept in exchange for written clarification that Serbian combatants were not solely responsible for the Yugoslav Wars.

The immediate consequence of this action was that Yugoslavia were ineligible for Euro 92. UEFA called up Denmark as Yugoslavia's replacements and the Danes famously cut short their summer holidays to win the tournament. It's another tantalising 'what if' moment for Yugoslav and Balkan football.

Red Star had played European football in every season since 1968 but like the national team they were banned from the 1992/93 Champions League. The squad saw the writing on the wall and they were scattered all over Europe. In addition to the six departures after the 1990/91 season another 16 players left for foreign sides after the sporting sanctions were imposed.

Chief among the departures were Jugović to Sampdoria, Belodedici to Valencia, Mihajlović to Roma and Pančev to Inter. Only Savićević would get an immediate chance to showcase himself in the Champions League though – he signed for AC Milan.

New Kids from the Bloc

IN 1989, UEFA had 33 members and organising its premier club competition was frankly a doddle. Wales didn't have a national league so there were only 32 potential champions to accommodate in the European Cup and with English clubs banned since Heysel in 1985 there were 31 entrants plus the holders to form a perfect knockout tournament.

By 1996, UEFA had swelled to 52 members as football struggled to keep up with the pace of post-communist political change. The first evidence of this can be found in the 1992/93 season when the European Cup had 36 entrants, at that time a record. For various reasons England, Estonia, the Faroe Islands, Germany, Israel, Latvia, Lithuania, Russia, Slovenia and Ukraine were all represented in 1992/93 despite being absent in 1989/90. Missing were East and West Germany (reunification), the Soviet Union (dissolution) and Yugoslavia (banned). Just to emphasise the pace of change, in the following season Albania, Belarus, Czech Republic, Georgia, Moldova and Wales were all added to the fold.

A preliminary round would be needed to reduce the 36 sides to a more mathematically conducive 32. All six of the countries competing in the European Cup for the first time were to begin their journeys towards the final in Munich at this stage and they would be joined by the champions of Ireland and Malta, two of Europe's weakest leagues.

KÍ Klaksvík (Faroe Islands) v Skonto Riga (Latvia)

Sixty-two degrees north, seven degrees west lie the Faroe Islands, a rugged, windswept archipelago of 18 islands, about equidistant between Norway and Iceland. There may be more unlikely places for a footballing revolution to begin but none spring immediately to mind. Fortunately, the visitors from Latvia knew a thing or two about revolution.

The Baltic republic had been at the vanguard of the movement against the Soviet Communist Party from within the USSR. When Moscow's grip on the republics was loosened following Gorbachev's perestroika and glasnost reforms, the first openly anti-communist organisation anywhere in the Soviet Union was formed in Latvia. Helsinki-86, named after the Helsinki Accords of 1975, began to organise in Latvia in 1986.

By 1987, peaceful demonstrations were regularly being held in Riga, Latvia's capital, and less than a year later these protests were being led by moderates in the ruling Latvian Communist Party. The restoration of independence was declared in May 1990 by the Latvian Supreme Soviet, affirmed by a popular referendum in March 1991 then internationally recognised in August 1991 following the failed coup d'état to remove Gorbachev. Twelve months later, Skonto were playing in the European Cup.

What made Skonto's representation of Latvia on this North Atlantic clifftop 2,000 miles from Riga all the more remarkable was that prior to 1991 the team didn't even exist.

Klaksvíkar Ítróttarfelag, commonly known as KÍ Klaksvík, had pipped B36 Tórshavn to the 1991 Faroese Championship on goal difference and their reward was to be the first team to represent the Faroe Islands in the European Cup.

Conquered by vikings around the year 800, brought under control of the Norweigan crown in 1035, handed to the King of Denmark after the Napoleonic wars, occupied by Britain during the Second World War – the Faroe Islands spent the best part of the last millennium wary of outsiders. They opted out of joining the European Union when Denmark joined in January 1973 alongside Ireland and the United Kingdom and didn't get around to joining UEFA until 1990.

When the Faroes did sign up there was not a single regulation-sized grass pitch in the entire country. This meant that the national team played its first competitive game in September 1990 over 800 miles away in Landskrona, at the southern tip of Sweden. The town of Landskrona had roughly the same population as the entire Faroe Islands and globally is known as one of IKEA's more upmarket sofa ranges.

The Faroes' opponents for that first match were Austria, who had just participated in the 1990 World Cup and despite the entire Faroese side being amateurs the islanders came away with a famous 1-0 win against a full-strength Austrian side.

The international press lapped up the underdog story as one of the greatest upsets in football history, encouraged no doubt by the comic image of the Faroes' goalkeeper Jens Martin Knudsen keeping the likes of Andreas Herzog and Toni Polster at bay while sporting an incongruous white bobble hat. Austrian coach Josef Hickersberger resigned the day after the loss.

By one measure the Faroe Islanders are the smartest people in the world. They have the most Nobel Prize-winners per capita of any nation or territory thanks entirely to Niels Ryberg Finsen, who was born in Tórshavn in 1860. He was awarded the Nobel Prize for Medicine in 1903 for his contributions to the study of tuberculosis luposa and the development of a radiation therapy. However, even the booksmart Faroese surely didn't fancy KÍ's chances of beating the Latvian champions, Skonto Riga.

Skonto were financed into being by Guntis Indriksons, a former KGB officer who was trying his hand at property and construction in the dying days of the Soviet Empire. After setting up his Skonto group in 1990, he founded the football team a year later and they immediately cantered to the national championship, conceding only seven goals in an 18-game season. Whether Indriksons' wealth reached the technical threshold of oligarchy or not, his plan was calculatingly capitalist for a former KGB man – he would attract top talent by being willing to pay his players more than anyone else.

Latvia was not a power in Soviet football. Only one side, FC Daugava Riga, ever played in the Soviet Top League and then only for seven seasons at various points between 1949 and 1962. Similarly, the furthest any Latvian side got in the Soviet Cup was the quarter-finals but there is a plausible case to make to say that Latvia could have been a World Cup semi-finalist back in 1938.

Latvia became an independent republic after the First World War and competed in the 1924 Olympic football tournament. The country then entered the qualifying tournament for the 1938 World Cup. After beating Lithuania 9-3 over two matches, Latvia were tasked with beating Austria, the 1934 World Cup semi-finalists and

1936 Olympic Games silver medalists, in a single game, in Vienna.

Despite being handed a raw deal by FIFA they performed admirably, taking the lead before losing creditably, 2-1. When Austria withdrew from the tournament in France on account of being annexed by Nazi Germany the Latvians were not extended an opportunity to replace them. Instead organisers invited England to participate – this despite England not even being a member of FIFA at the time. When that ruse failed, instead of inviting Latvia to France, FIFA gave Sweden a bye to the quarter-finals.

The counterfactual is especially tantalising because Latvia drew 3-3 with Sweden in Stockholm in their last meeting before the 1940 Soviet annexation, and also given Sweden's comfortable 8-0 victory over Cuba in the quarter-finals. Had Latvia been invited to France, could they have beaten Sweden on neutral ground and made it all the way to the semi-finals?

On 19 August 1992, four days after the inaugural English Premier League matches were played, the first game of the new UEFA Champions League took place in the Faroe Islands. By now there were two Faroese grounds that met UEFA's criteria but KÍ's home venue in Klaksvík wasn't one of them, meaning the game was played a short ferry ride away in Toftir on the neighbouring island of Eysturoy.

The Svangaskarð ground in Toftir is cut into the cliff face, which provides a natural amphitheatre and any particularly enthusiastic clearances have a chance of reaching the North Atlantic waves. The pitch was originally constructed from gravel but after the national team's win against Austria, locals decided to install a grass surface and upgrade the facilities so they could become the home of the national team. However, one amenity not yet installed was floodlights; consequently this was the first game in the inaugural season of the Champions League because it needed to kick off before any gloom set in.

Over 1,000 spectators filled the stands and hillsides to watch KÍ vs Skonto with both teams making their European debuts, which doesn't sound that impressive but it represented about 2.5 per cent of the entire Faroe Islands population. It would be the equivalent of around 1.15m people packed into Elland Road to watch the English champions.

Twenty-eight minutes into the match the deadlock was broken by Vitālijs Astafjevs, possibly the most famous player you've never heard of unless you're a huge Bristol Rovers fan. As a 21-year-old, Astafjevs was lured to Skonto from FC Daugava Riga with the promise of a professional contract including generous performance bonuses and he began repaying Idrinksons' investment with a tidy finish from the edge of the area and that also gave him a share of the claim to be the first goalscorer in the new Champions League format.

'I remember receiving the ball in space from the right-back. I took one touch to steady myself and shot from outside the box. It was a good finish but yes, it was a bit lucky. Of course it was lucky, it was the first goal,' he said.

Picking the ball out of the net wasn't the bobble-hatted Knudsen but a 22-year-old postman named Jákup Mikkelsen. Mikkelsen would go on to have quite the career, becoming the first Faroe Islander to win a league outside their homeland when his unfancied Herfølge BK side won the Danish Superliga in 2000. In 2012, Mikkelsen became the oldest international goalkeeper when he played against Iceland at the age of 42 and in between these events he even found time to be elected to the Klaksvík town council.

Whatever was said to KÍ at half-time worked and within a minute of the restart, striker Olgar Danielsen had drawn them level. But Skonto immediately hit back, scoring virtually from the restart to restore their lead, through Astafjevs again. A late goal gave Skonto a cushion for the return leg two weeks later. Not that Astafjevs was in a rush to leave – speaking years later he described the Faroes as an exotic and memorable country.

Between the two-legged European tie, Astafjevs would get to make his debut for the Latvian national team in a World Cup qualifier versus Denmark. Despite having come off the beach to win Euro 92 just a few weeks earlier, or perhaps because of it, the Danes couldn't break down the Latvian defence and left Riga with just one point for the 0-0 draw.

It could have been worse for Denmark as the Skonto front man Aleksandrs Jeļisejevs came closest to scoring with a left-footed stab from the edge of the area that clipped the outside of a statuesque Peter Schmeichel's post in the first half. That dropped point would eventually be the difference between Denmark and the Republic of Ireland qualifying for USA 94. Had Latvia not drawn with the Danes, the world would have been robbed of that Ray Houghton goal against Italy and John Alridge screaming 'fuck off you twat … dickhead … fucking cheat' at a FIFA technical delegate in their group match against Mexico. It's hard to imagine Kim Vilfort doing that with the same menace or ease.

Eighteen years later, when Astafjevs retired from international football he had amassed 167 caps, scored 16 times for his country, led Latvia to their first (and to date only) major championships and finished his career as the most capped European player of all time. His mark has subsequently been equalled by Iker Casillas and passed by Gigi Buffon and Sergio Ramos. When asked for comment about Casillas equalling his mark,

Astafjevs only half-joked, 'He is a keeper, I am a player.' He certainly was.

Notwithstanding his fine continental achievements, Astafjevs is best remembered in the UK for his four-year stint at Bristol Rovers. He was signed as Ian Holloway's Christmas present to himself in December 1999 with an eye to the 2000/01 season when he expected Rovers to be promoted to what is now called the Championship.

'The Latvian', as he was affectionately and lazily nicknamed, was as advertised; beguiling supporters of the Gas and dazzling opponents in equal measure as Holloway tried to swashbuckle his way out of the third tier of English football. Despite being top of the table in mid-March, Rovers went on a horrid run of form and took just ten points from their last 12 games, enduring the ignominy of slipping out of the play-off places on the final day of the season.

Worse was to follow the following year when the Bristol club was relegated to the fourth tier for the first time in their history. Astafjevs stayed loyal and played for a further two seasons at a level comfortably below his capabilities, exuding all the confidence an international number ten should against the mix of journeyman pros, faded stars and youthful what-might-becomes who populate the lower leagues. He greatly endeared himself to Rovers supporters in the process.

Back in 1992 Jeļisejevs took that confidence he got from rasping a shot against Schmeichel's post into the second leg versus KÍ as he opened the scoring within four minutes, much to the approval of the 12,000 Skonto fans through the turnstiles. Astafjevs netted the third on the night to take his European goal tally to three. Skonto ran out 6-1 winners on aggregate and earned their next assignment against Polish champions Lech Poznań.

The 1992/93 season wouldn't be the last time that Skonto would dine at Europe's top footballing table, however, as they would thanks to Mr Indriksons' largesse and the management skills of Aleksandrs Starkovs win 14 consecutive Latvian championships. No other men's European team can boast more consecutive titles, although KÍ Klaksvík's women's team can exert a measure of revenge for their men's side's defeat in 1992 at the hands of Skonto – they won the Faroe Islands women's league 17 consecutive times between 2000 and 2016.

Skonto's most famous European nights are two glorious failures from their latter attempts to make the Champions League group stages. In 1997/98 UEFA allowed the runners-up of top European leagues to enter the Champions League qualifying stages alongside the bona fide champions of smaller leagues, such as Skonto, who were the fortunate – or unfortunate, depending on your perspective – team to draw Louis van Gaal's Barcelona.

Skonto opened the scoring in the Camp Nou thanks to an outstretched Vladimirs Babičevs leg and some generous goalkeeping from Ruud Hesp. The Brazilian Giovanni pegged Skonto back but a fast sweeping counter-attack just after the break restored the Latvians' advantage, until Giovanni profited when Skonto failed to clear a corner effectively. Deep into injury time it looked like Barcelona would be travelling to Riga needing to win to qualify for the group stages but Igor Stepanovs, of future Arsenal infamy, leapt like a salmon to Superman punch an innocuous corner that was lofted towards the penalty area D. It was a moment of madness that Hristo Stoichkov punished from the spot to claim a 3-2 win. In the return leg, Luís Figo provided the cross for Sonny Anderson to register a 1-0 victory and wrap the tie up 4-2 on aggregate.

The other near miss came two seasons later. This time the amount of non-champions had swelled the numbers so much that three qualifying rounds were needed and after getting past Rapid Bucharest in the second qualifying stage, Skonto were paired with Chelsea, who had finished third in the Premier League the previous season. For over 170 minutes of the tie Skonto's defence stood firm but an eight-minute spell towards the end of the first leg at Stamford Bridge proved decisive with three goals in quick succession, including one of only three goals Chris Sutton scored in a Chelsea shirt.

Paul Ashworth, an Englishman who, like Sutton, came through the ranks at Norwich City, managed Skonto's rivals FK Ventspils to two runners-up finishes in the early 2000s and took over Skonto after after Starkhovs left to take the reins at Spartak Moscow. He said, 'All the best Latvian players of that era went to Skonto. Nobody was close in payments of salaries or bonuses; it was like Manchester United playing Rochdale in the same league.'

Despite being a regular bridesmaid to that Skonto team, Ashworth was full of admiration for the 'brilliant' job that Indriksons and Starkhovs did, saying of the 14 consecutive championships that it was arguable whether anyone has achieved more than Indriksons in world football.

Indriksons' influence even extended to the Latvian FA where he was made president in 1996. At times it was hard to distinguish between Skonto and the Latvian national team. Starkhovs managed both from 2001 to 2004 and when Latvia qualified for Euro 2004 and drew a finals match with Germany, the squad of 23 contained 19 current or former Skonto players. Indriksons has since withdrawn his money from Skonto and stepped down from his role at the FA, and the club has gone bankrupt, whereas the national team has dropped behind the likes of Andorra, Myanmar and Turkmenistan in the FIFA rankings.

'We played against Barcelona sure, but there's no chance for a game like that to happen now,' Astafjevs laments.

'I watch the Champions League on TV and I see there is no way a club like Skonto Riga could make it to the group stages. Today the Champions League is not for clubs from Latvia.'

Shelbourne (Republic of Ireland) v Tavriya Simferopol (Ukraine)

Prior to Latvia reasserting its independence, its national football team had never dined at the top table of Soviet football. The same couldn't be said for the Ukraine.

After the USSR dissolved and the Commonwealth of Independent States fulfilled its one tournament function at Euro 92, the question of how to divide up the Soviet Union's not inconsiderable footballing heritage arose. Both Ukraine and Russia felt they had strong claims to the history, titles and most importantly in the here and now, the UEFA coefficients.

Coefficient rankings are statistical formulae used for ranking and seeding teams in UEFA competitions. They take into account past performances over a period of five years and determine how many clubs and at what stage they enter different club competitions. Because FIFA and UEFA decided to anoint Russia as the sole successor country to the USSR, Ukraine found itself without a coefficient ranking, meaning that its teams were jointly the lowest ranked in Europe and had to begin this Champions League campaign in the preliminary round.

That coefficient decision was a body blow to Ukrainian football in the early 1990s as the Soviet Top League was well regarded. In the late '80s the Top League was the second best on the continent according to UEFA metrics, ahead of the Football League, Bundesliga and La Liga; only the fêted Italian Serie A was viewed as a stronger competition and the Soviet league enjoyed such an exalted position largely thanks to Ukrainian clubs and Ukrainian players.

In the previous 20 seasons, Ukrainian clubs had represented the USSR in the European Cup 12 times compared to just five from Russia itself (Armenia, Belarus, Georgia all represented the league once each). Twelve of Valeriy Lobanovskyi's Euro 88 squad who finished as runners-up to the Netherlands were Ukrainian compared to only four Russians, and Dynamo Kiev were by far the most successful Soviet side.

Dynamo were twice European Cup Winners' Cup winners (in 1975 and '86), twice European Cup semi-finalists, quarter-finalists a further five times and were the team that ended Bayern Munich's domination of the competition in the 1970s, dumping Maier, Beckenbauer and Rummenigge out in front of 102,000 fans in March

1977. At the time the Ukrainians had won as many European trophies as Hamburg, Manchester United, Porto and PSV Eindhoven had.

Dynamo even played a role in building the Ukrainian national consciousness prior to independence, switching from playing in their traditional blue shirts to yellow with blue shorts – the colours of Ukrainian nationalism. Versions of the yellow-and-blue flag had been used in Ukraine since 1848 but had been outlawed by the USSR, so it was quite some statement when Dynamo took the field against Russian opposition looking every inch the Ukrainian national side. In 1990 Kiev won the double, thrashing Lokomotiv Moscow 6-1 in the Soviet Cup Final and beating CSKA Moscow to the league.

Oddly, because the Soviet Cup Final was played in May and the league didn't finish until October, the double actually qualified Dynamo for two separate European competitions. They entered the 1990/91 Cup Winners' Cup and the 1991/92 European Cup as the representatives of the Soviet Union despite the fact that the Ukrainian parliament had declared the country independent in August 1991. On both occasions it took the might of Johan Cruyff's Barcelona to eliminate Kiev.

But when Irish league champions Shelbourne came to face off against their Ukrainian counterparts they were playing the relatively unknown Tavriya Simferopol rather than the famed Dynamo Kiev.

The 1992 Ukrainian championship, the Vyshcha Liha, was run on a very condensed basis with games only happening between March and June. Ukraine was looking westward and trying to align its footballing calendar with the majority of UEFA members. The idea was to run a condensed league campaign in the spring and then run a full season starting in the autumn.

To accommodate the tight timetable the league was split into two pools of ten teams; the winners would then play in a two-legged final to decide the overall champion and Ukraine's representative for the Champions League.

Dynamo Kiev were drawn in pool B alongside Dnipro, the only other Ukrainian team to get to the quarter-finals of the European Cup, while pool A was expected to be a battle between Black Sea team FC Chornomorets Odesa, who finished fourth in the 1991 Soviet Top League, and Shakhtar Donetsk from Donbass in eastern Ukraine. Tavriya were a second-tier club in the last year of Soviet football and had only been in the top flight once, back in 1981. To make their prospects worse they limped out of the Ukrainian Cup in the preliminary round.

By the time the play-off came around in June, the two-legged final had been replaced by a one-off game in Lviv, so that the national team could go on a tour of the United States. Footballing diplomacy was used to emphasise the two nations' growing friendship.

Dynamo had to play eight more games in the condensed calendar than Tavriya. Four came in the domestic cup competition and four were in the group stage of the 1991/92 European Cup – two against Barcelona followed by fixtures with Sparta Prague and Benfica.

The final was perhaps a game too far for Dynamo, who were now playing in a more traditional white. Kiev's best defender, Akhrik Tsveiba, was on international duty for the Commonwealth of Independent States in Sweden for Euro 92. Interestingly, Tsveiba is one of only two players to play international football for four different countries – the Soviet Union, the CIS, Ukraine and Russia.

As well as allowing Russia to bogart a UEFA coefficient that Ukrainians had largely built up, UEFA and FIFA allowed players from the former Soviet Union to play for any of the successor states regardless of where they were actually from, which in practice given that Russia had the coefficient and a place in the qualifying tournament for the 1994 World Cup (which Ukraine did not) meant that the best Ukrainian players like Andrei Kanchleskis and Viktor Onopko opted to switch their allegiance to Russia to further their international ambitions.

Back in Lviv, the title play-off was threatening to head into extra time, Dynamo's regular long-range shots were poorly calibrated and Tavriya weren't showing much in terms of urgency, quite content to soak up pressure and look to profit from a set piece or mistake.

This was exactly what happened when Sergei Shevchenko nodded home from an inswinging corner, much to the chagrin of midfielder Serhiy Kovalets and Lithuanian goalkeeper Valdemaras Martinkėnas who had a heated row as to who was to blame with neither ceding any ground. Not that Shevchenko cared; Tavriya had won the title and he had personally been awarded a new television and vacuum cleaner for his man-of-the-match performance. Meanwhile Tavriya as a club won $800 in prize money and a trip to Dublin.

Much like Soviet football, the 1980s was a boom time for the Republic of Ireland national team. Eoin Hand's group had heartbreakingly missed out on the 1982 World Cup in Spain on goal difference despite securing famous wins against the Netherlands and France in a tough qualification group. After Hand, England's 1966 World Cup winner Jack Charlton took up the managerial reins in 1986 and secured qualification for the Republic's first major tournament – Euro 88.

Ireland impressively topped a group featuring the 1986 World Cup semi-finalists Belgium, plus Bulgaria and Scotland, with only a small assist for Heart of Midlothian stalwart Gary Mackay, whose 86th-minute strike in Sofia was pure consolation for the Scots but meant that Ireland would be on the plane to West Germany instead of Bulgaria. Something about the luck of the Irish.

'Big Jack's' men more than held their own in the tournament, including beating England, and Ronnie Whelan's strike against the USSR is still replayed as one of the all-time great European Championship goals. They followed this up with a more straightforward qualification for the 1990 World Cup in Italy before eventually exiting in the quarter-finals at the hands of the hosts.

While the period is viewed nostalgically from a national team perspective, at a club level Irish football was in the doldrums throughout the 1980s. In the Republic's 1990 World Cup squad not only were there no players from the League of Ireland, but only four of the players had ever played in the competition. Kevin Moran appeared once for Bohemians in 1975 before transferring to Manchester United, where he was later joined by Paul McGrath after a standout season for St Patrick's Athletic. Liverpool, not to be out-scouted, recruited Steve Staunton (Dundalk) and Ronnie Whelan (Home Farm) after one and two League of Ireland seasons respectively.

If you were an Irish player of any talent the best thing you could do for your career was move to England or Scotland as soon as you practically could. Indeed, before

Major League Soccer and other well-paying foreign leagues became popular pre-retirement destinations, you were much more likely to see a fading star in the country than a rising one. Three of England's 1966 heroes passed through in the 1970s with Bobby Charlton donning the blue of Waterford, Gordon Banks taking a turn in goal for St Pat's and Geoff Hurst briefly leading the line for Cork Celtic. Hurst's time in Cork didn't intersect with either George Best, the 1968 European Cup winner and only man from the island of Ireland to win the Ballon d'Or, nor Uwe Seeler, the legendary Hamburg striker who captained the West German side that Hurst's hat-trick vanquished at Wembley.

Irish clubs had only progressed beyond their opening European Cup contests on three occasions and hadn't done so since the 1970s. Waterford United beat northern neighbours Glentoran in 1970/71's first round then nine years later, Dundalk triumphed over Hibernians, but the Maltese club rather than the Edinburgh outfit who reached the semi-finals in the inaugural European Cup tournament. Sandwiched in between those notable campaigns was a walkover victory for Cork Celtic against Omonia Nicosia on account of Turkey's invasion of Cyprus.

Heroic failure was more the order of the day for Irish clubs in UEFA competitions, and none more so than when Dundalk held PSV Eindhoven in the first round of the 1976/77 European Cup. PSV had reached the semi-finals the previous season and would go on to lift the 1978 UEFA Cup but for 69 minutes at a packed Oriel Park they were behind thanks to what was described as a 'murderous left-footed 20-yard volley' courtesy of Seamus McDowell, a £150 signing from Sligo Rovers. PSV's prolific striker Willy van der Kuijlen equalised late in the game to salvage a draw. In the return leg, Van der Kuijlen dutifully opened the scoring after 19 minutes while two-time World Cup finalist René van de Kerkhof helped himself to four goals as part of a 6-0 scoreline.

Although, to borrow a phrase from Norman Lamont, the British Chancellor of the day, there were green shoots of recovery that could be seen in Irish club football in the early 1990s if you looked hard enough. St Pat's had managed to hold Romanian champions Dinamo Bucharest to a 1-1 draw in Dublin just 16 months after Bucharest's eternal derby foes Steaua had contested the 1989 European Cup Final. However, true to form, the away leg saw a 4-0 reversal and another first-round elimination. The following year, Dundalk had managed a 1-1 draw at Honvéd, bringing back a vital away goal, but the Hungarians comfortably won the second leg 2-0.

Tavriya's destination was confirmed to be Dublin rather than Dundalk when Shelbourne's Brian Flood sealed the Shels' first title for 30 years with a 40-yard strike in a last-day decider. Shelbourne were managed by Pat Byrne, who was the last League of Ireland player to be capped by Ireland in a competitive international. Byrne, a legend of the Dublin football scene from his stints with both Bohemians and Shamrock Rovers and a plentiful smoker in the dugout, made the short trip to Drumconda and helped turn around Shelbourne's domestic fortunes. They were confident that this time they had a chance to get over that first European hurdle and hopefully secure a glamour tie in the next round.

Unusually, the Shels' line was led not by an Irishman but an Englishman called Garry Haylock. Haylock, in his early 20s and originally from Bradford, had been on Huddersfield Town's books when Eoin Hand was the Terriers' manager and initially he had joined Shels on a three-month loan.

'The League of Ireland was tough physically which is why Eoin sent me there in the first place as he thought I was soft. He was probably right,' Haydock said.

The following season Haylock returned on a long-term loan and was Shelbourne's top scorer in the title-winning campaign.

'I had the carrot of going to Australia pre-season and then playing in Europe so I signed a years contract,' he continued.

'We had a lot of players and staff who had played lots of games in some very strange places so the Tavriya game was just another country ticked off for them. I was very excited though. Ukraine was totally unknown and in the early 90s foreign travel was still quite novel especially where I was from.'

The first leg in Dublin nearly got off to the dream start when Haylock hit the post after less than a minute played.

'I should have scored,' he wistfully remembers. After that scare Tavriya, as expected, were content to play out the remaining 89 minutes. 'We should have won the game but we suffered with an inferiority complex,' said Haylock, for whom the return leg evokes stronger memories with the hotel being described as 'shocking', the food as 'horrible' but the stadium as 'impressive'.

The Lokomotiv Stadium in Simferopol had hosted several important USSR matches, including the decisive fixtures that secured qualification for both Euro 88 and Italia 90, and was relatively modern, being constructed only 25 years prior. The official attendance was reported as just over 10,000 when contemporary accounts describe the ground as being packed close to its 30,000 capacity. The discrepancy is possibly explained by the decision to let serving soldiers in for free.

Not to be outdone, Shelbourne's enterprising and colourful chairman Ollie Byrne even managed to turn the away leg into a PR coup by offering the chance for two lucky fans to join the team in Ukraine. The prize was won by a couple who treated it as their honeymoon. Sadly for the newlyweds they found the local vodka undrinkable and the Tartar-based cuisine impenetrable. Perhaps they should have consulted *Lonely Planet* which damned Simferopol with the faintest of praise: 'The Crimean capital is not an unpleasant city, but there is no point lingering here.'

That sentiment was taken to heart by the home team who raced into a two-goal lead after just 15 minutes. Sergei Shevchenko, whose goal had won the league title, gave Tavriya the lead, before his strike partner Talyat Sheikhametov doubled it. Shelbourne's Padraig Dully pulled one back on the stroke of half-time, leaving the entire second half to be played out with increasing tension as just one goal for the Irish side would take them through on away goals.

'In injury time Dessie Gorman cut in from the right,' remembers Haylock, 'and could have squared it to me to tap in but Dessie went for goal, put it over and we were out.'

Modern-day Crimea is even more inhospitable to western visitors than it was in 1992. Following the Russian annexation in 2014, Simferopol has been blockaded by the Ukrainian government that retains *de jure* if not de facto authority over the area, and the Irish Department of Foreign Affairs strongly advises against all travel to the area, as does Garry Haylock.

In 2015 UEFA organised a Crimean league after blocking Russian plans to incorporate Crimean teams from the annexed territory into the Russian league system. In a pleasing echo of history, TSK Simferopol, the successor club to Tavriya, were the first Crimean champions – and they too have struggled to repeat that initial success.

After winning the first Ukrainian league, Tavriya never once finished above fifth in subsequent seasons with their best campaign coming in 2009/10 when a cup victory qualified them for the Europa League play-off round.

There was a measure of revenge for Shelbourne the following season when competing in the 1993/94 Cup Winners' Cup. Shels drew Ukrainian opposition in the preliminary round for the second season running but this time the away leg would be first. Travelling to the picturesque Lviv, with its UNESCO World Heritage-listed old town, was an upgrade on Simferopol and in all honesty would have made a better honeymoon destination.

After securing a 1-0 defeat in the first leg Shels took Karpaty Lviv back to Tolka Park and put on an impressive display (please go seek out these highlights on YouTube, if not for Brian Mooney's 30-yard effort then for RTE's use of Indiana Jones-style graphics and backing music). Shelbourne scored three unanswered goals and not even an 88th-minute goalkeeping error could trouble them.

In the next round, despite another long-range Mooney goal, Shelbourne lost 5-1 on aggregate to an impressive Panathinaikos side who were only two years away from achieving a Champions League semi-final berth themselves.

And 1993/94 would be the last European high point for Irish club football for a while. Cork City were the League of Ireland's champions and they managed to successfully navigate the preliminary round, progressing thanks to an away-goals victory over Cwmbran Town of Wales. They remain the last Irish side to reach the first round of the European Cup and they nearly went one better.

Paired with Galatasaray, Cork managed to return from Istanbul with a vital away goal. Despite only being founded in 1984, Cork had a small amount of European pedigree. They had drawn with Bayern Munich in the 1991 UEFA Cup, and while it was not a vintage Bayern by any means the Germans still contained star power in the form of Steffan Effenberg, Christian Ziege, Thomas Berthold and the Brazilian forward Mazinho.

Dave Barry, a player who would absolutely be a candidate to be featured on the peerless Twitter account 80s Footballers Ageing Badly (@80saging), scored against Bayern and was responsible for the away goal in the Ali

Sami Yen Stadium, albeit via a large deflection. A 1-0 victory at Turner's Cross would see them through to the last 16 and quite frankly they were worth at least that.

Barry's midfield partner Declan Hyde had a rasping goalbound volley deflected over the bar by a defender's head and Anthony Buckley hit the side-netting when it was easier to score. Then Galatasaray hit Cork on the break with 15 minutes to go, snuffing out any chance of a dream last-16 encounter with a Manchester United including the Cork native, Roy Keane. Tugay Kerimoğlu, the future Blackburn Rovers favourite, slid in Kubilay Türkyilmaz, the Swiss striker who later scored a penalty against England at Euro 96, for the breakaway goal.

Irish sides have twice since then been a tie away from making the Champions League group stage. In 2004, Shelbourne triumphed over KR Reykjavík in the first qualifying round on away goals before the unlikely figure of English centre-back Davy Rodgers volleyed home a looping cross from outside the penalty area to beat Croatia's Hajduk Split 4-3 on aggregate. Shels were rewarded with a meeting against Deportivo La Coruña, who had reached the Champions League semi-finals the year previously. For 149 minutes they kept the tie scoreless, but eventually the Galicians had too much and ran out 3-0 winners. Meanwhile, Dundalk lost a play-off against Polish champions Legia Warsaw in 2016/17 for the right to be walloped by Borussia Dortmund and Real Madrid in that year's Champions League group stages.

Tavriya Simferopol would play FC Sion of Switzerland in the first round proper.

Valletta (Malta) v Maccabi Tel Aviv (Israel)

Prior to 1992 it could be argued that the best performance from a Maltese team in the European Cup was a 4-0 aggregate defeat of Hibernians by Manchester United in the first round of the 1967/68 tournament. It took United 180 minutes to score four goals against Hibernians but only 120 to put the same number past Benfica in that year's final at Wembley. Alternatively, it could be the one and only aggregate victory that Silema Wanderers managed against ÍA Akranes the Icelandic Champions in 1971.

Maltese teams would regularly need the number of goals conceded to be printed in brackets next to the score to assure people that a score hadn't been misprinted. Ipswich scored 14 (fourteen) against Floriana in 1962/63, Grasshopper Zürich bagged 13 (thirteen) against Valletta in 1977/78 and two years later Honvéd put 11 (eleven) past the same opposition. The past two seasons had seen ten-goal aggregate wins for Rangers and Benfica respectively and even the Cypriot champions Omonia Nicosia once took the liberty of reaching double figures against their Maltese European Cup opponents, Rabat Ajax.

So it's fair to say that Valletta were very much the underdogs in their match versus Maccabi Tel Aviv. Not only were Valletta representing the second-lowest ranked league system in all of UEFA (ahead of only Luxembourg), they would be taking on a club that had twice won its continental championship.

Geographically, Israel is indisputably west Asian and that may be the beginning and the end of the consensus when it comes to discussing the nation and its football. As Israeli champions, Maccabi Tel Aviv twice won the Asian Football Confederation's Champion Club Tournament in 1969 and 1971. They might have won in 1970 too had they been invited as holders, but they had missed out on automatic qualification thanks to local rivals Hapoel winning the Israeli league by one point. However, that 1971 success would be an ominous portent as they won the final when Iraqi side Al-Shorta refused to play in protest to what they saw as the Israeli occupation of Palestine. Just three years later, a coalition led by Arab nations voted to kick Israel out of the Asian Football Confederation, casting the country into the footballing wilderness, hopping from confederation to confederation just in order to be able to compete.

Ahead of the 1978 World Cup, Israel were given a special geographical qualifying grouping with south-east

Asian countries and even then North Korea boycotted the tournament rather than compete against them. For the 1982 event, Israel attempted to qualify via the European pathway, but found a group featuring Scotland, Northern Ireland, Sweden and Portugal too formidable. In 1990, Israel won the Oceania confederation tournament ahead of Australia and New Zealand but subsequently lost to Colombia 1-0 in a final two-legged play-off round. A combination of woodwork, squandered chances and Rene Higuita ensured that Israel didn't make their first World Cup since 1970.

However, a virtuoso Ronny Rosenthal performance helped put him in the shop window for an unlikely move to English champions Liverpool, eventually becoming the first non-British player signed by an English club for more than £1m. Rosenthal played a key role in the Merseysiders leapfrogging Aston Villa including scoring a perfect hat-trick in his first start, against Charlton Athletic, to win what turned out to be Liverpool's last championship for 30 years.

How FIFA would have managed Israel at Italia 90 is a tempting hypothetical to ponder. Had Israel taken Colombia's place in Group D they would have been pitted against the national sides of two countries who didn't recognise it as a state – Yugoslavia and the United Arab Emirates. There would also have been a third match against West Germany, at a time when the

Israeli government was voicing concerns about German reunification.

The 1992/93 season saw the debut of Israeli club sides in the Champions League and Cup Winners' Cup, before becoming a full member of the European confederation in 1994. Although as early as 1976 Israeli clubs were being invited to play against European teams in the Intertoto Cup (then not under the auspices of UEFA).

As the 1991/92 Liga Leumit champions, a title won at a canter with a goal difference of +53, the honour of being Israel's first representatives in official European club competition fell to Maccabi Tel Aviv. Tel Aviv handled the away leg in Ta' Qali like seasoned pros with Avi Cohen (not the 1980s Liverpool player of the same name, who also played for Maccabi Tel Aviv) and Avi Nimni scoring the goals. Cohen had contributed 20 goals from right-back in the title-winning campaign before being voted Israeli footballer of the year; whereas Nimni was just at the beginning of a three-spell Maccabi career that would eventually yield 174 goals for the club, who eventually retired his number eight shirt.

In their European bow, Maccabi were managed by a 37-year-old Avram Grant, who had ended Tel Aviv's 12-year championship drought in his first season and later would assemble Maccabi Haifa's title-winning side that became the first Israeli team to progress to the

Champions League group stages in 2002/03. And he would also famously get within a missed John Terry penalty of being a Champions League-winning manager when in charge of Chelsea for the 2008 final against Manchester United.

Tel Aviv's return leg against Valletta was put beyond doubt when Meir Melika scored after 24 minutes with a rasping drive from the edge of the six-yard box which found the roof of the net, sealing a tie against Belgian champions and 1978 runners-up Club Brugge.

Olimpija Ljubljana (Slovenia) v Norma Tallinn (Estonia)

The late 1980s and early '90s was not only a time for tumult for the Soviet Union but also Yugoslavia, Europe's other multinational communist state.

In truth, Yugoslavia had been bound together almost singlehandedly by Josip Tito (himself of dual Croat and Slovene ancestry), who led the partisan resistance to the Axis powers during the Second World War and then served as the country's prime minister and later president until his death in 1980.

His death gave rise to increasing ethnic tensions and competing nationalisms that spilled over following the 1989 revolutions in other parts of Europe. Multi-party elections were fought in 1990 with communist leaders being re-elected in Serbia and Montenegro, while republics like Croatia and Slovenia voted for nationalists in opposition to Serbian domination of Yugoslavia.

Politics was making its way to the football pitch too, and there was a famous riot that prevented a game between Dinamo Zagreb and Red Star Belgrade from being played. In Slovenia, the Slovene players from the top club from the country's capital – Olimpija – were flexing their political muscle. They orchestrated the removal of their successful coach by refusing to train under him, not in response to poor results or egregious conduct but because he was Serbian.

On 25 June 1991, Slovenia and Croatia declared their independence from Yugoslavia, events that set off a decade of war and genocide on the European continent with repercussions still being felt in football and beyond today. Kosovo, which was admitted as an UEFA member in 2014, is recognised by only half of the members of the United Nations and its teams are prohibited from playing games against Serbian and Bosnian teams for fears of violence and unrest.

Slovenia escaped relatively lightly from the Yugoslav Wars, with its portion of the conflict being referred to as the 'Ten Day War', resulting in fewer than 100 casualties on both sides. By October 1991 the last vestiges of the Yugoslav state had left their borders and in June 1992 Slovenia were playing their first recognised international match, against Estonia (a 1-1 draw), then in

August Iztok Čop and Denis Žvegelj placed third behind Britain's Steve Redgrave and Matthew Pinsent in the coxless pairs rowing to win Slovenia's first independent Olympic medal.

Just three days before that historic first Slovenian match in Tallinn, what remained of Yugoslavia had been expelled from Euro 92, a competition that many fancied them to win thanks to a now blossoming golden generation who had won the 1987 World Youth Championship, lost on penalties in the last eight of Italia 90 and propelled Red Star Belgrade to a European Cup triumph in 1991. We also know with the benefit of hindsight that the Danish side that replaced the Yugoslavs in Sweden did go on to win the tournament against a less than vintage crop of opponents.

There must have been a sense of déjà vu though when Olimpija Ljubljana's Champions League debut again pitted Slovenia against Estonia in the shape of Norma Tallinn. Six of the Slovene national team that played in that first international would also line up for Olimpija, though not Igor Benedejčič who despite scoring Slovenia's first international goal had to content himself with appearing as a substitute in a comfortable 3-0 victory. The goals came from Zoran Ubavič, Nedeljko Topić and Damir Vrabac.

The return trip to Tallinn wouldn't alter the complexion of the tie. Olimpija won 2-0 to progress, already making this a much more successful foray into Europe than their only other campaign which had ended in a 9-2 aggregate first-round defeat to Benfica in the 1970/71 Cup Winners' Cup.

However, it was a rare setback for Norma who won the first two post-independence Estonian championships without losing a game. The 1993/94 league was just out of Norma's reach, losing a play-off final, but they did win the Estonian cup to secure a third consecutive season of European football, where they would face Slovenian opponents again in the shape of Maribor, who mercilessly put Norma to the sword with a 14-1 aggregate defeat that foreshadowed the woes to come. At the end of that season, Norma finished bottom of the Estonian top flight with just ten points and a goal difference of -42 and a subsequent relegation saw the club dissolved.

Meanwhile, Olimpija's prize for overcoming Norma was substantial.

The Rossoneri

ARPAD ELO was born in Hungary just after the start of the 20th century, fortuitously moved to America a year before the First World War engulfed central Europe and grew up to be a professor of physics. Elo's passion was chess. He was the Wisconsin state champion eight times and considered one of the best players in the United States – something he wanted to mathematically quantify.

Elo set about devising a rating system for chess which was adopted by FIDE – the governing body of chess in 1970. Each player had a numerical rating, the higher figures indicating the better players. When a strong player came up against a weaker opponent, if he won then he would gain relatively few rating points as that outcome was expected. However, if the weaker man won against the favourite he would gain a relatively large amount of points. Crucially, these points were won from each other, making the system closed and individual contests within it zero-sum games.

While all results mattered in deciding a player's rating, the formulae weighted more recent contests and created a self-correcting system where if an individual was rated too lowly or highly their future performances against expectations would account for the apparent error.

The Elo rating system revolutionised chess. The conferment of Grandmaster status transformed from a subjective award to an empirical one. Elo's ratings system was also applicable to other closed games like European club football. The establishment of the European Cup and later on the Cup Winners' Cup and UEFA Cup allowed for national leagues to be benchmarked against each other and points to be exchanged.

Looking back we can see that, according to Elo, Wolverhampton Wanderers were not Europe's best team on 13 December 1954 but were merely tenth. They were behind four Austrian sides, Kaiserslautern, AC Milan, Juventus, Real Madrid and Barcelona.

With the preliminary round out of the way the 1992/93 tournament had its final 32 teams representing Europe (and beyond), and in a sense the competition proper was ready to begin with a panoply of sides spread across the continent; from Beşiktaş in Istanbul to Víkingur in Iceland. But if Elo was to be believed, the tournament had a clear favourite – AC Milan.

AC Milan were clear atop the Elo rankings with a 1,989 rating, which was the highest for a club side in over 30 years. The Rossoneri had won the previous season's Serie A title without losing a single match. At the time Serie A was widely considered the toughest league in the world and Elo agreed with seven Italian teams being ranked in the top ten of European clubs (AC Milan, Juventus, Torino, Sampdoria, Napoli, Roma, and Inter) but not only had Milan won the Scudetto, they won in style, scoring 74 goals, a 30-year high for the competition.

Italy had an entirely deserved reputation for aggressive, defensive football, known as *catenaccio*. In Italian, *catenaccio* means 'door-bolt' with the aim being to prevent goalscoring opportunities. Ascoli once managed to score only 14 goals in an entire season and still avoid relegation. In 1991/92, Serie A was still operating on a two-points-for-a-win basis and the much-needed back-pass and tackle from behind rules were still waiting to be implemented by FIFA. All told, this gave Italian defenders carte blanche to level the world's most expensive strikers with impunity.

Ian Rush's 1987 move to Juventus is often cited as a failure for its seemingly paltry return of seven league goals and for the quote that the player himself insists he never gave; it was reported that Rush said living in Italy 'was like living in a foreign country'. However, as Rush is at pains to point out to anyone who will listen – he top-scored for Juventus that season. Rush also outscored a host of world-class strikers including Roberto Baggio at Fiorentina (six goals), Rudi Völler at Roma (three) and Marco van Basten at AC Milan (three).

Like Rush, Van Basten struggled to adapt to Serie A initially after his move from Ajax. Tough Italian tackling gave rise to persistent ankle injuries and meant he only played 11 league games, contributing three goals before Euro 88 and that volley that changed his life.

By the summer of 1992 Van Basten was at the peak of his powers. He had just scored 25 goals in the Serie A to become *Capocannoniere* – translated as head gunner – for the second time, which he could pair with his two Ballons d'Or and two European Cups. His tally was higher than Hellas Verona, the 1985 league champions, managed across the whole 34-game campaign and only three fewer than city rivals Inter had managed.

While Rush was isolated in industrial Turin, Van Basten had some friends for company in the fashion capital of the world. To fans of a certain vintage,the phrase Gullit-Rijkaard-Van Basten rolls off the tongue as a singular entity entwined with each other at both club and national level.

Indeed, Ruud Gullit and Frank Rijkaard's lives meshed as early as their schooldays. Sons of Surinamese footballing fathers and Dutch mothers, Gullit and Rijkaard were born within days and miles of each other in Amsterdam, in September 1962. They began playing for the same DWS youth side and despite Ajax professing interest in signing both players Gullit ended up at FC Haarlem, although Rijkaard did join the capital club. The pair would make their international debuts in the same match, against Switzerland. Rijkaard started the game with Gullit replacing him for the second half. Simon Kuper, author of *Brilliant Orange*, claims the Swiss commentator didn't notice.

Gullit eventually convinced Rijkaard to leave Ajax in the summer of 1986 with Rijkaard going as far as signing a contract with PSV Eindhoven before changing his mind. The two rival clubs came to an agreement that Ajax would pay PSV a fee to keep Rijkaard.

Gullit and Van Basten arrived in Milan first, in the summer of 1987. At the time Italian clubs were limited to just two foreign players on each side. The Dutchmen's arrival meant the departure of two English players, Ray Wilkins and Mark Hateley.

Italy had been historically very welcoming to foreign footballers. In the 1950s clubs were fully professional and there was no maximum wage in contrast to England. Welshman John Charles – *'Il Gigante Buono'*, The Gentle Giant – is still revered by Juventus fans to this day. Meanwhile the Fiorentina side who were the first Italians to qualify for a European Cup Final in 1957 featured Julinho, a Brazilian winger, and a host of Swedes and Danes, who could only play amateur football in their home countries, were to be found knocking around the Italian top flight.

Following Italy's failure to qualify for the 1958 World Cup in Sweden and their lacklustre performance in Chile four years later the Italian Football Federation decided to ban foreign players from its league. This policy remained in place until 1980 when one foreigner per team was permitted, increased to two in 1982 and eventually three in 1988.

The rule change gave Milan the green light to add a third Dutchman. Rijkaard had fallen out with Johan Cruyff at Ajax, storming off the training pitch and vowing never to play for Cruyff again. You have to wonder whether the old master saw something of his younger self as the indignant Rijkaard refused to budge.

There can hardly have been a culture shock so profound as walking off a Johan Cruyff training ground and walking on to an Arrigo Sacchi one but that's what awaited both Rijkaard and Van Basten when they made the switch from Ajax.

'I think the way that Cruyff treated the team is exactly what football players like. He would talk about the game in a way that made it fun to play. If you play, you want to attack, right? It was always about creating something, it was always positive,' Van Basten said.

'In Italy, with Sacchi, it was different. It was about building up from the back with the defence. It was a completely different way of coaching football. Cruyff was more adventurous and spectacular. Sacchi was more disciplined.'

Gullit was never an Ajax player but he did get part of his footballing education from Cruyff when they played together at Feyenoord.

'He was 36 when he came to Feyenoord. There were moments when I thought, "Okay, now I'm going to get the ball off him" – but I couldn't. I was thinking, "36? Imagine how good he must have been at 24?"

'At the end of the year he told me, "Ruud, you need to make others around you play better." I was thinking, "Okay, I still have to give attention to my own career. How can I help others?" But when I went to PSV and then Milan the puzzle suddenly fitted together. I remembered everything Johan had said.'

In 1987, Ajax had secured a fee of around three million guilders (about what they paid to keep Rijkaard) for Van Basten, who had scored 128 goals in 133 league matches. PSV, armed to the teeth with corporate lawyers from Philips, demanded a world-record transfer fee as the price of parting with Gullit, who was under a long-term contract. After an intense boardroom battle, wealthy owner of AC Milan, Silvio Berlusconi, agreed to pay 18 million guilders (£6m), a world-record fee. It was £1m more than Napoli paid Barcelona for Maradona in 1984 and a statement of intent to the rest of Italy that Milan were back.

If you were told that the Italian police once arrested the AC Milan club president and two Rossoneri players during half-time of a match, you would be forgiven for picturing Berlusconi's trademark smile and wondering how he charmed his way out of that mess. But this particular action pre-dated Berlusconi's involvement with Milan by nearly six years.

On 23 March 1980, Italian police conducted an operation into alleged match-fixing by players and officials across Italy during half-time intervals to prevent the suspects from colluding in their alibis. After the dust settled Milan were forcibly relegated to Serie B.

Jan Ceulemans, the Belgian playmaker who starred for Club Brugge as they won the Belgian First Division in 1980 and with Belgium as they finished runners-up at Euro 80 in Italy, was due to become Milan's permitted foreign player, but instead backed out of the deal after posing with the iconic red-and-black striped shirt of Milan. He would go on to captain his country to a World Cup semi-final and the Rossoneri signed a 29-year-old Joe Jordan instead.

Milan escaped Serie B at the first attempt but then suffered more ignominy by being relegated again – this time on pure sporting merit.

Nils Liedholm was brought back as manager in 1984/85 and was inherited by Berlusconi when his purchase of the club was finalised in 1986. Liedholm was a legend at the San Siro. He had guided Milan to their most recent Scudetto in 1978/79, won the 1982/83 Scudetto with Roma and had just lost the European Cup Final on penalties to Bruce Grobbelaar's wobbly legs. Liedholm was also part of the Swedish triumvirate Gre-No-Li (also featuring Gunnar Gren and Gunnar Nordahl) that led Milan and Sweden to considerable success in the 1950s. They were very much the Gullit-Rijkaard-Van Basten of their day.

Despite brashly unveiling himself as the new Rossoneri owner by arriving via a helicopter at the city's Arena Civica in front of 6,000 fans, complete with the 'Ride of the Valkyries' entrance music, Berlusconi was persuaded to give the steady-as-we-go Liedholm another season and predictably the team finished a disappointing fifth. Most damningly, his style was too dour and conservative for the showman owner. Milan scored less than a goal per game in Liedholm's second spell in charge.

That's not to say a young Berlusconi wasn't impatient and his first foray into the transfer market was a super-aggressive capture of Roberto Donadoni. The 22-year-old Atalanta winger was close to finalising a transfer to Juventus until Berlusconi came in towards the conclusion of the deal and doubled the asking price. Neither Donadoni or Atalanta could say no and Juve, not for the last time, had her nose put out of joint.

'His dream was ambitious ... to win by having fun and playing well. That the beauty of the game is not in conflict with the victory,' reflected Arrigo Sacchi, who would be Berlusconi's choice to lead his revolution.

Berlusconi's pursuit of Sacchi, described by *Football Italia* alumnus James Richardson as the 'hairless nerd of calcio', happened by accident. Sacchi's Parma side had been drawn in the same Coppa Italia group as Milan and beat them 1-0. Berlusconi was impressed and told Sacchi he would follow his career closely. When they met again later that season in the knockout rounds, Serie B Parma again claimed the scalp of the Milanese.

Sacchi remembers: 'Within ten days, Berlusconi approached me about the job, not just because my team had won but because we had deserved to.'

Berlusconi's ambition was clear and he told his prospective new employee, 'We have to become the greatest team in the world.'

Despite the superficial differences between Berlusconi and Sacchi, the two men were more alike than perhaps either could have known. They shared a common disdain for orthodoxy. The grand and the old were not things to be admired and awed but questioned and challenged. Berlusconi had already done it with his media companies and now with his backing Sacchi would take on perhaps the grandest Italian dynasty of all – the Agnelli family, who owned Fiat and ran Juventus.

Juventus, nicknamed the Old Lady of Italian football, were the reigning champions of Serie A when Berlusconi bought Milan. Juve's most recent title was their 22nd overall and 21st since the Agnelli family took over the club in 1923. They were also (at the time) the only club to have won all three major UEFA trophies, winning the 1984 Cup Winners' Cup and the 1985 European Cup in addition to their 1977 UEFA Cup triumph.

To paraphrase Alex Ferguson, Milan's challenge was to knock Juventus off their 'effing perch'. The only problem was that the media didn't think Sacchi up to the task. He had barely played at any real level and his past occupation as a shoe salesman was often brought up to deride his suitability for the role. His new striker Van Basten inadvertently coined a nickname for him when asked about his rumoured arrival.

'Sacchi?' Van Basten shrugged. 'I don't know anything about him. Do you?' That was enough for the Italian press to dub Sacchi as 'Signor Nessuno' – Mr Nobody.

Signor Nessuno responded with one of the all-time withering one-liners: 'I never realised that to be a jockey you had to be a horse first.'

If Donadoni was Berlusconi's player on the Rossoneri then Carlo Ancelotti was Sacchi's man on the pitch.

'The most difficult negotiations we had was for Ancelotti because the doctor told us he had a knee invalidity of 20 per cent, but I asked Berlusconi to buy him anyway, saying we would win the league with him, and in the end he listened to me,' said the boss.

Ancelotti might not have had the legs to be a Milan player but he had the brain, evidenced by his subsequent success as a manager, to be a Sacchi one.

'I never looked at the feet of my players. I looked at their spirit, their availability, their modesty, their intelligence and their enthusiasm,' Sacchi said.

Things didn't get off to a tremendous start. The collective was prioritised over the individual and the players didn't initially warm to Sacchi's unusual training methods. After a poor run of results, including a UEFA Cup exit at the hands of Espanyol and murmurings of discontent among the playing staff, the owner rallied to this manager's defence with a short but impassioned speech: 'This is the coach I have chosen and those who follow him will stay here, those who do not follow him will leave.'

The biggest swipe at orthodoxy came when Sacchi did something considered heretical to Italian football – he abandoned the *libero* in favour of a flat back four. The *libero* was a foundation piece of *catenaccio*. If the full-backs and the half-backs didn't get you then the *libero* (translated as 'free man' because of his lack of man-to-man marking duties) would. All the great Italian sides had formidable *liberos*. Helenio Herrera's 'Grande

Inter' side, which won back-to-back European Cups in the 1960s, had Armando Picchi; Giovanni Trappatoni's Juventus had Gaetano Scirea, who had also captained Italy to World Cup glory in 1982.

Sacchi had a player adept at being a *libero* in Franco Baresi. Indeed, Baresi was Scirea's understudy for the Italian national team during the early 1980s but while Baresi had the positional intelligence and passing acumen of a *libero*, he also had the physicality and pace to play as a centre-half.

The flat back four was also a necessity to enable Sacchi's true innovation – pressing. Intense pressing was Sacchi's default, where the goal was to disrupt the opposition's play, but he could also demand 'total pressing' – an all-out assault on regaining possession; 'partial pressing' where gaining possession was not the aim and even 'fake pressing' was used if he felt his side needed to recuperate.

Hours and hours would be spent on shape without the ball. Sacchi's theory was that there should be no more than 25 metres between defence and midfield. In that dense a space, there's no role for a 'free man' and given the high defensive line needed to maintain that compactness he demanded his defenders become masters of the offside trap. In Baresi, Paolo Maldini, Alessandro Costacurta and Mauro Tassotti he could have asked for no finer pupils.

While his ideas mostly revolutionised how defenders played, they were implemented with attacking intent. Sacchi wanted to have men in front of the ball when it was won, so they could exploit opponents on the transition. A tenet of Saachi's approach was that all 11 players should always be in an active position, with or without a ball.

According to journalist Gabriel Marcotti, the combination of a flat back four, zonal marking, a high defensive line and pressing made Arrigo Sacchi the last true tactical innovator in European football before Pep Guardiola got his hands on Barcelona.

After Van Basten's injury the formation evolved from a 4-3-3 to a 4-4-2. Gullit had been playing as part of the front three on the right but the reigning European Footballer of the Year was moved inside to play as a second striker. Against defending champions and league leaders Napoli on 3 January 1988, Gullit put in a virtuoso performance as part of a 4-1 victory, scoring one and assisting another. The result was vital in pegging back Maradona and Careca's Neopolitans, who would have opened up a seven-point cushion had they won in the San Siro – in the days of two points per win that might have been insurmountable.

The return fixture at the San Paolo on 1 May 1988 was virtually a title decider. It certainly would have been had Napoli won as the Neopolitans led Milan by one point with three games remaining. Berlusconi wanted to impose a sex ban on his players for the final month of the season so they could be physically prepared and mentally ready to win the title. Gullit, the outspoken Amsterdammer who grew up in an environment where he could say exactly what he thought, told the club owner, 'I can't run with my balls full.'

Pietro Paolo Virdis, who had deputised for Van Basten for much of the season, opened the scoring for Milan. Maradona's equaliser was a beautiful free kick, one of those exquisitely placed efforts where the goalkeeper ends up haplessly wrapping themselves around a post while trying to claw it away.

With the game intriguingly poised at 1-1 with around quarter of an hour left, Gullit grabbed the bull by the horns and fed in a pinpoint cross for Virdis to score his and Milan's second. Then came a blistering one-man counter-attack where Gullit picked up the ball from Galli's throw-out and thundered down the pitch with it seemingly attached to his feet before gliding past the last defender and squaring for Van Basten to thump home into an empty net. It is probably safe to say that he had ignored Signor Berlusconi's advice. A last-minute consolation from Careca proved irrelevant and Milan drew their next game at home against Juventus but Napoli lost away to Fiorentina, sending the Scudetto north.

Napol's end-of-season collapse is the subject of much conjecture. The speculation is that too many Napoli fans had backed the club in the neighbourhood black market betting shops, the '*totonero*'. Alongside drug trafficking, gambling formed a vital part of the income of the Camorra (a mafiosa-like organisation in Campania) and they were said to be on the hook for approximately 200bn lira.

It's certainly true that Napoli failed to win any of their last five league fixtures and blew a four-point lead, but they did have a difficult run-in with games against Milan, Sampdoria, Juventus, Fiorentina and Verona. If true, it would certainly be ironic if the *totonero* that brought about Milan's downfall eight years previously resulted in them becoming champions in 1988.

After club football returned from its summer hiatus in 1988, Milan had acquired two European champions. Gullit and Van Basten scored the goals that allowed the Netherlands to win their first international trophy and not long after they were joined at the San Siro by a third, their countryman Frank Rijkaard, although his arrival in Milan had to compete for headlines with Inter signing Lothar Matthäus on the same day.

Berlusconi was desperate for Milan to perform well in the European Cup. Milan had won the tournament twice in the 1960s, becoming the first Italian side to do so in 1963, and he would be compared less favourably to other presidents should he not also take the Rossoneri to the summit of the European game. He was also uncharacteristically terrified.

Milan had a terrible recent record in Europe and hadn't been past the first round of the European Cup since 1969/70; they had been dumped out of other UEFA competitions recently by the underwhelming likes of Espanyol of Spain and Waregem of Belgium.

Speaking to *World Soccer*, Berlusconi summed up his thinking by saying, 'The European Cup has become a historical anachronism. It is economic nonsense that a club such as Milan might be eliminated in the first round. It is not modern thinking.'

Berlusconi had been particularly affronted by the pairing of Real Madrid and Napoli in the first round of the 1987/88 tournament. In the same draw, Lillestrøm of Norway got Linfield of Northern Ireland, and Shamrock Rovers of the Republic of Ireland met Omonia Nicosia of Cyprus. He might have had a point.

Fortunately for Silvio, Milan received a kind draw and in the opening round of the 1988/89 edition they were paired with Levski Sofia, the Bulgarian champions. Bulgarian clubs had performed well in the competition in the early 1980s with CSKA Sofia reaching a quarter-final and semi-final in consecutive seasons, and neighbours Levski knocking out Bundesliga champions VfB Stuttgart in 1984/85's first round. But this Levski side was a depleted force from the team that won the Bulgarian A League. Manager Vasil Metodiev had retired and leading scorer Nasko Sirakov, who had finished third in the European Golden Shoe standings, was transferred to Real Zaragoza. Sirakov would have been familiar to Italian audiences for his equalising goal against the Azzurri in the opening game of Mexico 86, where both national sides eventually exited at the round of 16.

Milan won 2-0 away from home in the first leg before Marco van Basten put on a show in the return leg at the San Siro, scoring four in a 7-2 aggregate victory. It would not be the last time Van Basten scored four times in a European match.

The next two ties saw the Milanese ride their luck. First they beat Red Star Belgrade on penalty kicks and Donadoni was especially fortunate. He had been knocked unconscious during a challenge and his airway had been blocked but a quick-thinking Red Star physio broke his jaw to no doubt save his life. Remarkably, Donadoni only missed three Serie A matches, coming back less than a month after his near-death experience to play in the Derby della Madonnina against a surging Inter who were top of the table. He was also instrumental in Milan's 1-0 aggregate victory over Otto Rehhagel's Werder Bremen in European Cup quarter-finals, buying a cheap penalty from Scottish referee Eddie Smith, which Van Basten converted.

This victory set up a mouth-watering semi-final between Milan and Real Madrid. It would be their first meeting for 25 years but history was against Sacchi's men as Madrid had won each of their previous three European Cup meetings – the inaugural semi-final in 1955/56, the final in 1958 and the quarter-final in 1963/64.

Real were in a golden period. They had won back-to-back UEFA Cups in the mid-1980s when that tournament was arguably more difficult to win because of the strength in depth of the competing teams. They had won their third of what would be five consecutive La Liga championships, powered by 'La Quinta del Buitre', a group of five homegrown players who graduated from the famed Madrid academy, La Fábrica – Emilio Butragueño, Sanchís, Rafael Martín Vázquez, Míchel and Miguel Pardeza. Importantly, their great rivals Barcelona were nowhere. They had just finished La Liga an unfathomable 23 points behind Real in the days of two points per win.

Some 95,000 vociferous fans were in attendance at the Bernabéu to witness the first leg, which was a robust contest. Real's German midfielder Bernd Schuster was setting the tone with his physicality but the sides looked evenly matched. Hugo Sanchez, the great Mexican forward, opened the scoring after an uncharacteristic lapse in concentration from Tassotti left him unmarked at a corner. Both sides had seemingly legitimate goals ruled out for offside. Gullit's effort from a Donadoni square ball where the Dutchman was three to four yards behind the Italian was particularly egregious but a draw was rescued thanks to a fine Van Basten diving header, in off the underside of the crossbar from about 16 yards out (well worth your time on YouTube). Tassotti provided the cross for some measure of redemption.

'We suffered, it wasn't an easy game,' said Baresi later. 'We could have fallen apart [after the disallowed goal], instead, we managed to play how we wanted. Back in the dressing rooms, we were all satisfied, if not with the result, with the performance.

'Of course, in the locker room, Sacchi told us that we hadn't achieved anything yet, but we were about to play a really tough second leg.'

The tie returned to Italy with Milan favourites, albeit not overwhelmingly. If Real had some reason for trepidation, it would have been that they had played four European games at the San Siro in the past decade – all against Inter – and drawn just one, with three defeats. It was not a happy hunting ground for them.

The night started in unusual fashion on the terraces. Referee Alexis Ponnet stopped the game after 90 seconds for the teams to pay tribute to the victims of the Hillsborough stadium disaster in England, which led to the deaths of 96 Liverpool supporters. First there was silence, then applause, and lastly a moving rendition of 'You'll Never Walk Alone' filled the San Siro night. If what was happening in the stands was surreal, what happened on the pitch was nigh on unexplainable.

Carlo Ancelotti uncorked a 30-yard screamer to give the Rossoneri the lead. Two beautifully worked crosses were met with headers from Rijkaard and Gullit and a shell-shocked Madrid went in at half-time trailing 3-0. The fourth goal was worth all the guilders Berlusconi had paid to assemble the team. Rijkaard fed Gullit, who then headed down for Van Basten to rifle the ball into the net. Donadoni put the exclamation point on affairs with another long-range shot for a goal, beating Paco Buyo at his near post. It was 5-0 with only 59 minutes on the clock – a rout.

Berlusconi apologised to his opposite number Ramón Mendoza for embarrassing Madrid and went into the Real dressing room to deliver this pep talk: 'Do not worry. We are proud of having beaten Real Madrid because it is the best football club in the world. You have a good fortune which we do not have and that is – that whether we win the European Cup or not – we shall never, ever be like you.'

Milan would need to win the European Cup against 1986 champions Steaua Bucharest in order to re-qualify for the tournament the next season and to have bragging rights in their own city. Rivals Internazionale had comfortably won the Scudetto with a record points total thanks to the goals of Aldo Serena, the all-round brilliance of Lothar Matthäus and a miserly defence featuring Walter Zenga, Giuseppe Bergomi, Andreas Brehme and Franco Baresi's older brother, Giuseppe.

The final was played in front of 97,000 fans at the Camp Nou. Never had a Barcelona crowd cheered on a team in all white as loudly. With travel from the Eastern Bloc severely restricted, the entire crowd was cheering on Milan, be they local or 'Milanesti'. Not only had Milan vanquished Real but they were taking on Steaua Bucharest who were persona non grata in the Catalan capital after beating Barcelona in the 1986 final – denying them their first European Cup.

Steaua had the wonderful playmaker Gheorghe Hagi, the Maradona of the Carpathians, but he struggled to have any influence on the game and was forced deeper and deeper by Milan's press in his attempts to possess the ball. Tassotti and Angelo Colombo were operating an incredibly effective high asymmetric press on the right-hand side to counter Steaua's preference for playing the ball out from the back through their left-back Nicolae Ungureanu.

The game as a contest was over quickly. By the time Gullit tapped into an unguarded net on 18 minutes Milan had already missed four or five good chances and Gullit himself had also struck the inside of the post. Van

Basten headed in a second from six yards out before
Gullit rifled a shot past Silviu Lung in the Steaua goal
from the edge of the area. To ensure there was no hint
of a comeback, Van Basten added a fourth a minute into
the second half. Milan could have easily by more but
they had all they wanted – the European Cup.

The players celebrated on the Camp Nou pitch,
lifting Sacchi into the air and posing for a team photo
with club president Berlusconi. The challenge now was
to defend the title.

Of the Italian sides to have won the European Cup,
only Milan's city rivals Inter had managed to claim back-
to-back titles, in 1964 and 1965. Inter won their first in
Vienna's Praterstadion (now known as the Ernst-Happel-
Stadion) by beating Real Madrid 3-1 and their second
against Benfica, 1-0 in the San Siro.

Come the end of an intense, shortened season, to
allow the Italian national team to prepare for the 1990
World Cup they were hosting, Milan would face Benfica
at the Praterstadion with footballing immortality on
the line. Retaining the trophy was a hallmark of being
a great side. Di Stefano's Real Madrid, Cruyff's Ajax,
Beckenbauer's Bayern, Paisley's Liverpool all won
multiple consecutive European Cups.

How the Rossoneri got to the final was quite the
achievement. They played almost the entire season
without Gullit, who missed 50 games and 283 days with

a knee injury. Rijkaard, who had begun life at Milan in defence before switching to a holding midfield role, was now required to take up the number eight shirt and fill Gullit's creative void.

Almost cruelly, UEFA's balls paired Milan and Real Madrid once more, this time in the round of 16. Less than six months after their 5-0 thumping Real were back at the San Siro and it was more of the same. Within 14 minutes Madrid were two down and manager John Toshack was replacing Schuster to bring on a sixth defender.

Van Basten crossed to Rijkaard for the opening goal on nine minutes, a powerful header that was reminiscent of Gullit's to win Euro 88. A few minutes later Rijkaard's pressing caught Martin Vazquez in possession and sent Van Basten through on goal. Buyo rushed out of his goal and scythed the Dutch striker down. The sanction was a penalty which Van Basten converted but in truth Real should have been down to ten men. That was pretty much the high point of Milan's European campaign until the final. Instead of kicking on and putting the tie out of reach, they allowed Madrid to escape from the San Siro only 2-0 down. The Spaniards won their home leg 1-0 but that was not enough to progress.

Next Milan would face Belgian champions KV Mechelen. Mechelen had pulled off a shock Cup Winners' Cup victory two years prior by beating Cruyff's

Ajax in the final. They were a workmanlike team with players that would later go on to be household names like goalkeeper Michel Preud'homme, Belgian international Leo Clijsters (father of tennis champion Kim), future Newcastle star Phillipe Albert and Marc Wilmots. But it was to everyone's surprise that after 180 minutes they were deadlocked with Milan 0-0 on aggregate. A scuffed free kick in injury time during the first half of extra time fell into the path of Tassotti to cross for Van Basten to tap in. Not for the last time in 1990 would Preud'homme be left rueing late extra-time goals.

Away goals were needed in the semi-final to get past Bayern Munich as Milan plumbed the depths of their squad to get past the German champions. Stefano Borgonovo, a striker, joined Milan in 1986 from Como but had spent three seasons out on loan before becoming a squad player for the 1989/90 campaign, scoring twice in 13 league appearances. Borgonovo won a questionable penalty late in the first leg, which Van Basten converted, and ended up stabbing home the decisive away goal in Munich after a fortunate ricochet off Maldini bypassed the Bayern defence.

In the final they would be facing Sven-Göran Eriksson's Benfica side but first they had the Scudetto to wrap up. After starting the season with four losses in their first ten games, including to unfancied Ascoli and Cremonese, Milan had gone 17 games unbeaten, winning an improbable 15 of those to lead the league but lately their form had dipped with losses to Juventus away and Napoli at home meaning the title hung in the balance with two games remaining.

On matchday 33, Sunday, 22 April, Napoli raced into a three-goal lead in Bologna, piling pressure on Milan who needed to better their rivals' results over the final two games. With their match in Verona level at 1-1 going into the last half-hour, Milan lost their heads, starting with Sacchi who managed to get dismissed from the touchline and needed police riot shields to protect him from the hometown reaction. Rijkaard and Van Basten followed their coach down the tunnel for early baths and when Verona scored with a minute to go, Costacurta joined them for labelling referee Rosario Lo Bello a 'cheat'. The only bright spot on the day for Milan was that Gullit was back, playing for almost 35 minutes as a substitute.

The final was 'a poor game', Eriksson reflected years later. 'Milan was not at their best and we didn't have the strikers to break down the defenders of Milan. I had a Brazilian one [Valdo] and a Swedish one [Mats Magnusson] but we were not quick enough to get in behind them. We defended very well and they only had one chance to score, but they scored, which was a pity.'

That goal came from Frank Rijkaard via an intelligent Van Basten movement and through ball. Rijkaard was surging into the space Van Basten had just vacated and he cooly finished past the keeper. Sacchi later said they practised the move in training around 30 times.

Gullit had managed to play the 90 minutes but he was not fully fit and was a diminished force compared to the year prior. The two Dutchmen would fall out the next month with Rijkaard thinking he had done enough given Gullit's fitness to wrestle the creative midfield role from him for the national team at the 1990 World Cup. Coach Leo Beenhakker disagreed and Rijkaard was deployed more defensively in a forgettable campaign only remembered for Rijkaard's spat with Rudi Völler of West Germany in the round of 16.

The next year was frustrating for Milan as they finish runners-up to Sampdoria in the league and lost to Olympique Marseille in the quarter-finals of the European Cup, and for the first time since 1986 a non-AC Milan player won the Ballon d'Or – the trophy didn't have far to travel though, as it was won by Matthäus at Inter.

Since Rijkaard's arrival in 1988 the team had been largely settled, with the only major change being Sebastiano Rossi replacing Giovanni Galli in goal. Even if Sacchi didn't tire of his players, at least some of them tired of him. The constant sessions without the ball, relentless focus on fitness and repetition of predetermined movements became harder to embrace when the rewards were fewer.

Costacurta, a stalwart of 20-plus seasons in the red and black, labelled Sacchi 'a crazy freak', a term he insists is loaded with affection. The legendary defender explained: 'it was difficult to accept the heaviness of his training; we didn't understand if he was a genius or a fool.'

At the end of the 1991 season, Van Basten went to Berlusconi and told the president he would have to pick between him or Sacchi. For the first time Berlusconi gave in to player power but officially put Sacchi on a sabbatical rather than release him to be free to ply his trade for a rival. The president wanted to ease Sacchi into the Azzurri job, where he could bring prestige to the national team without affecting the Rossoneri's prospects.

Long-time midfield allies Ancelotti and Donadoni, who have both since managed at the highest levels, concur – Sacchi changed Italian football.

'Sacchi started a revolution in Italian football at mental and tactical level,' said Donadoni. 'We had our style of playing and we were trying to impose it on all opponents.'

Ancelotti agreed: 'Arrigo completely changed Italian football – the philosophy, the training methods, the intensity, the tactics. Italian teams used to focus on defending – we defended by attacking and pressing.'

In Sacchi's place, long-time Milan assistant coach Fabio Capello was appointed but even Capello acknowledged that he changed very little for the 1991/92 season. It was Sacchi's players and system, freed from the tyranny of his management, and the results were glorious.

Milan won the league without losing a single game, becoming the first Italian side to do so. In the process they scored 74 goals and had a goal difference of +53, with Van Basten accounting for 25 of those goals. Most importantly they were back where they felt they belonged by representing Italy in the European Cup.

Luck of the Draw

THE SUMMER of 1992 was another significant milestone in the liberalisation of European football. Not only did the Premier League in England start but the limit of having more than three foreigners in a squad was removed by the Italian Football Federation.

Teams would still be limited to three foreigners on the pitch at any given time in accordance with UEFA regulations but this meant that the richest clubs like Milan could afford to stockpile insurance policies for their star players like Gullit, whose absence had keenly been felt when he missed almost a whole season with a knee injury.

The big spenders in the Premier League were Blackburn Rovers who spent a combined £7.3m on Alan Shearer, Graeme Le Saux, Stuart Ripley, Kevin Gallacher and Henning Berg – five players who would be stalwarts of their eventual Premier League title win in 1994/95. Shearer's £3.6m fee was a British record.

Italian clubs signed 13 players in the summer of 1992 for fees in excess of that figure: Sinisa Mihajlović to Roma, Brian Laudrup to Fiorentina, Paul Gascoigne to Lazio, Darko Pančev, Igor Shalimov, Mattias Sammer and Ruben Sosa to Inter, Gianluca Vialli and David Platt to Juventus and Jean-Pierre Papin, Gianluigi Lentini and Dejan Savićević to Milan.

The focus on attacking players to unlock defences was made even more imperative because this season more goals were expected. FIFA and the International Board had introduced a new rule preventing goalkeepers from handling a ball that was deliberately kicked to them by one of their own defenders.

To emphasise this new focus on attacking, the world transfer record was broken three times in two months. First, Milan signed Papin from Olympique Marseille for £10m, eclipsing the £8m Juventus paid for Roberto Baggio after Italia 90. Papin was Marseille's key striker and had a superb European record having been the top scorer in the European Cup for the previous three seasons. He was also the reigning Ballon d'Or holder and was not a bad backup to Marco Van Basten.

Juventus one-upped them by signing Vialli from Sampdoria for £12.5m, while Milan retaliated by signing Lentini from Torino for £13m. Lentini was an attacking winger from the future, combining pace, trickery, shooting and heading ability. He was the main creative force in the

Torino team that lost the 1992 UEFA Cup Final to Ajax but the 'Papa' was not a fan. Pope John Paul II called the transfer fee 'an offence against the dignity of work'.

Modern Champions League draws are lavish, televised affairs hosted in the auditorium of UEFA's shiny Nyon headquarters in Switzerland. Multilingual hosts have stilted banter with the audience of club representatives who have flown in on private jets. Glossy video packages extolling the virtues of the host city are produced and famous former players are presented as ambassadors for the final and to assist with the drawing of the balls. They have become an ever more complex process with various seeding pots, coefficients, prohibited country pairings and adverse weather provisions.

Back in July 1992, it was a much simpler affair with 32 balls, one bowl and two UEFA men in suits – one to pick the ball, the other to verify and read it out. The unseeded draw offered romance and peril in equal measure.

While many assume this was always the way of the European Cup era, it should be noted that the very first tournament back in 1955/56 *L'Équipe* didn't even go to the extent of having a draw but instead produced a predetermined seeded bracket. It conveniently placed Real Madrid and AC Milan, the two sides that Hanot had suggested were stronger than Wolverhampton Wanderers, in the opposite side of the bracket to French champions Reims.

The 1992/93 draw had a very unfamiliar feel, not least that teams were now not just competing for the glory of winning the European Cup but they wanted to nab a spot in the lucrative Champions League group stages.

Over the previous ten seasons, clubs representing 24 different countries had reached the quarter-final stages of the European Cup (Austria, Belgium, Belarus, Bulgaria, Czechoslovakia, Denmark, East Germany, England, Finland, France, Greece, Italy, the Netherlands, Poland, Portugal, Romania, Russia, Scotland, Spain, Sweden, Turkey, Ukraine, West Germany and Yugoslavia). Extending the qualifying period back into the 1970s would add multiple quarter-final appearances for clubs from Croatia, Hungary and Switzerland too. In 1992/93, for the second successive season there was no traditional quarter-final round and instead it was replaced by the group stage – renamed as the Champions League. This led to the promise of shared television revenue and bolstered gate receipts and going on recent history at least 75 per cent of the field could feel relatively optimistic about making the Champions League stages.

However, importantly for the drama of the competition, none of the biggest teams could feel entirely comfortable that they would indeed reach the last eight. Italian clubs had made the quarter-finals eight times in the previous decade but considering Italy had 13 entrants to those ten competitions on account of winning three editions of the tournament that's still a 38 per cent failure rate, or 33 per cent if you excuse Juventus knocking out Hellas Verona in the 1985/86 second round.

The best performing leagues on this metric would be the Bundesliga, La Liga and the Soviet Top League with 70 per cent of the nations' European Cup entrants in the previous decade reaching the quarter-finals.

In contrast, between 2011 and 2020 only ten countries were represented in the Champions League quarter-finals. Spain alone provided 25 of the 80 quarter-finalists in this period, only having fewer than two in one of the ten most recent seasons (2018/19). The big five European leagues (England, France, Germany, Italy and Spain) combined to account for 89 per cent of the quarter-finalists. In the ten years prior to 1992/93 that figure was 39 per cent. Just nine quarter-final spots over a decade were claimed by the rest of Europe – Portugal (four times), Cyprus, Netherlands, Turkey and Ukraine once each.

Many of the tent poles that made the European Cup recognisable were missing in 1992/93. Yugoslavia's exclusion from international sport meant that there was no Red Star Belgrade, depriving the contest of the allure of its second most recent winner. Additionally, there was no Soviet team to appear next to a hammer and sickle flag icon for the first time since 1966 and no East German side for the first time since 1956.

Even though the Berlin Wall came down in November 1989 and the reunification of Germany became official in October 1990 this was the first tournament without representation from East Germany. The DDR lived on through Hansa Rostock as the Oberliga was allowed to complete its 1990/91 season. Rostock won their first and East Germany's last championship and had the surreal experience of representing a country that no longer existed in the 1991/92 European Cup. Fortunately for them, Johan Cruyff's 1991/92 Barcelona team weren't sufficiently stymied by the logical fallacy and they managed to beat Rostock in the first round. That was the last the eastern part of Germany would have to do with the Champions League until Red Bull Leipzig became somewhat unwelcome guests in 2017/18.

According to the Elo rating system, Milan were the best side in the 1992/93 competition and the continent with defending champions Barcelona standing a close second in the cup and third across the continent. In a further tier of viable contenders, English champions Leeds United were ranked 11th by Elo, Olympique Marseille were 13th, Porto 14th, PSV Eindhoven 15th and VfB Stuttgart 16th. Had they been allowed to compete, Red Star Belgrade were 21st in Elo and would have been the eighth-highest ranked side in the first Champions League.

The first ball drawn out for the first round in 1992 was AC Milan. The Italian champions were returning to the European Cup under Fabio Capello's stewardship after taking a year's hiatus and they were drawn against the winner of a qualifying round match – that would prove to be Olimpija Ljubljana.

The next balls paired Polish champions Lech Poznań with Skonto Riga while 1988 European Cup winners PSV Eindhoven were paired with Lithuania's Zalgiris Vilnius. Then Barcelona, the reigning European and Spanish champions, were invited to play Viking, the Norweigan champions from Stavanger.

When match 14 was pulled from the bowl as IFK Gothenburg of Sweden versus Turkish champions Beşiktaş, had there been an audience in that auditorium it would have been murmuring, perhaps even going as far as to be abuzz. The four remaining clubs yet to be drawn were the champions of England, France, Germany and Northern Ireland – Leeds United, Olympique Marseille, VfB Stuttgart and Glentoran respectively.

It was exactly the situation that clubs and the broadcasters feared. Leeds, Marseille and Stuttgart would have been pencilled in for the Champions League stage at the start of the campaign, alongside Barcelona, Milan, Porto and PSV. Whatever happened next, one of the favourites for the title and biggest TV markets for the competition would be losing its champion in the first round.

Glentoran were next out and the East Belfast side would be at home in the first leg against Marseille, although the wait for that name to be confirmed would have felt a lot longer than just a few seconds.

Marseille, for whom the adjective enigmatic might very well have been coined, were perhaps due a bit of luck. They had lost the 1991 European Cup on penalties, a year previously the Phocaeans were denied at the semi-final stage by an obvious handball goal which allowed Benfica to reach the final on away goals, and famously no French side had ever won Gabriel Hanot's tournament.

That left Stuttgart and Leeds to be paired in the final tie. Between 1974 and '84 the European Cup was the exclusive possession of English and West German sides and four of those 11 finals featured both English and German representation. Now one of them would be out of Europe before the clocks went back.

This was a scenario that Leeds manager Howard Wilkinson envisaged. As a pundit for the BBC's 1992 European Cup Final coverage, Des Lynam had asked him how much he was looking forward to playing in the 1992/93 tournament. Wilkinson prophetically said, 'Initially it's a magnificent feeling to be alongside some of the names that will be in the hat, and then when the draw comes out maybe it's not such a tremendous feeling.'

The full draw for the first round was:
- AC Milan (Italy) vs Olimpija Ljubljana (Slovenia)
- Lech Poznań (Poland) vs Skonto Riga (Latvia)
- PSV Eindhoven (Netherlands) vs FK Žalgiris (Lithuania)
- FC Barcelona (Spain, holders) vs Viking (Norway)
- Rangers (Scotland) vs Lyngby (Denmark)
- Slovan Bratislava (Czechoslovakia) vs Ferencváros (Hungary)
- Kuusysi (Finland) vs Dinamo Bucharest (Romania)
- Maccabi Tel Aviv (Israel) vs Club Brugge (Belgium)
- Austria Vienna (Austria) vs CSKA Sofia (Bulgaria)
- Sion (Switzerland) vs Tavriya Simferopol (Ukraine)
- Union Luxembourg (Luxembourg) vs Porto (Portugal)
- AEK Athens (Greece) vs APOEL (Cyprus)
- Víkingur (Iceland) vs CSKA Moscow (Russia)
- IFK Gothenburg (Sweden) vs Beşiktaş (Turkey)
- Glentoran (Northern Ireland) vs Olympique Marseille (France)
- VfB Stuttgart (Germany) vs Leeds United (England)

According to the statisticians, some of the pairings were spectacularly uneven. In nine of the 16 ties one side had a greater than 90 per cent chance of progressing: Lech Poznań, Dinamo Bucharest, Club Brugge, AEK Athens, AC Milan, CSKA Moscow, Porto, Olympique Marseille and Barcelona. In fact, the probability of CSKA, Porto and Marseille going through was greater than 99 in 100, while the odds of Viking upsetting Barcelona were calculated at one in 1,000.

The least predictable ties were Stuttgart vs Leeds (who had a 50.4 per cent chance of progressing), Austria Vienna (56.7 per cent) vs CSKA Sofia and Rangers (58.3 per cent) vs Lyngby.

The European Cup wasn't the only show in town this season for fans looking for top-class European football on their televisions. In the south-west of Spain, Sevilla were putting on a host of glamorous international friendlies to mark and monetise the signing of Diego Maradona.

After his drugs ban and falling out with Napoli, Maradona had wanted to go home to Argentina and play for Boca Juniors once more but Boca couldn't afford the transfer fee. Marseille, who he nearly joined in 1989, did have the funds but they also had concerns about his fitness.

Sevilla emerged as contenders because they were managed by Carlos Bilardo, who coached Argentina when Maradona lifted the 1986 World Cup. The only snag was Sevilla couldn't justify the $4.5m demanded by Napoli, and that's when Silvio Berlusconi stepped in. Berlusconi gave Sevilla the money to buy Maradona on the condition that they would play a series of high-profile friendlies and Berlusconi would be given the broadcast rights.

Beginning with a game against the German giants Bayern Munich, who had not qualified for Europe that season, Sevilla and Berlusconi made use of midweeks normally reserved for European competitions to offer counter-programming to official UEFA matches. Further games against Porto, Paul Gascoigne's Lazio and a homecoming against Boca Juniors were arranged. If Berlusconi could make money from friendly matches, no wonder he wanted to expand the Champions League.

All 16 first legs of the first-round ties were played on the same day – Wednesday, 16 September – with kick-off times staggered according to the host club's preference. The majority of the UEFA Cup and Cup Winners' Cup first-round matches were also played on that Wednesday evening, which meant that for English viewers who had just seen top-flight football disappear from terrestrial television there was a direct head to head between Leeds's game against Stuttgart on ITV (Brian Moore and Ron Atkinson) and Liverpool's Cup Winners' Cup tie against Apollon Limassol of Cyprus on BBC1 (John Motson and Trevor Brooking). Fans of Sheffield Wednesday, who wanted to see their match against Spora Luxembourg, and their 38-year-old Trevor Francis player-manager give himself a debut in the UEFA Cup, had to buy a ticket.

If you were watching on BBC not only did you see the rare sight of Paul Stewart, Liverpool's new £2.3m signing, scoring – he would only score one other goal in four years at the Reds – but you saw barely 12,000 people rattling around Anfield in an atmosphere that could be best described as hospitable. This was not the atmosphere awaiting APOEL Nicosia fans as they took the trip across the Mediterranean to face AEK Athens in the Champions League.

Some 28,000 fans had packed into the Nikos Goumas Stadium in Athens for the encounter. For context that's 8,000 more than attended the AEK-Olympiacos derby that season. Olympiacos were and still are the most successful side domestically but Panathinaikos had historically been Greece's most successful team in Europe. Managed by three-time European Cup winner Ferenc Puskás, they had lost the 1971 European Cup Final to Cruyff's Ajax and got to the semi-finals in 1985, losing to Liverpool.

AEK were the third-biggest team in Greece as measured by titles and support but had some European pedigree themselves. In 1976/77 they had knocked out Dinamo Moscow, Derby County, Red Star Belgrade and Queens Park Rangers on penalties en route to the UEFA Cup semi-final. More encouragingly, Panathinaikos had been in the 1991/92 group stage, making them one of the last eight sides in the European Cup.

At the time Cypriot teams were seen as first-round fodder in European competitions. The national team had only ever won two competitive games (vs Switzerland in qualification for Euro 68 and versus Northern Ireland in qualification for the 1974 World Cup in West Germany). In qualification for Euro 92 the Cypriot national team played eight and lost eight – even the Faroes beat them.

In club play their record was somewhat better with Cypriot teams advancing to the second round of the European Cup six times, almost always at the expense of a fellow minnow from nations such as Ireland, Malta or Luxembourg. However, if looking closely you could see signs for optimism. In 1986/87, an APOEL side that included former European Cup winner Terry McDermott beat Helsinki JK to make the second round and in 1991/92 Apollon defeated Universitatea Craiova of Romania to reach the same stage. It was the first time that a Cypriot side had beaten a team from a significant footballing nation.

This was the first continental meeting between AEK and APOEL but curiously not the first competitive game between them. From 1967–74, when Greece was run by a military dictatorship, the Greek Alpha Ethniki (A League) operated on a Panhellenic basis and the previous season's Cypriot champions were invited to take part.

Sadly for the junta and the Cypriots also, their champions spent almost the entire period propping up the table, until the 1973/74 season when APOEL earned the right to represent Cyprus in the league. APOEL caused a few red faces in Greek football by finishing 13th – becoming the first Cypriot team to avoid relegation, doing so thanks to a 3-1 last-day victory against AEK. However, in the summer following the Turkish invasion of northern Cyprus the Greek junta fell, making way for the re-establishment of democracy, and with Panhellenism being viewed negatively from its military associations the two countries untangled their football leagues.

To add to the familiarity, in charge of APOEL was Polish coach Jacek Gmoch, who led Panathinaikos to that 1985 European Cup semi-final and had also been AEK manager for a spell.

Whatever Gmoch said to APOEL worked as they flew out of the traps. Perhaps he reminded them of Greece's snub to Cyprus in that year's Eurovision Song Contest. Greece only awarded the Cypriot entry ten points, favouring Linda Martin's Irish entry 'Why Me?'

Yiannos Ioannou, APOEL's all-time leading scorer with 264 goals in 504 appearances, should have put them ahead early on, and only a desperate block prevented him from doing so. From there AEK grew in confidence but found Andros Petridis in goal in inspired form, and when it wasn't Petridis stopping AEK it was the post. This was the type of goalpost that you don't see anymore, with a black band at its base, which evokes such strong memories of the 1978 World Cup in Argentina. Years later it emerged that those Argentinian posts were a quiet symbol of resistance to their own military junta – they were painted black to represent a black armband for all the Argentines who disappeared.

Eventually, AEK did go ahead. Toni Savevski, their Macedonian midfielder, unleashed a long-range shot that Petridis beat away only to see the rebound bicycle-kicked into the net by Alexis Alexandris. Cue the flares that Greek football is famous for – appropriately yellow to match AEK's colours. But they wouldn't be able to take a lead to Cyprus as a gorgeous bit of skill by Loukas Hadjiloukas wrong-footed the whole AEK defence and he calmly bent the ball past Antonis Minou in the AEK goal, to the joy of a sizeable travelling support.

Excluding two ties against Maltese and Irish teams, it was the first time a Cypriot team had not trailed after the away leg of a European Cup tie.

The return leg followed the same pattern of the first encounter with APOEL starting brightly. Andreas Sotiriou hit the post when one-on-one with the goalkeeper then AEK took the initiative when Refik Šabanadžović, their Yugoslav defensive midfielder, found the top corner with a left-footed half-volley from all of 25 yards out. Šabanadžović was by far the most credentialled player on the pitch. He had started four games for Yugoslavia at the 1990 World Cup, although his sending off in the quarter-final may have cost his national side a place in the last four, and had won the 1991 European Cup with Red Star Belgrade.

As APOEL chased the game to find the goal they needed, Alexandris pounced on a mistake and scored for AEK for the second consecutive game. Now APOEL needed three goals to go through. They got one from a hopeful long hoof that was allowed to bounce in the penalty area, Siniša Gogić heading home, and added a second from substitute Kostas Fasouliotis, who oddly wore the number 13 shirt as an outfielder. Fasouliotis then performed the trademark move of David Platt at the time by running into the net to retrieve the ball and sprinting to the centre spot with it under his arm. APOEL had five minutes left to make history, but it wasn't to be and they suffered a valiant defeat on away goals.

APOEL might not have made their name in the first Champions League but eventually they would provide the biggest underdog story of the new era when they reached the quarter-finals in 2011/12. If it was difficult for Cypriot teams to make the latter stages in the European Cup it was supposed to be impossible in the Champions League. In the mid-1990s the Cypriot champions weren't even allowed to compete in a qualifying round for entry into the Champions League group stages. When that indefensible position was reversed in 1997/98, it took some time for the Cypriots to reacclimatise to top-level competition. APOEL made the final qualifying round in 2002/03 where they once again lost out over two legs to AEK Athens. In 2008/09 Anorthosis Famagusta beat Pyunik of Armenia, Rapid Vienna and Greek champions Olympiacos to become the first Cypriot side to qualify for the Champions League group stage. Anorthosis may have finished bottom of the group but they gave a strong account of themselves, gaining six points from their six games. Their highlights were a famous 3-0 victory over Panathinaikos, and three draws with Inter Milan and Werder Bremen. They stood a real chance of qualifying for the knockout stages up until the final matchday.

Three years later APOEL went one better, beating Slovan Bratislava and Wisła Kraków to reach the group stages and then topping their group that featured Porto, Shakhtar and Zenit St Petersburg. The fairytale continued after Christmas when APOEL beat Lyon on penalties after trading two 1-0 scorelines over the two legs, before they finally succumbed to the might of Real Madrid in the quarters.

AEK Athens would go on to meet the winners of the PSV Eindhoven vs FK Žalgiris fixture, which was won as expected by the Dutch champions and 1988

European Cup winners. Despite missing Brazilian forward Romário for the home leg, PSV still ran out 6-0 winners. Ronald Koeman's brother Erwin opened the scoring before left-winger Juul Ellerman helped himself to a hat-trick. The goal of the tie came from Arthur Numan, the future Rangers left-back, whose long-range swerving shot made it six. Numan would repeat the trick in the second leg in Vilnius before Romário, back from injury, made it 8-0 on aggregate.

Milan threatened to rout Olimpija Ljubljana, going 2-0 up inside seven minutes. Eventually, they settled for a 7-0 aggregate score with Van Basten (two), Albertini, Papin, Massaro, Rijkaard and Tassotti getting on the scoresheet. Albertini's goal is worth seeking out. It's a sweetly hit 25-yard volley on a ball dropping from a great height, not dissimilar to Paul Scholes's famous volley against Aston Villa in 2006. Albertini's wasn't as powerfully struck but the control and the technique were there.

Ljubljana, alongside all the other qualifying round survivors, would exit the competition in this first round proper. Maccabi Tel Aviv lost 4-0 on aggregate to Club Brugge, while Skonto Riga went down 2-0 to Lech Poznań but gained a creditable 0-0 draw at home in the second leg. Shelbourne's conquerors, Tavriya Simferopol, were drawn against FC Sion. Sion had won the Swiss title for the first time in their history in 1991/92 but all that did was put their best players in the shop window for other clubs. Sion's three top scorers and their manager Enzo Trossero all left in the summer of 1992. Yugoslav Mirsad Baljić went to FC Zürich, homegrown striker Giuseppe Manfreda moved to Neuchâtel Xamax and 1990 World Cup finalist Gabriel Calderón returned to France. They needed reinforcements and went looking in Brazil. In 1992, there were Brazilians playing European club football but outside of Portugal it was almost exclusively internationals with significant pedigree playing at top clubs, such as Romário at PSV, Careca at Napoli and Carlos Mozer at Marseille. Examples of lesser luminaries such as Mirandinha, the first Brazilian to play in England with Newcastle, were fewer and further between.

Countries as big and as football-mad as Brazil had an abundance of talent that was not likely to win international caps but could still do a job for European club sides, often at a discount compared to local players. Switzerland had much more lax work permit regulations than most of the rest of Europe at the time and its clubs were able to offer contracts to players who weren't regulars for their national sides. This was something that AC Milan cottoned on to when they signed Giovane Elber in 1991 and almost immediately loaned him to Grasshoppers of Zürich in the hope he could develop and eventually become a Rossoneri player. Elber never got a chance in Milan but in 2001 he did help Bayern to win the Champions League.

In 2020, 824 Brazilian players played professionally in Europe. Sion had been at the forefront of that innovation when they signed four Brazilians during the summer of 1992. They found a striker at the unfashionable Goiás Esporte Clube named Túlio, who had been brought to Goiás by a young Luis Felipe Scolari. He was the top scorer in the 1989 Campeonato Brasileiro, had once been capped by the Seleção and cost Sion almost £1m. With him Sion brought three of his compatriots for company – Marcio Orvela, Luis Carlos and Roberto Assis – who would later be better known as Ronaldinho's older brother/agent.

Two goals from Túlio, one from Assis and a further from future Newcastle and Everton right-back Marc Hottiger gave Sion a 4-1 first-leg advantage. In Crimea, Túlio would again bag a brace en route to a straightforward 7-2 aggregate score. Sion's Brazilian investment was paying off.

The move also worked out well for Túlio, who would use his time in Switzerland and goalscoring exploits to garner a move to Botafogo where he would top-score twice in the Campeonato Brasileiro, and win the 1995 championship. His domestic form earned him the Brazilian number nine shirt during the 1995 Copa América, partly because Romário and national coach

Mário Zagallo had one of their regular disagreements. The only downside for Sion was the attendance. A modest crowd of 5,500 poured into Stade Tourbillon, when the stadium's capacity was 15,000 and Super League matches averaged nearly double the gate Tavriya drew. But they were by no means the only club to struggle to sell out in the first round.

Only 14,000 saw Milan's first-leg victory over Ljubljana, less than 20 per cent of the San Siro's 1992 capacity. Austria Vienna clearly hoped for a bumper crowd when switching their tie from their 10,000-capacity Franz-Horr-Stadion to the 50,000-capacity Ernst-Happel-Stadion, which had hosted the 1987 and 1990 European Cup finals. The 7,000 paying punters through the turnstiles would have been a disappointment for the club but at least the players delivered on the pitch, winning 3-1 against CSKA Sofia with future Southampton manager Ralph Hasenhüttl scoring an impressive goal.

One club with no trouble in the attendance stakes was Glasgow Rangers, who sold over 40,000 tickets for the visit of Danish Champions Lyngby. Rangers had a proud European heritage. In the European Cup they made the semi-finals in 1959/60 and reached the quarter-finals on four other occasions, while they were three times finalists of the Cup Winners' Cup, winning once. That victory did come with a two-year ban (reduced to one on appeal) from UEFA competitions for a pitch invasion by their fans before the final whistle was blown.

Rangers had just won their fourth of nine consecutive Scottish league championships in 1992, but their previous three seasons in the European Cup had been abject. A first-round elimination to Bayern Munich had been followed a second-round exit to Red Star Belgrade (after playing Valletta of Malta in round one) and going out in the 1991/92 first round to Sparta Prague.

Perhaps, the Ibrox faithful were understandably concerned that if they missed the Lyngby game there wouldn't be another European match for them to go and see. This was long before the days of play-off round losers or third-placed group stage finishers dropping into the Europa League. Indeed it was long before the Europa League. They need not have been worried though. Despite their performance being described by *The Independent* as 'less than convincing', Mark Hateley and Peter Huistra gave them a 2-0 lead that they were able to defend in Denmark. Better European nights awaited Ibrox.

As an unfashionable champion, Lyngby, who won the Danish Superliga for only the second time in their history, had suffered the same fate as Sion with Europe's more glamorous clubs picking off their best players. This was only exacerbated by Denmark winning Euro 92. The majority of the Danish-based players had new overseas clubs by the time they reported for pre-season training. Three of the four squad members Lyngby provided the national team had departed for Borussia Mönchengladbach, Olympique Lyon and Pisa.

Could the Norweigan or Swedish champions fare better than their Scandinavian cousins? Both Viking and IFK Gothenburg were underdogs – Viking had a one in 1,000 chance of beating the reigning champions Barcelona, whereas IFK's odds were somewhat better, given about a 25 per cent chance against the Turkish champions Beşiktaş.

Turkey were on a footballing journey from their nadir of two separate 8-0 defeats at the hands of England in the 1980s to finishing third at the 2002 World Cup. In club football they were improving too. Beşiktaş had reached the quarter-finals in 1986/87 and Galatasaray had gone one better in making the semi-finals in 1988/89 with an impressive victory over Arsène Wenger's Monaco side containing Glenn Hoddle and George Weah.

For one of the IFK team, Jonas Olsson, the game against Beşiktaş was extra special as it was his first match in two and half years, because of a tumour in his foot.

He later said, 'Fortunately, it was a benign tumour. After many months of waiting, it was decided that it had to be operated on. Roger [Gustafsson] gave me the opportunity to be part of the fight back and I made a comeback in the first match against Beşiktaş. It was an incredible feeling to be able to play again.'

Olsson, a reliable defender, came on as a 52nd-minute substitute to replace centre-half Ola Svensson, but he could have been called upon sooner had the referee sent off Svensson for grabbing a handful of Mehmet Özdilek's shirt as he was through on goal. Think Ronald Koeman on David Platt that night in Rotterdam but without the added ignominy of Graham Taylor muttering to the linesman that 'his friend' had cost him his job.

If there had been any muttering from the Beşiktaş bench it would have been in a lilting Lancastarian accent as they were being managed by former Coventry and Leicester boss Gordon Milne. Milne had no worries for his job; he had guided the Black Eagles to three consecutive Turkish league titles with their most recent claimed without defeat.

IFK left-back Tore Pedersen was lucky not to give away a penalty before Olsson's fellow substitute Kaj Eskelinen opened the scoring with a delightfully struck half-volley from the edge of the box. In the last ten minutes the former Empoli and Bayern Munich striker Johnny Ekström gave IFK a rather undeserved two-goal advantage to take to the banks of the Bosphorus.

The old İnönü Stadium on the European side of Istanbul was an undeniably beautiful venue. Situated in the Dolmabahçe area of the city, it was a classic European bowl-like ground with a running track, but what made it special was the views from the top rows of the Yeni Açık Stand. The Dolmabahçe Palace, Dolmabahçe Clock Tower and the Bosphorus were all visible, making it the only stadium in the world from which a football fan could view two continents in Europe and Asia.

Olsson remembers the match in Istanbul: 'There was a magical atmosphere in the arena. It was packed several hours before the match and the referee had to postpone the match for ten minutes due to all the smoke from fireworks and flares. The noise from Beşiktaş fans was extremely loud and deafening.'

Fortune again favoured IFK when after ten minutes a poor inswinging corner was met by even poorer defending. UEFA kindly credited Eskelinen with the goal but in truth it was Riza Çalimbay, the Beşiktaş captain and stalwart of 645 appearances across his career, who got the last touch in the goalmouth scramble. Owing to the away goals rule, Beşiktaş now needed to score four; the task was beyond them and their 31,400 sell-out crowd. They won the match 2-1 but exited the competition.

More heartache would follow that season for Milne with Galatasaray pipping his side to the Turkish league on goal difference, which some Beşiktaş fans look suspiciously on thanks to an 8-0 Galatasaray victory away at MKE Ankaragücü on the final day. It was a sliding doors moment as Galatasaray used that victory and their subsequent appearance in the 1993/94 Champions League group stage to propel themselves to a decade of dominance, winning seven league championships, the UEFA Cup in 2000 and making the Champions League quarter-finals in 2001 with home victories against Rangers, Monaco, Deportivo La Coruña, AC Milan, Paris St Germain and Real Madrid. Certainly, Alex Ferguson would have preferred a trip to see his old pal Gordon in November 1993 rather than the welcome he got from Galatasaray fans.

If the 3/1 shot from Sweden could win, how about the 1,000/1 shot from Norway taking on FC Barcelona? Barcelona had the 'Dream Team', a moniker applied to the reigning European champions with a wink and a nod to the other Dream Team, which had starred in the 1992 Summer Olympics held in the city. Michael Jordan, Larry Bird and Magic Johnson lit up the basketball court and played with an expressive, attacking style that was much too strong for their opposition.

Hristo Stoichkov, Michael Laudrup and Ronald Koeman were the Michael, Magic and Larry of Johan Cruyff's side. Stoichkov had announced himself to Barcelona fans with three goals for CSKA Sofia against Barcelona in the 1989 Cup Winners' Cup semi-final; Laudrup had rehabilitated his reputation at the Camp Nou, becoming one of the world's most admired forwards after disappointing as 'the next Platini' at Juventus, and Ronald Koeman was Cruyff's representative on the pitch. Koeman played under Cruyff at Ajax and was a believer in total football. As you might be if you score 239 career goals from defence or midfield.

The Dream Team emerged from Barcelona's lowest ebb. In 1986 the club had unexpectedly lost the 1986 European Cup Final on penalties to Romanian club Steaua Bucharest and two years later the players participated in what's known in Catalonia as the Hesperia Mutiny.

Barcelona were attempting to circumvent La Liga regulations around wages and would sometimes have two contracts with players; one for their football and one for their image rights. Spanish tax authorities were none too pleased to discover this and when the club suggested that the players themselves should make good with the authorities, neither were the players. Towards the end of the 1987/88 season the playing squad and coach Luis Aragonés issued a manifesto calling for the president of the club, Josep Lluís Núñez, to resign.

It read, 'President Josep Lluís Núñez has deceived us as people and humiliated us as professionals ... we've lost all confidence in the president. We feel totally cheated by the president. The president doesn't have any respect for the fans. He's always tried to buy us off and separate us. This historic club, with values that the Catalan people have always represented, has been dehumanised in this form.

'In conclusion, even though a petition for the [president's] resignation is the right of the club's members, the squad are suggesting said resignation.'

Núñez refused, but with club elections looming in the summer of 1988 he couldn't be certain of being president much longer. So he picked up the phone and dialled Amsterdam.

Johan Cruyff had been managing Ajax since 1985, and had won two Dutch Cups and the Cup Winners' Cup although the Eredivisie had escaped him. But Núñez wasn't especially interested in Cruyff the manager; he needed Cruyff the icon, the man who lifted Catalan spirits when he joined in 1973. Cruyff's first victory was a public relations coup when he let it be known he opted for Barcelona over Real Madrid because he didn't want to play for a club so closely linked to the fascist regime of Generalissimo Francisco Franco. Cruyff led Barcelona to their first title in 14 years, punctuated with an emphatic 5-0 victory in the Santiago Bernabéu. Naming his son Jordi (a Catalan name) didn't hurt his popularity either.

Bringing in Cruyff enabled Núñez to win the 1988 presidential election but the Hesperia Mutiny meant that almost the whole playing squad had to be turned over. Fourteen players left that summer and that suited Cruyff as he got to recruit for his system.

Not only was Cruyff one of the greatest and most skilful footballers to ever play the game, he was a significant thinker on the game of football and devotee of Rinus Michels's total football philosophy. Cruyff said, 'In my team, the goalie is the first attacker and the striker the first defender.'

He espoused a 3-4-3 formation with a midfield diamond that opened up passing channels to exploit space between opponents' flatter banks of defenders and midfielders. Key to his system was Koeman, who operated as the sweeper/*libero* in a three-man defence. Koeman not only had the ball-playing skills to act to keep possession but also instigate moves with direct balls to the wide forward players.

It's going too far to say that the Barcelona Dream Team was as dominant as their basketball equivalents, and they needed away goals to beat Kaiserslautern in the 1991/92 European Cup second round, with José María Bakero rising at the far post with a header with just 15 seconds left in normal time to prevent their elimination. In the group stage they lost to Sparta Prague and needed extra time to beat Sampdoria – but they did play beautiful football. Cruyff insisted on that.

It was Koeman who scored the only goal at Wembley during the 1992 European Cup Final, with an edge-of-the-area free kick that evaded three charging Sampdoria defenders to zip past Gianluca Pagliuca. Outside of

Madrid and Liguria, the football world was largely content to see Cruyff's Barcelona finally crowned champions of Europe and even more pleased when they covered their hideous light orange kit for the trophy presentations with traditional blue and garnet stripes.

Fast forward four months and they were beginning the defence of a trophy they had spent 32 years trying to acquire at home to Viking, the Norwegian champions from Stavanger.

Norwegian teams could only boast five European Cup match victories in the history of the competition. Three times these came against Linfield of Northern Ireland, one against fellow Nordic minnow Repias Lahti of Finland and Fredrikstad Fotballklubb had beaten Ajax, but that was way back in 1960, only a few years after Dutch football permitted professionalism and before Michels and Cruyff transformed the capital club.

Norway's best result in any European competition up until that time also featured Barcelona. Lyn of Oslo reached the quarter-final of the 1968/69 Cup Winners' Cup, beating the Turkish and Swedish entrants in a competition somewhat marred by five Eastern Bloc withdrawals due to the geopolitical situation following the Prague Spring in 1968.

Lyn's appearance in the quarter-finals posed a bit of a dilemma as pitches were typically unplayable in winter. The solution was that they would play their

home leg against Barcelona at the Camp Nou. Despite this disadvantage, Lyn managed a creditable 3-2 defeat in the first leg. The 'away' fixture was scheduled for nine days later, Saturday, 8 February 1969. They drew 2-2 and went out, but Barcelona needed late heroics from defender Gallego, who scored twice in the last 15 minutes to keep them in the competition.

However, to put this into its full context the greatest Norwegian triumph in European football was swiftly followed by its biggest embarrassment. The same Lyn side just seven months later lost to Leeds United 16-0 on aggregate with Leeds bagging ten in the first leg at Elland Road.

History wasn't the only thing lining up against Viking, as their recent form was woeful. Most sides competing in the European Cup have won their domestic league the previous spring, but as football in the Norwegian winter is a tricky prospect the Tippeligaen is contested from April to October meaning that the Viking side competing against Barcelona were a full year removed from their title. Results in the meantime hadn't been kind and with only four games of the Norwegian season remaining they were second from bottom and five points adrift of safety.

Nando, Koeman, Juan Carlos, Bakero, Julio Salinas and Stoichkov were rested from the team that had won the trophy at Wembley. It was not unreasonable for

Cruyff to make six changes given both Viking's form and La Liga's insistence on scheduling Barcelona to play away at Atlético Madrid on the following Friday evening, just 48 hours after their opening European Cup match. Whoever said Spanish authorities favour Madrid clubs over the Catalans? Certainly, Stoichkov seemed to benefit from the rest by scoring twice in the opening eight minutes as Barcelona won 4-1 away in the Vicente Calderón Stadium.

Cruyff's assessment of the worthiness of his opponents was shared by the sparse 35,000 crowd that made the Camp Nou seem empty, a full 62,500 shy of the previous week's league attendance against Real Madrid.

On the hour mark most of those who had bothered to part with their pesos were whistling to show their displeasure – the game was a slow 0-0 affair with the organised Viking side proving stubborn for Michael Laudrup and co. to break down. In fact, the side from Stavanger came closest to breaking the deadlock. Counter-attacks twice led to one-on-ones with Andoni Zubizarreta; Øyvind Mellemstrand, on the end of a lung-busting run from his normal right-back position blasted wide, while a young Egil Østenstad should have done better when slipped in.

Catalan blushes were spared in the 87th minute when all 5ft 88.5in of Guillermo Amor found himself unmarked on the penalty spot as he rose salmon-like to power a header past the otherwise excellent Lars Gaute Bø in the Viking goal.

Could Viking do the unthinkable? Perhaps they would go one step further than their fellow Scandinavians, Åtvidaberg, who as Swedish champions in 1973/74 took the eventual winners Bayern Munich to penalties in the first round. Bayern featured Franz Beckenbauer, Gerd Müller and Sepp Maier less than 12 months before they delivered the World Cup to West Germany. Bayern won the European Cup that year, after signing Conny Torstensson from Åtvidaberg, who had impressed against them. Torstensson scored four key goals for Munich in their quarter-final and semi-final ties to add to the two he scored against them in the first round. A classic case of 'if you can't beat 'em, join 'em'.

In between the two Barcelona-Viking legs was an international week and Norway beat the Netherlands 2-1 in Oslo, a victory which would eventually set up their qualification to USA 94 and condemn Graham Taylor to doing Yellow Pages commercials. Former Viking and current Tottenham Hotspur shot-stopper Erik Thorstvedt helped keep the Dutch to a solitary Dennis Bergkamp effort. Meanwhile, Ronald Koeman made the mistake of being caught in possession on the edge of his own penalty area to provide for the winning goal for Rosenborg's Goran Sorloth.

A week later, with Cruyff now taking no chances, Koeman would be asked to lead his club team back to Norway to try to hold on to a slender 1-0 advantage. Alongside Koeman, Juan Carlos, Stoichkov and Bakero were recalled to the starting line-up. Goals, however, were still at a premium. With the game still deadlocked at 0-0 and time running out Cruyff suddenly discovered a pragmatic streak, withdrawing Stoichkov in a defensive change. The 12,000 Viking fans packed in the Stavanger Stadion were in great voice, urging their team to find a goal in the final minutes, but they only had one chance of note, a free kick that was lofted into the penalty box and bounced around until it found the arms of Andoni Zubizarreta. Barcelona were through unconvincingly, narrowly avoiding being the first holders since Nottingham Forest lost to CSKA Sofia in 1980 to fall at the first hurdle of their European Cup defence.

The Old Enemy

PUB QUIZZERS will know that Howard Wilkinson is (at the time of writing) the last English manager to win the top flight when he won Leeds United's third First Division championship in 1992, the club's first title since the days of Don Revie. Since then four Italians, two Scots, a Portuguese, a German, a Chilean and a Spaniard have managed the various Premier League winners.

Born in Sheffield, Wilkinson spent time in the Sheffield United youth ranks before transferring to Steel City rivals Wednesday in 1962 where he struggled to crack the first team and made just 22 appearances during his four-year spell at Hillsborough. After failing to make the 1966 FA Cup Final side, Wilkinson transferred to Brighton & Hove Albion where he enjoyed more success, playing over 100 times for the south coast club. He ended his career at part-timers Boston United, where he juggled playing, managing and a job teaching – from which he earned his Sgt Wilko nickname (a nod to the Phil Silvers character Sergeant Bilko).

After managing Notts County, and then former club Wednesday to a respectable fifth-placed finish in the First Division, Sgt Wilko dropped down to the Second Division to take the Leeds job, also luring Gordon Strachan from Manchester United, Lee Chapman from Nottingham Forest and Vinnie Jones from Wimbledon to make the move with him. In 1990, Leeds won the Second Division and then remarkably finished fourth in their first top-division campaign since 1982.

Chairman Leslie Silver authorised some summer reinforcements to the squad with two £1m-plus deals. England international left-back Tony Dorigo joined from Chelsea and Rod Wallace, a speedy supporter striker arrived from Southampton – giving Leeds a classic big man, little man front partnership. Wallace would contribute 11 goals in the league and help Chapman get another 16. Meanwhile, Steve Hodge, another England international, joined for £900,000 and he added seven league goals from midfield, although in his book, *The Man with Maradona's Shirt*, Hodge claims Wilkinson didn't fancy him and just 12 starts across the campaign despite a fee of almost £1m would back up that theory.

In February, another £900,000 was spent on Eric Cantona, a man for whom the word 'mercurial' was surely invented. Two months earlier Cantona had retired from football. After he had thrown the ball at a referee, a French Football Federation disciplinary panel banned him for a month. In response Cantona walked up to each committee member in turn and called them an 'idiot'. His ban was doubled and his last bridge in France had been burned. National team manager Michel Platini took on the role of unofficial agent, pitching him to various English clubs including Liverpool. After Cantona had impressed on a trial at Sheffield Wednesday, Leeds took the gamble on him with the fans quickly warming to his laconic style of play. In truth though, Cantona didn't have too much to do with the title win, contributing only three goals and mostly appearing from the bench. It was secured by the British spine of the team, especially the midfield of David Batty (England), Gary Speed (Wales), Gary McAllister and Gordon Strachan (both Scotland) and an unbeaten home campaign, aided and abetted by vociferous Elland Road support.

Twice before had Leeds been English champions and each time they had gone deep into the European Cup. In 1969/70 they announced their arrival at Europe's top table with a 16-0 shellacking of Lyn, the Norweigan champions. Further 6-0 and 2-0 aggregate victories over CSKA Sofia and Standard Liège meant that they reached the semi-finals without conceding a goal, setting up the first English-Scottish tie in the European Cup.

Celtic were the first northern European team to win the European Cup in 1967 with the famous Lisbon Lions, who beat Inter Milan 2-1 with a side that all came from the surroundings of Glasgow. English press unkindly suggested Celtic were a side on the decline. They had needed a coin toss to get past Benfica in the second round, but fortunately for the Bhoys their luck in Lisbon didn't desert them.

Manager Don Revie was asking his side to compete on all three fronts and deliver a treble. Leeds were tired though. Their FA Cup semi-final against Manchester United had taken two replays to sort and in the run-up to a European Cup semi-final they had to play six games in 15 days. Within two minutes of the first leg starting, Gary Sprake had conceded his first goal in Europe that season and that was enough for Celtic to take a lead back to Glasgow. Unbelievably, the Football League, run by Alan Hardaker, who was not a Revie favourite, made Leeds play a game away against West Ham the day after that first leg.

Four days before the return, Leeds played 120 minutes in the famously brutal 1970 FA Cup Final against Chelsea. Celtic moved the second leg to Hampden Park to accommodate more fans and they succeeded in selling 136,505 tickets, a record official attendance for a UEFA club match which is never likely to be beaten.

Billy Bremner, a lifelong Celtic fan scored on 14 minutes for Leeds, a long-range effort that pinged in off the post, but a five-minute period after half-time sealed the game. John Hughes got across Jack Charlton to head home a low near-post cross to make it 1-1 on the night, although at this point an away goal would still have sent Leeds through. Hughes, a giant of a centre-forward, then clattered into Sprake with a two-footed challenge which left the goalkeeper's bone protruding through his skin. David Harvey came off the substitutes' bench and his first act was to pick the ball out of the net as Bobby Murdoch scored to send Celtic through to a final they would ultimately lose to Feyenoord.

Five years later, Leeds were back in the European Cup under Revie, although they hadn't been strangers to European success in the intervening years. In 1971 Leeds won the Inter-Cities Fairs Cup, the precursor to the UEFA Cup, and in 1973 they finished runners-up to AC Milan in the Cup Winners' Cup but lengthy European campaigns had taken their toll on Leeds, who finished third in 1973 after three years of finishing as runners-up in the First Division. In 1973/74 Revie made the decision to concentrate on the league, fielding weakened sides in cup competitions, and his tactics worked. Leeds comfortably won the title while losing only one game at home but in July 1974 Revie was tempted away from Elland Road by the lure of managing England proving greater than another shot at the European Cup.

Famously, the Leeds board turned to Revie's rival Brian Clough when looking for his successor. David Peace the author of the novel *The Damned United*, imagined Clough addressing Revie's men: 'Well, I might as well tell you now. You lot may all be internationals and have won all the domestic honours there are to win under Don Revie. But as far as I'm concerned, the first thing you can do for me is to chuck all your medals and all your caps and all your pots and all your pans into the biggest fucking dustbin you can find, because you've never won any of them fairly. You've done it all by bloody cheating.'

Forty-four challenging days later Clough was relieved of his Leeds duties before he had the chance to exact revenge for his own European Cup nightmare when his Derby County side had made the semi-finals in 1972/73 only to lose to the Old Lady of Turin. 'Juventus bought the referee,' Clough told his biographer Tony Francis. 'Of that there is no shadow of doubt. I was cheated.'

Stepping into the breach left by two of England's top managers was Maurice Lindley, a long-time Revie confidant and scout whose previous managerial experience was ensuring that Crewe Alexandra finished bottom of the Third Division (North) for three consecutive campaigns. Yet Leeds were able to get past Swiss champions FC Zürich with Allan Clarke (three), Peter Lorimer and Joe Jordan providing the goals.

By the time that Leeds were playing Újpesti Dózsa of Hungary, former England right-back Jimmy Armfield had been appointed. Armfield, who had been a one-club man as a player with Blackpool, had just won the Third Division with Bolton Wanderers. Under Armfield's guidance, Leeds comfortably beat Újpesti and Anderlecht of Belgium in the quarter-finals, before securing a famous victory over Barcelona in the semi-finals.

Wearing their all white kit that was instituted by Revie in tribute to Real Madrid's Los Blancos team that won the first five European Cups, Leeds found themselves playing in the face of 111,000 Catalans cheering on Johan Cruyff, Johan Neeskens and Charly Rexach as if the English side were their El Classico rivals. It was a task made no easier by Gordon McQueen's decision to thump a Barcelona player in full view of the referee. Yet ten-man Leeds beat Cruyff's Barcelona with Lorimer scoring in the Camp Nou to add to Elland Road strikes from Bremner and Clarke.

The final was held in Paris, where holders Bayern Munich were after back-to-back titles, although they too had endured a torrid season, finishing in the bottom half of the Bundesliga and sacking their European Cup-winning manager Udo Lattek. His replacement was Dettmar Cramer, who was appointed with the personal recommendation of Franz Beckenbauer – a favour returned for 12 years earlier when Cramer had insisted the DFB revoke their ban on young Beckenbauer for fathering a child out of wedlock.

Leeds fans will tell you that Beckenbauer handled the ball in the penalty area, Clarke was felled by the Kaiser for a stonewall penalty that wasn't given and that Lorimer had a perfectly good goal that was chalked off. And they would be right. They're less likely to mention that Terry Yorath should have been dismissed after just two minutes for a leg-breaking tackle on Swedish international Bjorn Andersson, which was outrageous even by the standards of the day.

The legitimacy of Lorimer's goal was not disputed by Bayern midfielders Franz Roth or Ranier Zobel, but it was by Beckenbauer. He raised his arm vertically to indicate an indirect free kick, which would be the consequence of an offside. French referee Michael Kitabdjian had awarded the goal but Beckenbauer convinced him to consult with his linesman who had sprinted back to the halfway line, indicating his agreement with the decision. Nevertheless, these two men who had each been convinced of the goal just moments earlier managed to confer and decide that Herr Beckenbauer was right – Leeds had been offside.

As Leeds tired both physically and of poor refereeing, the West Germans capitalised with Roth and Gerd Müller scoring late to give the Bavarians a 2-0 victory.

Former Bayern player Paul Breitner said, 'A referee's decision cost them [Leeds] the final.'

If luck runs in threes then Beckenbauer enjoyed three helpings of it during the match and was soon lifting his third major trophy in the space of 12 months. Two European Cups and one World Cup, as the song doesn't go, and he and Bayern would add a third consecutive European Cup just 12 months later.

It was not Kitabdjian's first refereeing controversy. He was the referee for a play-off between Morocco and Tunisia in Marseille to decide who would progress to the final stage of African qualifying for the 1970 World Cup. The match, much like the two-legged tie beforehand, was a stalemate and under FIFA rules at the time would be decided by the toss of a coin.

The coin was propelled skyward by Kitabdjian, and as it reached the top of its arc and gravity triumphed over thrust it began its rapid journey towards the turf. The Tunisians celebrated and thought that they were advancing. Except that they weren't. Kitabdjian declared the coin toss void and retreated to the privacy of the Stade Velodrome dressing room and emerged to let the world know that Morocco had won the toss of the coin. How this didn't start a war or a minor naval skirmish, to this day no one knows.

Leeds fans were not going to be as placid as the Tunisians, though, and they rioted – first in the stadium, with at least one supporter attempting to reach the referee at the conclusion of the match and countless others deciding to smash their Parc des Princes seats off their hinges. Missiles that were thrown from the Leeds end broke one photographer's arm and claimed the eyesight of a camera operator.

They then fought the French police before finally running amok throughout the City of Light. Journalist Chris Hunt said, 'The followers of Leeds United – or at least a maniacal percentage of them – killed the spirit of soccer.' The *Yorkshire Post* headline was 'Shame of Paris' and UEFA agreed, banning Leeds from its competitions for four years. Not that it mattered in the end, as Leeds's own domestic performances had excluded them from Europe for that period.

It actually took them a further 13 to return to the premier competition of European club football, and like the bully at school you just can't seem to avoid, the Germans were waiting for them on their return.

Leeds's First Division title victory had been secured when Liverpool beat their nearest rivals Manchester United with Yorkshire Television cameras ensconced to capture the scene in Lee Chapman's living room as he, Cantona, David Batty and McAllister (in a shirt and tie) watched their triumph sipping cups of tea.

Stuttgart's championship came in decidedly more dramatic fashion. They entered the last day of the

Bundesliga season in second place, level on points with both Borussia Dortmund and Eintracht Frankfurt, whom they trailed significantly on goal difference. All three teams were playing away but whereas Stuttgart were playing Bayer Leverkusen, who were contesting the UEFA Cup places, their rivals were facing teams in the relegation zone in the shape of Duisburg and Hansa Rostock.

With 15 minutes to go the title was going to Dortmund as Frankfurt were drawing away at Rostock and VfB were level 1-1. Matters looked even bleaker when future Ballon d'Or winner Matthias Sammer was sent off for Stuttgart for sarcastically applauding the referee, leaving ten men to chase a goal and a championship.

Andreas Buck, a pacy winger playing that day, remembers: 'Leverkusen sensed their chance to win so that they could move into the UEFA Cup and over-ran our goal. In one of our relief attacks four minutes before the end, Guido Buchwald headed the 2-1 for us. Suddenly we were first!'

Buchwald, the captain, rose to the occasion, literally. His towering far-post header sent the VfB fans into raptures and on a collision course with their English counterparts. 'The joy was huge because the championship came so unexpectedly,' adds Buck.

Before the real action started, fate brought the two champions together in the pre-season Makita

Frank Rijkaard, Marco Van Basten and Ruud Gullit, AC Milan's three Dutchmen.

Bernard Tapie celebrates the 1988/89 Ligue 1 title with Jean-Pierre Papin, Gaetan Huard and Franck Sauzée.

Arrigo Sacchi on the training ground with Daniele Massaro.

Tapie's head to head debate with Jean-Marie Le Pen of the National Front.

Silvio Berlusconi with the European Cup after Milan's 1990 victory over SL Benfica.

Basile Boli and Abedi Pele react to Red Star Belgrade's victory over Marseille in the 1991 European Cup Final.

Svangaskard Stadium, Toftir, Faroe Islands – where the first match of the 1992/93 Champions League season was played.

Papin saying goodbye to Marseille fans before his transfer to Milan.

The TV scrum around Maradona after the Seville v Bayern Munich friendly, 28 September 1992.

Carl Shutt and David Batty celebrate Leeds United's victory over Stuttgart in Barcelona.

Mark Hateley and Marcel Desailly competing for the ball at Ibrox, November 1992.

PSV vs AC Milan, December 1992 – the last time the three Dutchmen played together for club or country.

International Tournament. Gordon Strachan, who was on co-commentary duty for the competition for ITV alongside John Helm, recalls: 'Howard had the idea to play Gary [Speed] as a sweeper in Europe as the back-pass rule had just come in. We tried it in the Makita game. Let's put it this way, I never did co-commentary again and Gary never played as a sweeper again either.'

Leeds won 2-1 with £2m summer signing David Rocastle scoring the winner, but Speed was seemingly at fault for the Stuttgart goal scored by Fritz Walter, who never got international recognition despite consistently notching up double digits in the goals column. He had top-scored in the Bundesliga during Stuttgart's championship season ahead of future Leeds favourite Tony Yeboah, then of Eintracht Frankfurt.

With the first leg in Stuttgart, Leeds needed to be on their game from the off at the Neckarstadion. The stadium had hosted two the European Cup finals of 1959 and 1988 and once saw over 100,000 supporters pack inside to watch Germany's first international match after the Second World War, but in September 1992 its capacity was reduced to just 36,000 to allow for construction work to take place in time for the summer's 1993 IAAF World Athletics Championships.

Buck concedes the athletics track robbed the Neckarstadion of some of its atmosphere compared to other 'pure football stadiums', admitting also that

Stuttgart fans could sometimes be a little reserved. Still, the venue held no fond memories for England fans as it was where the Republic of Ireland beat England 1-0 in Euro 88. None of the Leeds side had played that day but English fans might have wished Tony Dorigo had, as it was fellow left-back Kenny Sansom's miskick that set up Ray Houghton's goal.

The match was the first competitive meeting between English and German club sides since the 1985 Cup Winners' Cup semi-final between Everton and Bayern Munich, and the first club meeting since the 1990 World Cup semi-final was decided on penalties.

Eyes weren't solely on England; both countries were perceived to have a hooligan problem at the time but the stakes were higher for English clubs, who were only in their third season back in European club football following the lifting of the ban imposed following the 1985 Heysel Stadium disaster. The Football Association and the Foreign Office keenly observed the proceedings.

If the media were discussing pre-match tactics then it's likely they meant police tactics. Chief Superintendent John Ellis of West Yorkshire Police travelled to Germany to warn his counterparts of the 'unofficial' fans from whom trouble was expected. There were also fears that the tie could attract neo-Nazi organisations, who had been increasingly prominent in the wake of German reunification, or that Bayern Munich supporters could get involved having waited 17 years to cross paths with Leeds fans again since Paris.

The reality is that the vast majority of the 'unofficial' Leeds followers were just there to watch their team and had been put off joining the official coach party from Yorkshire by a combination of cost and logistics. The club organised coach trip, a 34-hour round journey, which was timed to arrive only an hour before kick-off and depart again immediately after. It was hardly surprising that some fans wanted to fly short haul and see more of Germany than the autobahn. Despite Leeds's objections, Stuttgart sold the 'unofficial' fans tickets so their journeys weren't wasted and the game passed off peacefully with few incidents.

Both sides were slightly altered from their championship-winning line-ups. Eric Cantona had replaced Rod Wallace as Chapman's secondary striker, while Mel Sterland, an overlapping right-back who Peter Drury, then of BBC Radio Leeds, describes as 'ahead of his time', sustained an ankle injury at the start of the 1992/93 season, leaving Leeds short of a recognised replacement. Wilkinson's answer for this tie was to play David Rocastle, their record summer signing, in Sterland's position. It was his competitive debut for Leeds but not a European Cup debut for Rocastle as he had played for Arsenal in the 1991/92 competition against Austria Vienna and Benfica, in his more usual position on the right wing.

Gordon Strachan was the only other British player with European Cup experience but that came 12 years earlier playing for Aberdeen. Strachan was, however, a Cup Winners' Cup winner having been a part of the famous 1983 Aberdeen team who beat Real Madrid 2-1. Cantona, too, boasted European Cup experience but appeared twice against Dinamo Tirana and once at Lech Poznań for Marseille before he fell out of favour (as was his want) and lost his place in the side to Abedi Pele.

However, Stuttgart's big fear was Cantona's striker partner Lee Chapman. The 36-year-old Stuttgart coach Christoph Daum said in his pre-match press conference that Chapman was his 'headache'. 'I just don't have a player to deal with him – especially his power in the air,' Daum maligned.

At the time German football had an inferiority complex to the British game's physicality. Everton had out-muscled Bayern in the 1985 Cup Winners' Cup semis, much like their great rivals Liverpool had done to Borussia Mönchengladbach in the 1970s. Alan McInally, who was a respected pro in England and Scotland, became a cult hero in Bavaria as an imposing target man. Likewise, British teams perceived their German opponents to be more tactically advanced and situationally aware.

While Leeds had added to their team on paper, Stuttgart were diminished. Star midfielder Matthias Sammer had left Germany in exchange for ten million Deutschmarks to follow a well trodden path from the fatherland to Inter Milan. In 1989, Andy Brehme, Jürgen Klinsmann and Lothar Matthäus were Inter's West German answer to their city rivals' three Dutchmen and while they won the 1990 World Cup for their country, the return for Inter in three seasons was limited to the 1991 UEFA Cup. Still, when it came to the time to replace Matthäus, the German experiment had gone down well enough for Inter to select his heir apparent from Die Mannschaft.

Losing a player of Sammer's ability would have been more palatable to Stuttgart fans had he lasted for more than six months in Italy. He could not settle and despite a decent return of four goals in 11 Serie A matches he requested a transfer back to Germany due to homesickness. Borussia Dortmund won his signature, paying half of what Inter paid to Stuttgart, and the rest is history.

The move worked out well for both parties. Sammer scored ten goals in the second half of the 1992/93 for Dortmund but he really shone when Ottmar Hitzfeld converted him to a *libero* as part of his 3-5-2 system. Sammer was named German Footballer of the Year in 1995 and 1996, then captained a Germany side built around his talents to victory at Euro 96, where he was named the tournament's best player. The Ballon d'Or followed, a rare honour for an ostensibly defensive player, and his club career reached its zenith when he won the following season's Champions League with Dortmund. Cruelly, a career-ending knee injury meant that he would only play three more Bundesliga games for Dortmund before retirement.

While Sammer was a big loss, Stuttgart still had Guido Buchwald, an inspirational captain and tenacious defender. He had drawn the assignment to man mark Diego Maradona in the 1990 World Cup Final. 'I shut him down, and back in Germany they started to call me "Diego". He was the best in the world at that time, and because I marked him so well in that game, his name became my nickname,' boasted Buchwald.

Buchwald had marked Maradona out of the World Cup Final but his coach wasn't convinced he could handle the physicality of Chapman.

Also a threat as shown in the Makita Tournament was Walter and he was ably supplied by two pacy wingers, Buck and Ludwig Kögl, who played for Bayern Munich in the 1987 European Cup Final aged just 21.

The first leg was a cagey affair in the opening stages and Leeds edged the first half. Cantona, twice, and Strachan forced decent saves from Eike Immel but half-time arrived without either side ever really threatening to trouble the scorers. Early in the second half it became apparent that Cantona had a problem as his movement was severely impaired by a hamstring injury. It was the sort of injury that in modern football the player would go down for to indicate they needed to be subbed. However, with very of-the-time sensibilities, Cantona played on, essentially on one leg until Leeds could ready his replacement, former Spalding United striker Carl Shutt.

Cantona's hamstring may have failed him but that didn't stop him attempting a crossfield pass using his injured leg. The ball was easily intercepted and you can hear Wilkinson on the TV broadcast shout, 'Eric, fucking hell!' He was right to be worried, too, as the intercept went left to Kögl, who couldn't fail to find Walter with a through ball when Chris Whyte, the covering centre-back, tripped over his own feet. A composed Walter delicately dinked it over an onrushing Lukic and Ron Atkinson purred on co-commentary about his 'classic finish'.

Then there was a headless 20-minute period where Leeds conceded two more goals, both of which had question marks involving the goalkeeping. A second came for Walter, bundling in a parried shot that Lukic probably should have pushed further away from goal. Lukic looked in two minds whether to catch or parry and consequently spilled Eyjólfur Sverrisson's shot into Walter's path. Sverrisson won and top-scored in the Icelandic league before his move to Stuttgart in 1989, but what made that unusual was that the league his Tindastóll club were winning was the Icelandic basketball league. His exploits for Tindastóll's football team couldn't get them a championship but did get him a move to Stuttgart.

Finally, Buck got in on the action, going past Fairclough at pace and firing a shot across Lukic. Alan Parry on commentary said 'that's a disaster now for Leeds' while Atkinson didn't mince his words, saying the two-time First Division champion was out of position and should have saved it.

It was the second national embarrassment that day for England as the game coincided with Black Wednesday, the day that interest rates briefly touched 15 per cent as the government desperately tried to defend Britain's position in the European Exchange Rate Mechanism. In the end, like the government, any defence that Leeds had was ineffectual.

In the away goals era of the European Cup, which had began in 1967, there had only been three teams who had overturned 3-0 deficits in their home legs. Barcelona were the first to do so, losing 3–0 to Gothenburg in the semi-final 1985/86, but winning 3-0 in the second leg and advancing to the final 5–4 on penalties. Werder Bremen came from behind to beat Dynamo Berlin in 1988/89's first round and Galatasaray had done the same in that year's second round against Neuchâtel Xamax of Switzerland. No side had done so against the calibre of the team as Stuttgart, however.

No one had told the Elland Road faithful who roared the opening kick-off as if it were a goal. The 20,457 in attendance were determined to make up for the absence of the 15,000 fans who would have been in the East Stand had it not been under reconstruction following the Taylor Report into stadium safety.

Amazingly, Cantona was fit. He had been seeing a specialist in Amsterdam to aid his recovery, so the only change that Wilkinson made was to bring in Scott Sellars for Rocastle. Sellars, a left-sided midfielder, necessitated a midfield rejig with Speed partnering McAllister in central midfield, Strachan playing on the right and Batty being relegated to right-back, a position he had been forced to play that summer at Euro 92 as England flailed around Sweden without a recognised player in that position.

Speed got the night off to a fine start, laying the ball off to Strachan who had drifted in from the flank. Strachan then floated the ball forward from just outside the centre circle to Cantona who cushioned a header expertly into the path of Speed, who did not have to alter his stride as he was arriving in the box and volleyed home. After his retirement, Speed described the goal as the best of his career. There was hope.

McAllister then had a shot blocked and Fairclough headed over from about ten yards out, but unfortunately for Leeds, Stuttgart scored next. Chapman misplaced a header and Slobodan Dubajić pounced on the loose ball. The Yugoslav sweeper sprang from the backline and carried it forward with that Continental ease that was viewed with both a mixture of awe and suspicion. Dubajić advanced at least 50 yards before a defender went to meet him, but a simple lay-off to Buck and a tame shot from outside the area levelled the contest on the night, and all but buried Leeds in the tie. Atkinson called out the defending as an 'absolute joke' and once more correctly criticised Lukic's positioning. It really was the softest of goals. Leeds would need to score another four to go through and they had less than an hour in which to do it.

Chapman bought a penalty off the Danish referee, Kim Milton Neilsen, when he wrapped his arms around Buchwald and made out that the centre-half had hauled him to the ground as he attempted to latch on to a Strachan cross. McAllister empathically converted the spot kick for Leeds to go into the break in front on the night but very far behind in the tie.

Leeds persevered and the modest crowd worth twice their number roared them onwards; there was a belief in the stands that it was possible. Strains of 'Marching on Together' were ringing around the ground when Strachan again provided a pinpoint delivery on 66 minutes. Two Stuttgart defenders sandwiched Cantona as Strachan's ball arrived but it broke kindly, leaving him one on one with an onrushing Immel. The ball wouldn't drop fast enough but thinking on his feet the Frenchman lobbed Immel with his knee. It looked ugly but it was a moment of genius for which he would become renowned.

A glancing near-post header from Chapman on 78 minutes levelled the score at 4-4 on aggregate but Buck's away goal still gave Stuttgart supremacy. Judging by the ashen looks of Immel and Maurizo Gaudino, after Chapman's header sailed between the keeper and front-post defender, they were not confident that Leeds wouldn't get the fifth goal they needed.

Strachan, 5ft 6in tall, 35 years of age and fuelled on a diet of porridge, bananas and seaweed tablets, was the orchestra's conductor, playing a key role in each of the Leeds goals on the night. Chapman called him the 'heart and soul' of the team and he used all of his experience and guile to drag Leeds back into the tie.

Swiss international Adrian Knup replaced Walter in a like-for-like swap after the fourth goal. Then Daum withdrew his support striker Gaudino for Yugoslav defender Jovo Simanic, figuring his 6ft 4in frame made him a perfect candidate to neutralise the aerial advantage Chapman was providing. Simanic was making his Stuttgart debut having toiled in the reserves since he moved to Germany to escape the chaos of early-90s Yugoslavia.

The subs worked and the German outfit were able to hang on. Leeds, emphatic winners on the night but nonetheless losers by the slenderest of away-goal margins, were free to resume their flattering title defence. *The Independent*'s report the next day said that it was 'an epic match, a heroic performance' and that it did much to repair the image of English football abroad. The newspaper even went as far to say that 'one more goal and Leeds would have consigned Lazarus to history's inside page'.

'For minutes the applause didn't stop at the stadium. The English are proud of their team. But they also respect our win after two crazy games,' recalls Buck, scorer of the decisive goal. 'We hug each other in the cabin. There is singing on the bus to the airport. I sit blissfully in my seat and look out into the night. My away goal really made the difference. I cannot believe it.' After the game, Daum sang Buck's praises, telling the German media that the winger should be in Berti Vogts's national side.

On the plane home, Buck said he noticed VfB's general manager Dieter Hoeneß, twice a European Cup runner-up with Bayern, pacing up and down the British Airways flight from Manchester with a pensive grimace. Daum had sunk into his seat, seemingly leaving all his energy in the stadium. He beckoned over assistant trainer Lorenz-Günther Köstner asking what was wrong.

'Andy,' Köstner whispered. 'We have a problem. A problem with the foreigners.' Köstner broke the news to Buck that they had played four foreigners but he implored the scorer, 'Don't say anything! Not a word to the press when we land. We'll play stupid first. Maybe no one even noticed!'

The introduction of Knup and Simanic for Walter and Gaudino meant that for eight minutes Stuttgart had four foreigners on the pitch, in Simanic, Knup, Sverrisson and Dubajić. This was against UEFA's rules. Did Daum and his backroom staff momentarily think the Swiss Knup was German? Or think that Gaudino, the son of two Italian migrants from Naples was not German? Or had they simply panicked and forgot the rules under immense pressure?

Stuttgart's plan to play dumb lasted as far as the baggage carousel, when German reporters began peppering the team with questions about the rule breach. The error had been spotted by eagle-eyed Leeds fans as well, who got through to the club the next morning. Leeds quickly asked UEFA for a 'clarification'.

Daum was being savaged in the German press. The *Stuttgarter Zeitung* proclaimed, 'If you want to compete with Real Madrid you must not act like the SV Hintertupfingen.' The point was only marginally undermined by that paper failing to notice that Barcelona were Spain's representatives in the European Cup that season.

It would not be Daum's last time in the eye of a media storm. In 2000, the German national side was at its lowest ebb. They had flopped out of Euro 2000, even losing to Kevin Keegan's England. Daum, who had transformed Bayer Leverkusen, was the obvious candidate to take on the challenge of getting Germany back to the top of world football, where they believed they belonged.

Daum's long-time nemesis Uli Hoeneß, the general manager of Bayern, made public decade-old rumours of drug addiction, adding allegations of extortion and use of prostitutes for good measure. The Hoeneß-Daum beef stemmed from an explosive TV studio debate in 1989 where they tore strips off each other. Initially, when Daum offered to undergo drug testing and Hoeneß retracted his most salacious accusations, it looked like this might end badly for the Bayern supremo but Daum's hair sample returned a positive result for cocaine. Franz Beckenbauer rescinded Daum's national team contract and Leverkusen dismissed him.

Back in 1992 the British tabloid sports media was gaga at the notion that the Germans had failed to be stereotypically efficient. When the news broke, ITN anchor Alistair Stewart joked that Stuttgart had more foreign reserves than the Bank of England. Leeds argued strongly that Stuttgart should be disqualified. Stuttgart, for their part, threw themselves at the mercy of UEFA, arguing plaintively that the substitution had no effect on the tie and less honourably that Leeds also had more than three foreigners on the pitch.

They pointed to Speed as a Welshman, in addition to the Scots Strachan and McAllister and France's Cantona. However, while colloquially known as the three foreigner rule, the actual rule allowed for three foreign players and two 'assimilated' players. Assimilated players were foreign players who continuously played with a national association for five years. The assimilated players had to complete three of those five years on a junior team. Speed had joined Leeds aged 14 and spent four years in the youth team before being called up to the seniors, and Leeds were well within their rights to play him alongside their three foreign players.

If you believe Leeds, UEFA took the coward's way out. After five hours of deliberations UEFA punished Stuttgart for wrongdoing, awarding the second leg to Leeds by a 3-0 scoreline, the usual result for a forfeit victory. Conveniently, this meant that the sides were tied 3-3. They also agreed that Stuttgart's accusations in respect of Speed were spurious and fined the club 10,000 Swiss francs. But instead of ordering the sides back to Elland Road for 30 minutes of extra time and possibly penalties, UEFA insisted on a replay, in Barcelona.

McAllister maintains that this was an unjust outcome and showed the power that the German FA had in UEFA at the time. He contended that if the shoe was on the other foot there was no way the British side wouldn't have been chucked out of the competition. Strachan, meanwhile, found out of Leeds's reprieve while watching his son play in a school football match.

It was the first play-off in the European Cup since the 1967 semi-final between Inter Milan and CSKA Sofia had ended deadlocked over two legs. Thanks to Inter offering CSKA a generous proportion of the gate money, the Bulgarian army side were persuaded to switch the play-off from Graz in Austria to the not-so-neutral venue of Bologna, Italy. Inter won 1-0 and went on to lose to Celtic's Lisbon Lions in the final.

Both sides had just a few days' notice to prepare for a winner-takes-all clash in the Camp Nou. At least relations between Leeds and the Football League had thawed since the Revie-Hardaker days, and the organisation agreed to postpone the second leg of Leeds's League Cup match against Scunthorpe to give them a better chance of success.

Just over 7,000 fans saw the replay in the cavernous 120,000-capacity Camp Nou. It's a wonder that any at all made the trip on six days' notice in a pre-Ryanair world. Despite the paucity of supporters in attendance, UEFA, still worried about hooliganism which hadn't occurred in the first two legs, categorised the game as 'Category A', meaning Barcelona had 5,000 stewards and staff in attendance.

Leeds made one change as Sellars was out. Fairclough was moved to right-back to counteract Kögl's pace with Jon Newsome coming into the side at centre-half and David Batty reverting to midfield. Fairclough was Wilkinson's third right-back in as many games. Another quirk of this tie is that Leeds wore three different kits – all blue in Germany, all white at home and all yellow in Catalonia.

Stuttgart also made just the one change with André Golke in for Gaudino in midfield, but this time they were taking no chances. Simanic wasn't even on the bench and would never play for the club again, scapegoated somewhat for a clerical error that was not his fault. His only action for Stuttgart being those eight fateful minutes in Leeds.

The breakthrough came when an attempted Stuttgart clearance only found Strachan, who after taking a few steadying touches let fly from 25 yards out and beat Immel with a fantastic strike. Asked to recall the goal when interviewed for this book Strachan said, 'Aye, that wasn't bad.' The lead was deserved but brief and not for the first time in the tie Dubajić was given a free pass to bring the ball out of defence. He found an overlapping right-back who crossed for Golke to head in.

The first 20 minutes of the second half were guarded. Buck described the period as 'like two old boxers, nobody wanting to make a mistake'. Tony Dorigo nearly sliced a clearance into his own net and Cantona was loping around the pitch having looked to have suffered a recurrence of his hamstring injury from the first leg. Wilkinson then broke with English football superstition and made a substitution while defending a corner. He withdrew Cantona on 75 minutes for the fresh legs of Carl Shutt, who Buck, as one of the two Stuttgart players not committed to attacking the corner, clocked as 'a pale guy with a brush cut and a weird running style'.

Shutt had just nipped to the loo, no mean feat at the vast Camp Nou. On the way he passed a shrine of the Virgin Mary and Jesus and, completely out of character for him, he prayed. When he returned to the touchline Wilkinson told him he was going on. He turned to fellow sub Rocastle and declared, 'Rocky, I'm going to fucking score here.'

The corner was dealt with and Dorigo brought the ball forward up the left flank and played it towards the fresh Shutt, whose first touch was heavy and looked to concede possession to Buck. Instead of just clearing the danger, Buck believed he had time to open his body and find a team-mate rather than the empty Camp Nou stands. He was wrong. The man with the weird running style was faster than he anticipated and dispossessed him with a block tackle.

Shutt was through and he declined to square to an unmarked Strachan screaming for the ball, then beat Günther Shäefer and nutmegged Immel for the decisive goal. A divine intervention indeed. Strachan half-jokingly says that it's a good job Shutt scored because if he hadn't done the Scot would be at the striker's house every morning for the rest of his life asking why he hadn't squared it. Leeds were euphoric and Stuttgart looked beaten.

'The moment I lost the ball. I knew he was going to score, it was over, and I screwed up,' lamented Buck, who admitted to being in shock and said he finished the game in a trance. He never did get the international call-up that Daum demanded but six years later he finally got to play in the Champions League group stage for Kaiserslautern in the 1998/99 season. Kaiserslautern topped a group featuring PSV Eindhoven, Benfica and HJK Helsinki but lost to Bayern in the quarter-finals.

The Leeds vs Stuttgart trilogy was one of the great European ties, won by the odd goal in 11 over the course of three matches. Dramatic shifts of momentum, superb performances and even allegations of skullduggery on the part of UEFA make this a compelling story even nearly 30 years after the event.

Wilkinson summed up the feelings from the Leeds camp: 'A magnificent night, a magnificent result and a terrific performance. Now we can look forward to a great all-British tie with Rangers.'

Davids vs Goliaths

WITH NEARLY 1,000 European Cup goals scored, over 250 matches won and 13 tournament victories Real Madrid are widely acknowledged as the kings of continental football. But Real are only one of over 500 different clubs to have competed in either the European Cup or Champions League. Gabriel Hanot's tournament was not intended to just be the sole preserve of the rich and famous.

Valletta of Malta (38) have scored more European Cup goals than 1982 champions Aston Villa (24); Dundalk (32) have played more matches than Nottingham Forest (20) and Everton (10) combined; Belfast's Linfield have more European Cup and Champions League campaigns (29) than Liverpool (25).

However, the indisputable basement dwellers in UEFA's eyes at least are Luxembourg with two of their clubs, Avenir Beggen and Union Luxembourg, being ranked 525th and 526th in the competition's history.

Avenir sit stubbornly at the foot of the all-time table with no wins, no draws and 12 defeats from their six participations. After losing 8-0 to AC Milan in their 1969 debut, they suffered consecutive 13-0 and 17-0 aggregate reverses to mid-tier continental powers Rapid Vienna and IFK Gothenburg in the mid-1980s, eventually settling for a cumulative goal difference of -55, only managing to score once in 12 matches.

Union's European record was slightly better before they were dissolved in 2005. They came into the 1992/93 competition on the back of a third consecutive domestic league triumph but their reward for those previous titles were 6-1 and 10-0 aggregate defeats to Dynamo Dresden and Olympic Marseille. In 1971/72 Union ran Valencia relatively close, falling 4-1 over two legs, and the 1962/63 14-0 aggregate loss to AC Milan is relatively forgivable because Milan went on to win the competition that season.

The country's first European Cup match flattered to deceive. Spora Luxembourg narrowly lost 4-3 away to Borussia Dortmund, before triumphing 2-1 in the return leg played in Luxembourg City. Had the away goals rule been in force at the time then Dortmund would have been eliminated. The Germans took no chances with the play-off, offering sufficient financial inducement for Jeunesse to agree to travel to Dortmund where they dutifully received a 7-0 drubbing.

Amazingly, neither Union nor Avenir are responsible for the single worst defeat in European Cup history but that dubious honour does predictably belong to a Luxembourg side. Stade Dudelange were one of three teams from Luxembourg's fourth-biggest city, Dudelange (population circa 15,000), the centre of the Luxembourg steel industry which accounted for much of the country's wealth. Stade pipped Union of Luxembourg City to the 1964/65 Championnat du Luxembourg by a single point, setting up a glamour European tie with two-time Portuguese winners Benfica in the following season's first round. The city of Dudelange, as well as the whole country, can be thankful that Eusébio, who was in the middle of his Ballon d'Or-winning season, only played in one leg of the tie, accounting for just four of the 18 goals that Stade conceded.

There might have been reasons for optimism at the Stade Achille Hammerel when the draw paired Union Luxembourg with the Portuguese champions FC Porto in the first round as the Luxembourg national side had recently drawn with Portugal. Given that they hadn't beaten another European side since a 2-1 victory over Norway in November 1973, the 1-1 draw was kind of a big deal.

The Luxembourg result was the first indication that the so-called 'Golden Generation' that won Portugal back-to-back World Youth Championships might not be all they were cracked up to be. Future Manchester United assistant and Real Madrid manager Carlos Quieroz's team that evening contained João Pinto, Paulo Futre, Fernando Couto, Vítor Baía, and an 18-year-old debutant named Luís Figo.

Fans had to reach almost three decades back into their memory banks to recall a Luxembourgish victory in the European Cup – a 5-4 aggregate victory for Jeunesse Esch over Finnish champions Haka in 1963. Albeit it was one attributable to an 84th-minute Haka own goal in the second leg. This is one of only two victories, both for Jeunesse, in Luxembourg's European Cup history.

In 1992/93 the 1987 winners Porto made light work of Union, racking up nine goals and conceding just the one over the course of 180 minutes. When Fernando Couto scored Porto's second from a free-kick routine that Union graciously didn't attempt to charge down and even more charitably John van Rijswijck in the Union goal allowed to let slip between his fingers, Couto could be seen laughing all the way back to the halfway line, his coiffured mullet bouncing in unison with his shoulders.

A similarly brusque dispatching of the Finnish champions from the vaunted Romanians was expected. Romania were represented by Dinamo Bucharest, who couldn't quite match their eternal derby foes Steaua for European pedigree but did have 13 previous European

Cup campaigns to their name and were semi-finalists in 1983/84, losing 3-1 on aggregate to Liverpool.

Kuusysi, from the city of Lahti, about 100km north of Helsinki, were representing Finland for the fourth time. Kuusysi were a financially troubled club for much of their existence. In the 1960s they had to briefly merge with local rivals Reipas and in the 1970s the situation became so dire that serious discussions were held about becoming a juniors only club.

Lahti benefited from the gradual liberalisation of the USSR and Finland's unique position as a Western market economy able to trade with the Soviets. With their 1,340km border with the USSR and a recent history of invasion and strife Finland were careful to balance themselves between Western and Eastern Blocs in the Cold War.

With the benefit of a booming economy, local businessman Martti Rinta was able to assume the role as the club's benefactor. He cleared their considerable debt and the 1980s were the golden period for Kuusysi. In 1982, they first played European football, representing the country in the 1982/83 Cup Winners' Cup; the next season was their European Cup bow – coincidentally, a first-round defeat to Dinamo Bucharest.

However, their greatest triumph came in 1986, where they reached the quarter-finals of the European Cup, becoming the first Finnish team to do so. Shockingly, they did this despite receiving difficult draws. In the first round they beat the Yugoslav champions Sarajevo home and away, while in the second they defeated the neighbouring Zenit Leningrad (now St Petersburg) 4-3 on aggregate before losing to eventual champions Steaua 1-0 over 180 minutes.

The 1990s weren't as kind to Lahti and consequently Kuusysi. The economic downturn of post-Soviet Russia was biting hard due to their geographic proximity. Unemployment in Lahti reached 18 per cent in 1992, up from just four per cent in 1990.

On the European pitch the side had reverted to Finnish stereotypes, providing little resistance to Swarovski Tirol (Austria) in the 1990/91 European Cup nor Liverpool in the 1991/92 UEFA Cup. Kuusysi did manage to win the home leg against Liverpool 1-0 thanks to a goal from their English striker Mike Belfield. The issue was that they were 6-1 down from their trip to Anfield. Belfield had played for Wimbledon in the lower reaches of the Football League before, like many English footballers, going to Scandinavia on loan, either for experience or game time during the summer when the domestic game was on hiatus. Unlike the rest, Belfield never left, living in Finland to this day. When Belfield eventually retired he was one of the top ten appearance makers in Finnish football history, and the only overseas player in that list.

In front of the smallest crowd of the entire 1992/93 European Cup/Champions League season, it was Belfield's job to lead the line against Dinamo and try to write another chapter of European history for the Lahti club. The 1,330 Kuusysi supporters in attendance were treated to a home victory courtesy of a Jari Rinne goal.

The return leg saw a wasteful Dinamo squander chance after chance. Sebastian Moga, Gabor Gerstenmaier, Sulejman Demollari and Nelson Mensah all should have brought Dinamo level before Gerstenmaier bundled in Dorinel Munteanu's parried shot to equalise with 15 minutes remaining. Munteanu was the stand-out player on the pitch, giving early evidence for why he became and remains Romania's most-capped player. His free kick was unlucky to find post rather than net. Demoliari and Mensah both missed open goals before the tie went to extra time.

The sense of farce only increased when Daniel Timofte managed to head the ball straight to Kuusysi goalkeeper Jyrki Rovio who had fallen over as the Dinamo cross came in. When Rovio was beaten, Kuusysi defenders managed to clear the ball off the line on three different occasions in extra time. Finally, the Kuusysi levee burst when another shot cleared off the line was returned with interest by Demoliari. Dinamo deserved their win but they made hard work of it.

Defeat to Dinamo wasn't the worst fate to befall Kuusysi in 1992. In December that year their financier Rinta died of a heart attack. According to his own estimates Rinta had spent several million Finnish marks on the club. After his passing, Kuusysi couldn't match their previous success (or budgets) and in 1996 were forced to merge with local rivals Reipas to stave off extinction. FC Lahti have stabilised themselves in the Veikkausliiga but are very much a mid-table club and their best finish in the past 20 years has been third.

But at least Finland and Luxembourg were represented in the 1992/93 campaign. And no list of European Cup minnows would be complete without acknowledging Albania. The long-term holders of the title of Europe's weirdest country, where beards were banned, only members of the government were allowed to drive cars and over 170,000 military bunkers were built, averaging almost six military bunkers per square kilometre of land.

Not surprisingly, when Albania's communist government collapsed in 1991 they had the poorest citizens in all of Europe. Per capita gross domestic product was just $260 per year in 1992. It would have taken 95,000 Albanians to club together their entire year's earnings to buy Gianluigi Lentini from Torino, while Italians 45 miles away across the Adriatic Sea earned more than $23,000 per year. Only 560 Italian annual salaries were needed to purchase a Lentini.

Albania had a hate-hate relationship with the European Cup – they hated being in it almost as much as UEFA hated having to invite them. In fact they only joined to annoy the Soviets. When long-time leader Enver Hoxha fell out with the USSR in 1960 for not being communist enough, the Soviets responded by cutting aid to Albania. Hoxha retaliated by entering the European Cup.

Previously, despite Warsaw Pact countries participating since the very first incarnation of the tournament, Albania and the USSR were the only two refuseniks when it came to the European Cup. Albania's decision to allow its champions Partizani Tirana to compete was primarily to embarrass and isolate Moscow.

Albanian sides didn't win any of their first three European Cup ties, against IFK Norrköping (Sweden), Spartak Plovdiv (Bulgaria) nor FC Köln (West Germany), but performed creditably, only losing by one or two goals on aggregate and remaining undefeated at home. Kilmarnock, winners of the 1965 Scottish championship on goal average ahead of Heart of Midlothian, perhaps discovered the reasons for this when they ran the list of 17 Nëntori Tirana 'registrations' past an English journalist familiar with Albanian football. He recognised the players but they weren't all 17 Nëntori players. Kilmarnock were effectively taking on the Albanian national side.

Then the boycotts started. Albanian sides withdrew or were banned by UEFA for withdrawing for 13 of the next 26 seasons. No one could quite work out why Norway had drawn the ire of Albania when 17 Nëntori refused to play Vålerenga. By 1967 West German clubs were now on the unacceptable list and another tie was nixed. However, games against Belgian, Dutch and Bulgarian sides could still go ahead.

In 1971 the Albanian authorities withdrew from a match against Austrian opposition and UEFA responded by banning all Albanian sides for a year. So aggrieved at their year's ban the country boycotted the European Cup for a further five seasons, although in their defence they only missed the 1977/78 tournament because they filled the paperwork a week late.

UEFA shouldn't have felt singled out by Albanian sporting recalcitrance. Albania was the only country to boycott every single summer Olympics in the 1980s. The 1980 games in Moscow were a non-starter, yet they joined in the anti-American counter-boycott of 1984's Los Angeles games, making them and Iran as the only countries to boycott both Olympiads. They then skipped the 1988 Seoul Olympics because they alongside Cuba recognised North Korea as the only legitimate regime on the peninsula.

Finally, in 1982/83 an Albanian side won a European Cup tie, 20 years after first attempting to, when 17 Nëntori beat Linfield of Northern Ireland on away goals. In the second round they drew Dynamo Kiev, the Soviet champions, and promptly withdrew. There was no accommodation possible as Hoxha considered the USSR as traitors to communism (and that was before glasnost and perestroika).

Northern Ireland themselves were no strangers to the minnows tag. Their champions had entered the European Cup since 1957 and only had six victories to show for it, against Icelandic, Irish, Luxembourgish (twice) and Norwegian (twice) opposition. Historically, they were just as likely to get a double-digit spanking as make it past round one but the passion for European football ran deeply and was strongly felt all across the six counties.

In July 1992, Barney Bowers, a sales rep from east Belfast, was relaxing on holiday with his family in Portugal when he received news from home. He was going to have to go to Marseille. Not for work nor on the next leg of his vacation though; Bowers would have to go to Marseille to captain Irish champions Glentoran against Olympique Marseille in the first round of the 1992/93 European Cup.

They would be Bowers's 22nd and 23rd European appearances in a Glentoran career that spanned back to 1981, and he would have had more if not for a severely

THE FIX

broken leg. His first personal experience with the
European Cup was in 1967 as part of a 25,000 crowd
when Benfica and the great Eusébio came to Oval Park
in the first round.

Bowers said, 'Eusébio and all those boys trained on
Victoria Park right next to the Oval. We had to be in
school but our mums popped down and got all their
autographs.'

Eusébio scored an 86th-minute equaliser which
turned out to be vital. The return leg in Lisbon was
drawn 0-0 and Glens simultaneously became both the
first team to stop Benfica scoring in a home European
game and the first side eliminated from the European
Cup on the new away goals rule. Benfica would go on
to beat Saint-Étienne, Vasas SC and Juventus en route
to the 1968 final, where another east Belfast lad would
deny them the title – George Best.

Bowers was taken to Derby County as a youngster,
living in nearby Spondon. He would sometimes go with
some of the other Derby players to watch their East
Midlands rivals Nottingham Forest's great European
nights and was there in 1980 when as champions for the
previous two seasons, Brian Clough's Forest crashed out
of the 1980/81 European Cup in the first round against
CSKA Sofia.

In 1981, Bowers returned to Northern Ireland and
his beloved Glentoran, who had just won the Northern

Irish championship. They were fortunate to draw the Luxembourg champions in the opening round and Progrès Niederkorn were duly dispatched 5-1 on aggregate. CSKA Sofia were their reward and Bowers had gone from punter to player in the space of a season. Glens lost the first leg in Sofia 2-0 in an evening tinged with tragedy for the death of the club physio Bobby McGregor, who aged 55 had a heart attack on the Sofia pitch.

Perhaps spurred on by McGregor's memory, the home leg produced what is commonly considered Glentoran's best European performance as Jim Cleary and Ron Manley got the goals to send the tie into extra time. Manley's wonderful solo goal remains etched in the memory of those lucky enough to be in attendance at the Oval that evening. The contest looked to be heading for penalties when a Sofia free kick took a wicked deflection off Terry Kingon in the Glentoran wall, completely wrong-footing Alan Paterson in goal. Had Glens progressed it would have set up a quarter-final with Liverpool that would have been the biggest club match in Northern Ireland's history. As it was, they at least had the satisfaction of seeing Sofia knock out the defending European champions, with CSKA becoming the first team to do that in back-to-back seasons (a record later matched by Real Madrid).

Glentoran's and Bowers's next crack at the top competition came in 1988/89, although they were a fixture of the Cup Winners' Cup in the intervening years. They drew the unenviable task of playing Russian champions Spartak Moscow, captained by Rinat Dasayev, who had just led the USSR to a runners-up finish at Euro 88. The Glens again returned from the Eastern Bloc two goals behind but in Belfast, Dasayev was called into action many times to save his side. Defender Terry Moore scored from a looping cross after half-time but as the Glens pushed for the equaliser they left themselves exposed to Spartak counter-attacks. Fedor Cherenkov scored with the last kick of the match to even deny Glentoran victory on the night.

So there was a measure of optimism around the Oval, one of Britain's most characterful football grounds, ahead of the visit of Marseille. Glens fans didn't necessarily expect a victory but going on recent showings they thought they might be able to cause some difficulties for the big-spending French outfit.

Tapie arrived by private plane and requested the Irish club source him a limousine for the one-and-a-half-mile journey from the airport to the ground. Marseille brought their own food, chefs and waiting staff with Glentoran club secretary Derek McKeague remarking that they wouldn't have had to have done that if they had drawn Leeds or Rangers.

The tie brought much-needed finance to Glens – the advertising boards alone were purported to be worth

£100,000 for the French companies wishing to reach Marseille's loyal fans via the television. The likes of Casanis, a Marseille based anise-flavoured pastis apéritif, commercial talk radio station RMC, and San Marina, a mid-range shoemaker most famous for women's boots, took advantage of the boards.

Also making the most of their commercial opportunities were the Glentoran players who, as semi-professionals, had to work on the day of the game. The lucky few got a few hours' dispensation from a kindly employer to join the team for their pre-match meal at 4.30pm instead of the normal 6.30pm for a weekday game.

The semi-professionalism extended to the broadcast coverage. Whoever was responsible for the BBC Northern Ireland graphics seemed to have taken down the Marseille team's name phonetically with Bowly, Sozee, Vaskez and Dechamp being presented to the viewing public instead of Boli, Sauzée, Vasquez and Deschamps. A small mercy that it wasn't Abedi Pelly (sic) wearing the number ten shirt.

Bowers was by now captain of Glentoran and well on his way to making an eventual 524 club appearances. Beginning as a goalscoring midfielder, his only concession to age was to drop a bit deeper as his career wore on and aged 33 he was playing at centre-half and marking a 32-year-old Rudi Völler, who was leading the line for Marseille.

'We were well pleased to have drawn Marseille. Glentoran had a good record at home in Europe so we didn't fear anyone at the Oval,' says Bowers. 'We played against big British sides in friendlies quite often so we had experience of playing Liverpool and Manchester United. We played quite good football, so the bigger they were the better it suited us.'

The 1992 version of the Glentoran team was one in transition. Manager Tommy Jackson was gradually putting the stalwarts of the 1980s out to pasture and bringing through new blood. Justifiably so, as the 1991/92 Irish championship determined, but Bowers admitted that consequently Glens 'were naïve in European terms'.

It was the 22-year-old John Devine, Bowers's centre-back partner, who committed the error that allowed Völler a one-on-one with Simpson to open the scoring after four minutes. In truth, Franck Sauzée should have broken the deadlock moments earlier from a similarly advantageous position. It looked like a long night ahead against the French champions and 1991 European Cup finalists.

The fans packed into the Oval's terraces didn't diminish their voice, cheering every interception and moment of respite as if it were a precious chance. The match resembled an attack vs defence training game for most of the first half. Bowers says, 'By the time we got into the game we were 4-0 down.'

Völler, Pele and Sauzée were the creative drivers of the team. The German provided intelligent movement and back-to-goal play, drawing the Glentoran defence out to positions where they were vulnerable. Pele, the reigning African Footballer of the Year from Ghana, had explosive pace, sublime ball control and could either beat a marker with power or guile, while Sauzée, a French international, enjoyed bossing a midfield.

Bowers calls Marseille the 'best team I ever played by a mile', but according to the captain they didn't let their technical superiority affect their sportsmanship. 'They were all very humble, very respectful guys,' he stresses. An example of this can be found from Völler who Bowers approached to confirm a shirt swap during the second half. The World Cup winner, responding in English, said 'no problem, no problem' but the security measures at the final whistle saw security and the RUC whisk the Marseille players off the field and Bowers thought that the chance had gone. But later on Völler made his way to the home dressing room to offer his shirt as agreed. Bowers was flabbergasted that he would bother and was also embarrassed as he had to tell Völler that he couldn't give him a shirt in return because the club needed it for a league game on the following Saturday. Again, Völler replied 'no problem, no problem'.

The foregone conclusion of the outcome didn't stop a hardy band of Glens fans following the team to the south of France, many by coach. Marseille, with the benefit of a 5-0 first-leg advantage and Bernard Tapie's deep pockets, rested Völler with François Omam-Biyik, famous for the headed goal that gave Cameroon a 1-0 victory over Argentina in the opening game of the 1990 World Cup, leading the line instead.

Akin to an elite sprinter negotiating the early rounds of an Olympic Games, Marseille burst out the blocks, scoring twice at the Stade Velodrome inside the first 12 minutes. Pele's bicycle kick was the pick of the strikes. With the cobwebs blown off they could slow down to an energy-saving jog and they eased to an 8-0 aggregate victory.

Sadly for Glentoran this would be their last crack at the premier European competition with UEFA legislating countries like Northern Ireland out of the Champions League.

In 1994/95 only the 'best' 24 nations were allowed to put forward their champions for the competition, which began that season with eight play-off games, followed by four groups of four, then reverting to its traditional knockout format. How the Luxembourg champions Avenir Beggen, with that country's abysmal European record, were judged worthier than the Bulgarian champions is anyone's guess. Levski Sofia had just provided seven members of the national team squad that reached the 1994 World Cup semi-finals and in recent memory there had been Bulgarian semi-finalists in the European Cup

By the time UEFA had backtracked on that unjust and indefensible reliance on algorithms it had allowed non-champions from bigger nations to enter. In 1997/98 Crusaders, representing Northern Ireland, had to negotiate two qualification rounds to win one of the 16 qualification spots for the Champions League group stage that only eight of 24 entrants pre-qualified for.

In 2019/20, Linfield would have had to negotiate four qualifying rounds for one of four 'champions path' places in a group stage that 26 of the 32 teams had pre-qualified for. UEFA is so sheepish about the mountain that sides like Linfield have to climb that it euphemistically calls the fourth qualifying round the 'play-off round'.

In the modern Champions League group stage, less than half the teams are their national champions. By design, as there are 15 spaces for domestic champions and 17 for non-champions, which is something Bowers disagrees with: 'I was always in favour of the champion of every country being part of the European Cup/ Champions League – that's the way it should have stayed.'

The Auld Enemy

THERE WERE only 12 days between Leeds United's victory in Barcelona and the first leg of their second round tie versus Glasgow Rangers. The short turnaround time was evident in the ticket stubs that provided entry to Ibrox for the clash against 'Stuttgart/Leeds'. The consensus in the English media was that Scotland's champions were not as good as Stuttgart and therefore Leeds were expected to secure one of the eight berths in the inaugural Champions League group stage, worth an estimated £6m.

Predictably, the tie was dubbed the 'Battle of Britain', as every post-war meeting of English and Scottish sides had been regardless of whether it was Dunfermline Athletic versus West Bromwich Albion or Glasgow Rangers versus Leeds United.

While most people accept the story that football, or at least codified football, was an English gift to the world, Irish historian Ged O'Brien argues that it is a thoroughly

Scottish game and a legacy of the highland clan system. Whatever the truth of the matter, it's indisputable that Scottish and English footballing ties run deep.

The Glasgow amateur club Queen's Park were semi-finalists in the first FA Cup, with their clash against Wanderers in 1872 pre-dating the first England-Scotland international by nine months. Ten years later it was Scotland's 5-1 victory over England that led to wide acceptance of the Scottish 'passing game' being superior to English kick and rush, and Scots were drafted in to form the spine of professional sides such as Preston North End, England's first invincibles.

If 'Battle of Britain' feels too much like hyperbole for a football match then at least take comfort in the moderation and temperance shown since the late Victorian era. In 1895, Heart of Midlothian and Sunderland, the respective Scottish and English champions, agreed to play each other for the 'Championship of the World'. A one-off match at Tynecastle was won 5-3 by Sunderland, and their squad that were entirely Scottish.

Despite the clear demarcation between English and Scottish football there continued to be occasional attempts to promote cross-border clashes. There was the British League Cup in 1902, the Empire Exhibition Trophy in 1938 and the Coronation Cup in 1953 – all three tournaments were won by Celtic. Naturally, Celtic were the opponents that Wolves invited to be the first club side to participate in a floodlit friendly at Molineux.

The first meeting in a UEFA-sanctioned competition between English and Scottish clubs also featured Wolves against Glasgow, but this time the blue half, as the two sides met in the semi-final of the 1961 Cup Winners' Cup. Rangers advanced to the final but lost to Fiorentina. The 1960s saw four Anglo-Scottish meetings in the Cup Winners' Cup with honours being divided evenly, before Celtic and Leeds met in the semi-final of the 1970 European Cup, the first clash between the two nations in the continent's premier club competition.

A 1980 meeting between Aberdeen and Liverpool was the only other instance prior to this Leeds-Rangers tie that English and Scottish champions had duelled it out in the European Cup. Liverpool won that tie comfortably, 5-0 on aggregate, and a young Dons manager named Alex Ferguson banned laughter on the six-hour coach journey back to Aberdeen. One of the players trying to stifle any giggles lest he receive a £10 fine was a 23-year-old Gordon Strachan.

The early 1980s was a barren period for Rangers, who had won the league in 1978 but wouldn't do so again until 1987. It was one thing to lose to Celtic but this Rangers vintage was being pipped to the title by the 'New Firm' – Aberdeen and Dundee United – as well. Graeme Souness was lured from Italy as player-manager and he (with the help of the UEFA ban) attracted a number of England internationals north of the border. First went Chris Woods and Terry Butcher, and soon followed by Trevor Francis, Ray Wilkins, Trevor Steven and Gary Stevens.

In 1989, Rangers won the Scottish title for the first of a record-equalling nine consecutive times. The 1992/93 season was their fourth successive European Cup campaign but they hadn't been happy ones, and two first-round exits coupled with one second-round departure was a disappointing return for the talent they possessed.

If Rangers had an English spine then whole strands of Leeds's DNA were Scottish. Some of the greatest players to pull on the white shirt of Leeds were from north of the border – Billy Bremner, Eddie Gray, Joe Jordan, Peter Lorimer and Bobby Collins to name just five. Gordon Strachan and Gary McAllister were keeping the saltire flying in West Yorkshire.

Strachan said he wasn't phased as a Scot going up against Rangers: 'It didn't bother me, Rangers fans have never liked me.' He added with typical Strachan mischief that 'Gary Mac' might have felt differently as 'he's a Rangers fan'.

The current Rangers assistant manager slightly disputes that characterisation: 'I'm a Motherwell fan. I grew up in Lanarkshire, played for Motherwell but everyone in my area had their team and also followed one of Rangers or Celtic. I was Rangers.'

Another midfielder with split loyalties was Stuart McCall, whose dad Andy used to play for Leeds. The younger McCall was born 'within a corner kick of Elland Road' and followed them home and away as a youth.

Fears of hooliganism were heightened given the all-British clash. Leeds and Rangers agreed to impose a ban on away fans for both legs. The decision was reached after meetings between police and officials of both clubs in Scotland and ratified by UEFA. While there were officially no away fans at either game, some players helped each other's families circumvent the ruling. McCall sourced tickets for McAllister's family to attend the first leg in Glasgow and likewise McAllister returned the favour to allow McCall's Yorkshire-based family to watch him at Elland Road.

Rangers were confident but not complacent. There was a lot of respect in particular for the Leeds midfield. McCall, whom Walter Smith started in an unfamiliar role on the left of midfield in an attempt to neutralise Strachan, believes 'we were probably up against one of the best midfields that an English side had ever had.

'They were all internationals – Gordon Strachan on one side, the late Gary Speed on the left and Gary McAllister and David Batty in the middle of the park.

204

That was probably as good a midfield four as had been about in the English league for a long time.'

'Nothing scared us,' recalled Rangers defender John Brown. 'When you are involved in Old Firm matches and you can play in those games without being overawed then you can play in any game.'

There was a febrile atmosphere at Ibrox for that first leg as 42,000 Rangers fans greeted the Leeds players with a wall of noise. Jim White, anchoring the STV coverage, claimed without a hint of bombast that it was 'the most eagerly awaited club match in 20 years'. White was harking back to Rangers's only European triumph, the 3-2 1972 Cup Winners' Cup Final victory over Dynamo Moscow.

McAllister said that while he was waiting for the kick-off he looked around at his midfield colleagues Batty, Speed and Strachan. The noise was so loud that they couldn't verbally communicate and instead just had to trade glances. 'I have never heard noise like it,' he would claim.

The Belgian referee blew his whistle to start the match and within four seconds the first skirmish of the Battle of Britain was initiated. Ian Durrant put in an old-school tackle on David Batty just to let him know he was there. No quarter was given and none taken. Durrant himself was no stranger to a physical challenge, having missed two and half years of his career following a horror tackle from Aberdeen's Neil Simpson.

After 40 seconds the first corner had been won and on 61 seconds Leeds were in front. Strachan's corner, floated in to the near post, was cleared by a Mark Hateley header but only as far as the edge of the area, where McAllister caressed a volley into the top corner of Andy Goram's goal. With no away fans to celebrate, McCall says 'you could hear a pin drop' inside the stadium.

The lack of crowd response made McAllister believe his strike had been disallowed at first – a cognitive dissonance borne from years of Pavlovian training to expect each goal to be greeted by at least a small pocket of support.

McAllister was left unencumbered to hit his strike because his international room-mate Ally McCoist, who was supposed to be marking him, had been ball-watching and drifted towards the corner delivery. A few words were exchanged before the game restarted.

Chris Whyte, the former Arsenal centre-half who had travelled the circuitous route to Leeds by way of spells in the United States's Major Indoor Soccer League and then time with West Bromwich Albion, put his own tone-setter in on McCoist with clattering from behind in the Rangers half that FIFA and the International Football Association Board would clamp down on before the 1994 World Cup. Even by the standards of the day Whyte was lucky not to be booked, with the Belgian referee making over-the-top 'no more' gestures with his arms. Whyte ignored the advice moments later as he sneakily tugged McCoist back by the shirt when potentially through on Lukic's goal. Rangers should have had a penalty.

On 20 minutes Durrant swung in a right-footed corner from the left. Lukic came to meet it, climbing over Dave McPherson and Richard Gough to punch the ball. The fist was more a glancing blow than knockout punch and the ball implausibly squirmed backwards, crossing the Leeds goal line despite Tony Dorigo's best last-ditch efforts.

The Stuttgart games had left question marks about Lukic but this was an out-and-out howler. One theory was that Lukic was blinded by Ibrox floodlights, which at the time Rangers believed were the most powerful in Europe. For what it's worth Lukic himself said, 'When I sat down and analysed that night, I came to the conclusion it was just one of those things. You can go through all the top keepers and pick out errors like that.'

Lukic's association with Leeds went back a long way. As a schoolboy growing up in Chesterfield and being courted by the club he travelled to watch Leeds beat Barcelona en route to the 1975 European Cup Final. His Leeds debut came in 1978 and he re-joined them in 1990 when they were promoted to the First Division.

After that self-inflicted wound, Leeds began to impose themselves on the tie. Jon Newsome headed against the post from a corner, while Strachan had a goal wrongly chalked off for offside. Quick one-twos with Cantona and Speed had played Strachan in but the attack was whistled dead as he was rounding Goram.

Rangers's English midfielder Trevor Steven, who nearly moved to Leeds that summer, provided the corner that gave his side the lead. He crossed, and although McPherson's header was saved well by Lukic, McCoist showcased the poacher's instinct that had won him the European Golden Boot the previous season. He wheeled away in celebration as well he might because it was his 25th goal of the season and it was only October. He had more words

Ibrox was somewhere between bedlam and pandemonium as the home side continued at a ferocious pace until the referee's whistle rescued a rattled Leeds after just over 45 minutes of action. McCall had nearly added a third on the stroke of half-time and Durrant was immense after being switched back to his left-sided midfield role.

After the resumption, a bit of the edge had been taken out of the game, or maybe it was just impossible to keep that level of intensity up for a full 90 minutes. The second half sputtered to its own conclusion with neither side wanting to worsen their position. Rangers would take a one-goal lead to Yorkshire but Leeds had the away goal.

The cold light of day brought the realisation that Leeds were still favourites to progress to the Champions League. Rangers manager Smith thought that 'we could, and should have scored more' and his star striker McCoist agreed: 'It is going to be very, very tough now. Leeds have such a good home record.'

The BBC's *Football Focus* team split down national lines with Gary Lineker saying he felt Leeds were favourites due to the away goal and Bob Wilson, the former Scotland goalkeeper, disagreeing with his guest.

'The English newspapers still wrote us off as no-hopers,' remembered Andy Goram. 'They all predicted that Leeds would give us a good battering down there. So when it came to the Gaffer's pre-match team talk he didn't have to say much. He came in with a big pile of press cuttings from the English newspapers and threw them into the middle of the floor. Smith said, "If this doesn't motivate you then nothing will."'

For the return leg, UEFA's post-Heysel phobia of terraces meant that the capacity at Elland Road had been cut to 25,000 but the demand could have filled Wembley.

There were thousands of Leeds supporters outside to welcome the Rangers coach. 'They were banging on our bus windows,' recalls McCoist. 'I was up at the front with Ian Durrant and looked out to see one of the boys who drinks in the Red Lion pub in Kinning Park. I'll never forget it. He looked up at me, opened his jacket to reveal his Rangers strip and gave me a salute! To this day it makes me laugh. That was him reporting for duty.'

David Rocastle was recalled to the Leeds team for the first time since the first Stuttgart match to deputise for an injured Batty and he produced immediately, with an incisive 40-yard through ball that split Brown and McPherson. Goram held up Cantona for a split second, enough for Brown to recover and block Cantona's shot, which had beaten his goalkeeper, with an outstretched arm. Penalty? Red card? Nothing. The Russian referee didn't see anything amiss.

Moments later, literally, Goram cleared upfield, Durrant challenged for the ball and Hateley, Rangers's English forward, added a nice touch of symmetry to the tie by opening the scoring with a spectacular left-footed half-volley from outside the box in the first few minutes against his nation's champions, echoing McAllister's effort two weeks previously. The match director was still showing a replay of the Brown incident when the goal was scored.

Hateley lolloped towards a bouncing ball outside the area and released the sweetest half-volley as he was moving away from goal. The shot was crisp and unexpected but not especially off centre. Lukic was again beaten when he shouldn't have been, ending up on his shoulders in the goalmouth with his legs in the air looking more like a yoga instructor than a goalkeeper. McAllister believed it was a good strike but one 'you'd want your keeper to save'.

Now Leeds would need at least two goals to take the tie to extra time – nicking a 1-0 wouldn't have been enough. Wilkinson's men attacked, channelling their play through Cantona, who had Brown on toast all evening. The French international created three great chances only to find Goram impenetrable as the last line of defence on each occasion. Whyte also had a header cleared off the line by McCall.

The next day, the *Daily Record* purred, 'Goram seemed to have wings as he leaped from one side of the goal to the other, maestro of his position and surely ending forever silly criticism from south of the border about Scottish keepers.'

Although Goram was very nearly not a Scottish keeper at all. Born in Bury to a Scottish father who was also a goalkeeper, Goram got his start at Oldham Athletic and impressed enough to be called into the England under-21 squad in 1983 but not enough to be capped by Howard Wilkinson, deputising for Dave Sexton. Had Wilkinson picked Goram, he would have been ineligible to play for Scotland under FIFA rules at the time and would have counted as a foreign player for Rangers. It was a sliding doors moment that played itself out in front of 9,000 supporters on a Tuesday evening in Newcastle.

Goram is one of only four players to play football and cricket for Scotland. 'If I had been an England Test selector, I would have picked Andy for the cricket team on the performance,' lamented Wilkinson.

Things were about to go from bad to worse for Leeds. By pushing men forward to get one of the two goals they needed to stay in the tie, they left themselves vulnerable to a superb Rangers counter. Hateley dummied to give space to Durrant who then advanced the ball to the big Englishman, and moving away from goal he whipped in a devastating far-post cross with his left foot that a flying McCoist headed in. It was 2-0 on the night and Leeds once more need four goals at home to progress, but this time there would be no reprieve. Hateley was another with Wilkinson connections as he had been coached by him at South Nottinghamshire School Boys.

Cantona scored a consolation goal in the last five minutes but Leeds's spirit was broken. The Elland Road faithful gave the visitors warm applause at the final whistle but that was nothing compared to the scenes in the away changing room.

Brown says, 'The door flew open and in walked Alex Ferguson. He went round us one by one, shook our hands and said how tremendous the result was. He was delighted we'd won to shut up the English press and show them what Scottish football was all about. He couldn't have been more chuffed.'

It's hard to believe now but Ferguson really needed a reason to be cheerful in the autumn of 1992. United were in tenth place in the nascent Premier League, on a seven-game winless run, including a home loss to Wimbledon for the first time, and they looked nailed on to continue their 25-year championship drought.

At the end of the 1991/92 season the goals dried up for United, allowing Leeds to pip them to the title. Ferguson missed out on Alan Shearer, who not for the last time opted not to sign for Manchester United; Paul Stewart chose Liverpool over his native Manchester and Sheffield Wednesday refused to part with David Hirst. The only striker he did sign, Dion Dublin from Cambridge United, broke his leg in September.

A striker was priority number one for Ferguson and Wilkinson needed a right-back. Mel Sterland's injury had exposed Leeds's lack of depth and having used four different right-backs in their five European games, signing some cover made sense.

Wilkinson had identified Denis Irwin of Manchester United as his preferred target. Irwin had played for Leeds in the mid-1980s before being allowed to join Oldham on a free transfer in 1986. Bill Fotherby, his chairman, dutifully put in the call. Fotherby's United counterpart Martin Edwards rebuffed the approach and enquired about the availability of Cantona and to his surprise he wasn't immediately told what he could go do to himself.

Leeds had evolved their style of play to more prominently feature Cantona and utilise his talents, to the chagrin of his fellow strikers Chapman and Wallace.

'Eric didn't like the way we played, but you can't change a whole team,' argues Chapman. 'Howard tried to change the way we played, to play through midfield. We'd won the title playing a certain way.'

The back-pass rule had necessitated some of the change. Booting the ball from hand up to the likes of Speed and Chapman to feast on the knockdowns became less viable, although it had worked in the Charity Shield, which Leeds won 4-3 against Liverpool with a Cantona hat-trick, but seldom since. After Rangers eliminated them from Europe they sat 14th in the Premier League.

Nîmes, the French side Cantona signed from, were due another £500,000 before the end of the calendar year and not making the Champions League group stage had left a big hole in Leeds's financial projections. Besides, Cantona wasn't happy and the whole dressing room knew it. He was feuding with assistant manager Mick Hennigan, the bad cop to Wilko's good cop.

Between the two Rangers games Leeds played Queens Park Rangers. Wilkinson left Cantona out of the starting line-up and the Frenchman said he wanted to 'go home'. Rather undiplomatically, his manager replied, 'Here's your passport, fuck off!' So he did, later faxing the club saying he wanted a move to either Liverpool, Arsenal or Manchester United.

Leeds couldn't hide the fact that Cantona was in the announced squad for the QPR game and then on the Saturday lunchtime he was nowhere to be seen.

'When he's not at training on the Monday, you can't keep it quiet. People knew he'd disappeared and that there had been a problem,' admitted Wilkinson.

Restored to the starting line-up for the second leg with Rangers out of necessity not love, there wouldn't have been a financial imperative or sporting rationale for Cantona to be sold had Leeds made the last eight in Europe. Of course, the rest is history, including four Premier League titles, two FA Cups, third place in the 1993 Ballon d'Or voting, becoming an inaugural inductee to the English Football Hall of Fame and member of the PFA Team of the Century. It is fair to say the move worked out for Cantona, Ferguson and Manchester United fans around the globe.

It may have even helped Leeds in the short term. After their calamitous title defence, the worst since the 1938 Manchester City side were relegated as defending champions, Leeds had two consecutive top-five seasons but the bloom was off the white rose. Wilkinson was booed off and quite disgracefully spat upon by his own fans at Wembley following a particularly insipid 3-0 defeat to Aston Villa in the 1996 League Cup Final.

That September, Eric the Red returned to Elland Road to hammer the final nail in his former boss's coffin. Cantona had already assisted two goals when he scored the Red Devils' fourth and celebrated in front of the same Kop he scored in front of against Stuttgart and Rangers. By Monday morning Wilkinson was sacked; the memories of Bournemouth, Bramall Lane and Barcelona no longer sufficient to sustain him and the Leeds faithful.

The Yorkshire club would rise once more in the 2000/01 Champions League; powered on by a golden generation of youth, the return of grizzled veterans like David Batty and an unsustainable attitude to debt, Leeds finally reached the group stage eight years after their first attempt.

Drawn in a 'Group of Death' alongside Milan, Barcelona and Beşiktaş, Leeds enjoyed several famous nights under the Champions League lights when beating Milan, putting six past the Turks and knocking out the Catalan side before beating Lazio and Anderlecht in the second group stage (a short-lived innovation that proved too much even for UEFA) and Deportivo La Coruña in the quarter-finals. Valencia ended their hopes of reaching their second European Cup/Champions League final with victory against them in the last four.

Eventually the debts had to be paid and the ensuing ignominy of relegation to the third tier of English football has meant that Leeds have now been absent from the Champions League for 20 years, but in the Marcelo Bielsa era there's at least cause for optimism.

Back in 1992/93, Rangers's odds were slashed at British bookies and they were as low as 5/1 to win the tournament.

East Meets Best

THE SOCIALIST economic system that existed in eastern Europe from the post-war period to the early 1990s was characterised by planned economies, public ownership of the means of production and strong political control. Decision-making was centralised and sport was often given a privileged status because of its ability to project strength; the reflected glory governments or ministries hoped to bask in or simply to distract the masses for a few hours each week.

When the communist governments fell, regardless of whether the political process was peaceful, the resulting economic shocks were violent.

Switching to capitalist market theories brought complete change to the economies of half the continent. Shortages all but disappeared but new types of economic uncertainties and inequalities emerged. Unemployment, recessions and a less equitable distribution of wealth and resources followed. Football mirrored life.

The continent's mid-sized eastern powers (football or otherwise) were diminished. Harsh economic realities meant that valuable assets were sold (and undervalued) because of a short-term need for foreign currency. Players were streaming westwards depriving the top Eastern Bloc clubs of the steady stream of talent they had previously relied upon to punch above their weight at continental level.

Many communist countries had rules in place to stop talented young players from leaving. For Yugoslavia and the USSR the age was 28. By then as a top player you had probably given ten years' service to your club(s) and country and it was only then that they would allow you to pursue the money on offer in Italy, Spain or Germany. For other countries the practice differed slightly but the principal was the same. The best players from a country would stay to play football even if it was not the choice they would have made in an open market.

Just ask Robert Maxwell. The former MP, newspaper tycoon, fraudster and occasional football club chairman tried to get two Czechoslovakian defectors registered for Derby County. The only problem was that Ivo Knoflicek and Lubos Kubik were registered to Slavia Prague. No matter how much Maxwell moaned or made up sob stories about how he financed their passage to England, the Czech club insisted on Derby paying a fair transfer fee. The FA, UEFA, FIFA and the Czechoslovak FA all lined up behind Slavia and the duo had to leave Derby without ever playing a game.

Back in 1992, just four of the 16 teams left in the European Cup second round were from the Eastern Bloc: Lech Poznań (Poland), Slovan Bratislava (Czechoslovakia), Dinamo Bucharest (Romania) and CSKA Moscow (Russia).

This number was down on the normal representation that they would enjoy at this stage of the competition. It wasn't uncommon for six or seven of the last-16 teams to come from the east, which was not bad considering they often only had eight out of the 30-plus entries.

Three Eastern Bloc teams made the eight-team group stage which established the finalists in the 1991/92 season – Red Star, Sparta Prague and Dynamo Kiev. This time around, only Poznań could be considered to have a good chance of progression against their opponents – IFK Gothenburg of Sweden. Slovan had drawn Milan, Dinamo met Marseille and CSKA faced Barcelona.

The story was being repeated across European football. Just two ex-communist sides made the last 16 of the UEFA Cup – Dynamo Moscow (Russia) and Sigma Olomouc (Czechoslovakia). At that point it was the fewest number of Eastern Bloc teams to have reached that stage, down significantly from 1984/85 UEFA Cup where east had parity with west and Videoton of

Hungary reached the final, losing to Real Madrid 3-1 over two legs.

UEFA and the east were always uneasy bedfellows, as were the USSR and most western-based international sports organisations. Much of sports administration at the time was overtly political.

It is tempting now to view the Olympics as a benign, classless event but the Olympic movement was overtly political. De Coubertin et al.'s notion of gentlemen amateurs had a profound impact on who was able to take part. The muscular nationalism that some in the Olympic movement espoused came from the same political tradition that pushed Europe into the Great War.

The Soviet Union had little truck with the 'bourgeois' games, whose ethos had just as much to do with the playing fields of English public schools as they did with ancient Olympia, and stayed well clear in the inter-war years of the 20th century. In football, the USSR national side only played occasional bilateral games against Turkey.

Instead they organised Spartakiads, named for Spartacus, the escaped slave leader from Greek mythology. International Spartakiads were games for 'labourers' but the USSR found themselves increasingly isolated.

In 1952 they relented and joined the Olympic movement. In their first games the Soviet Union finished second in the medals table behind only the USA, and although football was not one of their 71 medals they did give a good account of themselves, beating Bulgaria and losing to eventual silver medallists Yugoslavia after a replay.

Eight years later they were the first champions of Europe, winning the European Nations Cup in France. This time they benefited from politics as Spain refused to travel to the USSR for their quarter-final.

However, this pedigree wasn't initially replicated at European club level; no Soviet club sides entered UEFA tournaments until the 1966/67 season and UEFA never chose to hold one of its club finals in a Warsaw Pact country.

The European governing body did allow the 1973 European Cup Final to be played in Belgrade but that was as far east as it was comfortable travelling. Eventually, in 2008 Moscow hosted the Champions League Final, followed by Kiev in 2018 with St Petersburg scheduled for 2022. Poland and Azerbaijan have also hosted the Europa League Final.

In 1992/93 that favouritism for the bigger western clubs could be evidenced in the draw for the second round. The winners of these ties would form the Champions League groups and to provide the likes of Milan, Barcelona and Marseille a touch more of an advantage this time the draw would be seeded. Fortuitously for these plucky megaclubs, seven of eight would be drawn at home in the second leg for added benefit.

All of the remaining eastern European sides were unseeded, except Lech Poznań of Poland, and no one could quite work out UEFA's rhyme or reason, least of all IFK Gothenburg goalkeeper Thomas Ravelli.

'I do not know anything about these Poles. They were really seeded in the draw? It is unbelievable. I think we will get past them anyway,' were Ravelli's pre-match comments to *Expressen,* a Swedish newspaper.

For Ravelli's as well as readers' benefit, Poznań were founded in 1922 and named after one of three brothers who according to legend established three Slavic nations – Lech, Czech and Rus. Success evaded them entirely until the 1980s, when consecutive Polish championships were followed up by consecutive first round exits from the European Cup, although in their defence they drew Spanish and English champions on each occasion.

In 1990/91 they threatened to cause a serious upset against Marseille. Poznań won their second round home leg 3-2 and were 3-1 up until Chris Waddle pulled one back for the visitors. Unusually, the match was played on a Thursday rather than a Wednesday at Bernard Tapie's urging. He is alleged to have offered US$100,000 to postpone the game as well as offering to host the Poznań side in Marseille at his own expense in his hotel.

The second leg was highly anticipated. Marseille won 6-1 but many Poznań players complained of food poisoning. 'My head was spinning, my stomach felt tight. I felt a great powerlessness. I really wanted to play, but it just couldn't be,' recalled Dariusz Skrzypczak, who assisted the opening goal in Poland.

To make matters worse, Mirosław Trzeciak asked to be substituted after 15 minutes. He spent the rest of the match with Skrzypczak in the locker room, both shivering from the cold, and wrapped in blankets.

Until the final six minutes the game was poised at 3-1, meaning a Poznań goal would trigger extra time. Three Marseille goals in the final six minutes gave the scoreline an air of a thumping that it wasn't. The Poznań players complained that they ran out of energy due to illness.

IFK Gothenburg v Lech Poznań

Poznań won the Polish title again in 1992. This time, with millions of badly needed dollars at stake from Champions League qualification, they took their own chef to Sweden. Skrzypczak anticipated a physical match and said, 'It will be a fight, [IFK] represent the English style of football.'

The first leg was an even contest, deadlocked at 0-0 until Kazimierz Sidorczuk's weak clearance invited a speculative shot from Patrik Bengtsson. Sidorczuk was out of position from his rushed clearance and left an invitingly large area of his net unguarded that even Bengtsson's weak shot was able to find.

Still, 1-0 away from home was seen as a manageable result and the crowds poured in for the second leg, expecting to see the Poles make the Champions League group stage.

Masses were said in the churches and nearly 28,000 crammed into the Municipal Stadium with fans resorting to sitting on seatless sections of bare concrete or in the aisles in order to get a view of this historic moment.

Sadly, they were to be let down. Johnny Ekström opened the scoring with a simple tap-in, after Sidorczuk had done brilliantly to deny Stefan Rahn's bicycle kick. Poznań would now need three goals to qualify, and three became four minutes into the second half when Mikael Nilsson slotted home.

Jonas Olsson told me, 'After our second goal, it felt like Poznań gave up.' 'Mediocrity' was Ravelli's more cutting assessment, and he added, 'I spent the whole game leaning on the post. I had nothing to do.'

The Poznań fans agreed. Only around 5,000 stayed until the final whistle, mostly to demand the sacking of manager Henryk Apostel following the eventual 3-0 defeat.

Since 1992/93 Poland has only been represented in the Champions League proper three times. In 1995/96

Legia Warsaw gained a modicum of national revenge beating Gothenburg to qualify for the group stage and made the quarter-finals thanks to further victories over Rosenborg and Blackburn Rovers.

The following year, Widzew Łódź, semi-finalists from 1983, also won their play-off to reach the group stages, finishing a distant third behind Ajax and that season's eventual winners, Dortmund.

The only other Polish team to make the Champions League were the 2016/17 Legia side. Their famous 3-3 draw against the Real Madrid of Ronaldo, Bale and Benzema was played in front of an official crowd of zero as punishment for crowd disorder in an earlier 6-0 defeat to Dortmund.

Robert Lewandowski aside, it's never been easy to be a Polish fan of the Champions League.

Dinamo Bucharest v Marseille

More than 45,000 supporters poured into the Dinamo Stadium to watch the 'Câinii roșii' (Red Dogs) try to cause an upset against the heavily fancied Marseille. A tapestry of flags and flares greeted the teams as they strode out of the tunnel on a wet Wednesday in Bucharest.

The home side's twin playmakers, the left-footed Dorinel Munteanu and the right-footed Gabor Gersten-maier, looked to exploit space behind Marseille's wing-backs Eric Di Meco and Jocelyn Angloma. On commentary, Michel Platini, the recently departed French national team coach, was critical of their positioning.

Marseille's veteran boss Raymond Goethals had lined the team up in 3-4-3 formation with Casoni operating as sweeper between the centre-back pairing of Marcel Desailly and Basile Boli. While it started as 3-4-3 the system had the flexibility to resemble a 5-4-1, leaving Rudi Völler an isolated figure up front as Dinamo had the best of the opening exchanges.

For all their bright opening play Dinamo weren't able to test a 22-year-old Fabien Barthez, playing his first European Cup match away from home. With a full head of hair, Barthez was almost unrecognisable from the player who with the help of a Laurent Blanc kiss to the forehead before every match would help France win their first World Cup six years later.

Eventually Marseille came more into the match but their shooting was woeful and only two of their 14 efforts were on target. The goalless draw was a fair reflection of the ambition of both sides.

For the return at the Velodrome, Goethals rang the changes. Both full-backs were replaced but more importantly he reverted to the 4-3-3 formation that brought Marseille all their success. However, instead of Papin, Pele and Waddle it was Alen Bokšić partnering Pele and Völler.

Bokšić was a physical yet creative Croat who had scored the winning goal for Hajduk Split in the 1991 Yugoslav Cup Final to deny Red Star Belgrade an historic treble. He moved to Cannes the year prior but injury limited him to just one appearance.

It was a risk to replace Waddle, who had wowed the Velodrome crowd for three seasons, with a player who had barely played outside of Yugoslavia but it proved to be an inspired one. That he was a cut-price option owing to the risk would have also appealed to Tapie as the debts from years of profligate spending were starting to be called in. Bokšić repaid Tapie's investment by scoring 29 goals in all competitions for Marseille in 1992/93 including both against Dinamo to secure a Champions League berth.

Bokšić's first was a centre-forward's header showcasing his strength and power as he fought to reach a Boli cross he was second favourite for, nodding the ball back across the goal. The Velodrome rewarded him with rapturous applause for both the effort and the result.

The second goal was all guile and finesse. Manuel Amoros delivered a nicely weighted low cross from the right, the entire Dinamo defence bought Völler's dummy and Bokšić caressed the ball into the net.

It was needed too as Dinamo had missed two gilt-edged chances to get an away goal advantage. If you're being kind, Munteanu's cross for the first might have been a touch high but Zoltan Kadar was unmarked and shouldn't be heading over from the six-yard box.

After half-time Kadar tried to make amends by whipping in a dangerous front-post cross that his strike partner Ovidiu Hanganu managed to miss entirely. Any touch from Hanganu, who was a couple of yards out at the most, would have resulted in a goal.

Dinamo wouldn't make the group stages in 1992/93 and to this day they still haven't. Twice they've been a game away from qualification but have lost out to Manchester United and Lazio on those occasions.

Their eternal rivals Steaua have made seven group stages in their 16 participations in the Champions League era but they've never reached the knockout phases or come close to recapturing the heights of 1986 or 1989 again.

Steaua did have a memorable UEFA Cup run in 2005/06. After 120 minutes of the semi-final they were 3-0 up on aggregate against Middlesbrough with the benefit of two away goals. The unlikely duo of Stewart Downing and Massimo Maccarone put on a clinic to give Middlesbrough the four goals they needed to make the final.

The best effort from a Romanian team in the Champions League was in 2012/13 when even beating Manchester United 1-0 at Old Trafford wasn't enough to make the knockout stages. Cluj finished level on ten points with Galatasaray in Group H and even had a better goal difference but lost out on head-to-head tiebreaker rules.

Slovan Bratislava v Milan

Had the UEFA Super Cup existed in 1969 it would have been contested between Slovan Bratislava, the Cup Winners' Cup winners and AC Milan, the European Cup winners. Sadly, Anton Witkamp, the sports editor of Dutch newspaper *De Telegraaf,* didn't come up with the idea until the great Ajax side needed more ways to burnish their reputation.

The same Ajax were responsible for ending Slovakian hopes of a unique UEFA double in 1969 when they beat Spartak Trnava in the European Cup semi-finals. Ajax advanced to the final with a 3-2 win but that couldn't detract from Trnava's performance, the best from a Slovakian (or Czech) side in the European Cup.

And 1969 was a tumultuous year for Czechoslovakian society. The year previously, Slovak politician Alexander Dubček became leader of the Czechoslovakian Communist Party. He attempted to introduce 'socialism with a human face', a series of reforms to make the state more tolerant of political rights and slightly more social democratic as opposed to socialist.

The reforms were very popular in Czechoslovakia but terrified Moscow. The idea of a free press ran against their idea of a one-party state. After negotiations between Moscow and Prague failed, the Soviets invaded.

Dubček was arrested and instructed people not to take up arms against the invading forces but couldn't prevent a campaign of civil disobedience. Road signs were taken down or painted over to confuse the invaders.

On the football pitch, the ramifications were that UEFA segregated its competitions to avoid sending western teams into an internal Warsaw Pact conflict. Bulgaria, East Germany, Hungary, Poland and the Soviet Union withdrew their teams in protest.

The progress of two Czechoslovakian sides deep into the European Cup and Cup Winners' Cup was a great fillip to the people with the games broadcast for the whole nation on television and radio.

In April 1969, Dubček was eventually deposed as party leader and a process of 'normalisation' began undoing his reforms. The performances of Czechoslovakian club sides in European football normalised too, not again reaching the heights of the Prague Spring until after the Velvet Revolution.

The 1992 Slovan vintage was not of the same calibre but it did contain one gem. The Bratislavan side won the Czechoslovakian league in 1992 for the first time since 1975 courtesy of 19-year-old Peter Dubovský's 27 league goals.

Expectations were fairly high for Slovan as Sparta Prague had made the group stage the previous season. Sparta finished second in Group B and even beat eventual winners Barcelona 1-0 in the process.

Dubovský's impact for his hometown club sustained into their European campaign. He scored twice in the 4-1 victory over Ferencváros of Hungary in the first round. His second (and Slovan's third) was a particularly beautiful left-footed volley after meeting a far-post cross.

Slovan played a nice brand of passing football against the Hungarian champions and were sartorially elegant too, turning out in a two-tone, sky blue-striped kit that would appeal to Coventry City fans of a certain age.

The only black mark from the first-round victory was the violence meted out to visiting 'Fradi' supporters from heavy-handed policing.

Against Milan in the second round, Slovan ultimately justified their unseeded status but performed creditably. Milan entered on a 40-match unbeaten streak which they extended thanks to a solitary Paolo Maldini goal. At the San Siro, it took two world-class strikes from distance from Zvonomir Boban and Frank Rijkaard to break Slovan's resistance before Simone and Papin rounded out the scoring.

The velvet divorce split Czechoslovakia in two on 1 January 1993. The remainder of the Czechoslovak league was played out amicably and this time Sparta pipped Slovan despite Dubovský again topping the scoring charts.

Slovan would transfer to the Slovak Superliga for the 1993/94 season and participate in the UEFA Cup without Dubovský, who was pursued aggressively by Europe's top clubs. Eventually, the two willing to meet Slovan's valuation were Ajax and Real Madrid with the prolific striker opting for Spain. Real paid 500 million pesetas (about €3m) to complete the deal.

That choice would prove a mistake. At that time Cruyff's Barcelona were dominant in Spain and the Real hierarchy chopped and changed managers in an effort to reverse their fortunes. Benito Floro, who signed Dubovský and persevered with him as he was finding his feet in La Liga, was sacked following a 5-0 defeat to Barça and a 2-1 loss to Unió Esportiva Lleida, a tiny Catalan team playing what remains their sole top-flight season.

Caretaker manager Vicente del Bosque relegated Dubovský to the bench and his permanent replacement Jorge Valdano froze the Slovak out entirely when Raúl emerged. Had he gone to Ajax, a team with a far better track record of youth development, Dubovský could have been part of two Champions League finals in the mid-1990s.

Despite the setback Dubovský carved out a neat career in Spain after leaving Madrid. He moved to Oviedo where he became a crowd favourite before dying tragically young, aged just 28. On holiday in Thailand he fell from a waterfall on the island of Koh Samui, while trying to take a picture with his fiancée.

'Peter was a very talented and skilful player,' Dr Josef Venglos, the former Czechoslovakia and Aston Villa manager, said. 'A very modern player with excellent technical ability while being a good team player at the same time. In my opinion, he was up there with Zidane – he had the same graceful, aesthetic movement on and off the ball.

'He was definitely one of the top players of his generation, not only from Slovakia's point of view, but across the whole of Europe. He was Slovakian, but he played like a Brazilian.'

Slovan's prize for winning the inaugural Slovak league was a UEFA Cup berth rather than Champions League spot. UEFA restricted access to the Champions League in 1994/95 to only the 'top' 24 leagues. The Czech Republic kept Czechoslovakia's coefficient points, meaning Sparta qualified as Czech champions but Slovan did not as Slovakian champions and have never subsequently made it to the group stages.

Košice, Žilina and Artmedia Bratislava are the only Slovak teams to make the Champions League group stages with Artmedia being responsible for Slovakian club football's best moment since independence with a victory against Celtic.

A lot has been written retrospectively about the quality of that Celtic team – most of it unfair. That season they went on to win the Scottish League by 17 points, the year previously they had knocked Barcelona out of the UEFA Cup and the year afterwards they made the knockout stages of the Champions League. In between Artmedia battered them 5-0.

CSKA Moscow vs Barcelona

When taking the long view of history it may be hard to compare the sports club of the Red Army to an underdog, but in this time and place they very much were.

Russia was particularly badly affected by the post-Soviet economic turbulence. When the European Cup first round draw was made, 125 rubles could buy you a dollar. By the time CSKA and Barcelona met that figure had jumped to 368 rubles to the dollar, a near 200 per cent increase. Hyperinflation was hurting the economy. Prices rose by 2,520 per cent in 1992 as a result of deregulation and the Russian Central Bank was printing money at a record clip.

Barcelona, as previously chronicled, were the Dream Team, lining up with Cruyff, Laudrup, Stoichkov, Koeman, Guardiola et al.

Historically CSKA had focused their sporting resources on ice hockey and basketball to the detriment of football. The club's most successful period was immediately after the Second World War, winning five titles in six years. Between then and winning the final Soviet championship there was only one other title to report, in 1970.

The 1980s saw CSKA relegated to the second division and they only returned to Top League in 1990, making their ascent to the summit of Russian football all the more noteworthy.

European experience was thin on the ground. CSKA's only European Cup campaign ended in a second-round defeat to Standard Liège and their 1991/92 Cup Winners' Cup efforts were thwarted in the first round by AS Roma.

Not much could be gleaned from CSKA's opening-round victory either. The draw had paired them with the Icelandic champions Víkingur and over two legs the Russians won 5-2.

While Víkingur had been hosted at the 10,000-capacity Grigory Fedotov Stadium, the visit of Barcelona demanded a bigger arena so the first leg was played in front of 40,000 fans at the Luzhniki Stadium, the home of the 1980 Olympic Games.

Guardiola gifted CSKA the perfect start. Aleksandr Grishin caught Guardiola in possession and had a clear path to goal, which he gleefully took to open the scoring. But in the second half, Txiki Begiristain bailed out his friend, getting on the end of a sweeping move to take an away-goal advantage to the Camp Nou.

Three of CSKA's championship-winning team of 1991 – Dmitri Galiamin, Dmitri Kuznetsov and Igor Korneev – had already made the journey to Catalonia and signed for Espanyol. But the absence that was felt the most was Mikhail Yeremin. Yeremin was CSKA's title-winning goalkeeper who died from injuries sustained in a car accident one day after he had been part of a 3-2 Soviet Cup Final victory over Torpedo Moscow.

Given the economic climate, no Russian TV station could afford Barcelona's asking price for the broadcasting rights. After half an hour that frugality looked eminently sensible as Barcelona were two goals to the good through Miguel Ángel Nadal, and Begiristain again. 'We all thought it was done,' admitted Michael Laudrup.

CSKA manager Gennadi Kostylev made a first-half substitution as Grishin, the goalscorer from the first leg, was replaced by Dmitri Karsakov. It proved to be an inspired decision. Karsakov found Evgeni Bushmanov's surging run on the stroke of half-time and Bushmanov lashed the ball so firmly it hit the bar twice before crossing the white line.

Karsakov, playing without fear like only a young player can, laid the equaliser on a plate for Denis Mashkarin to score with a free header from inside the six-yard box. The provider then turned scorer with an audacious back-heeled finish that Cruyff would even appreciate and that was enough for CSKA to go through in what was a full-blown nightmare for the Dream Team.

Barcelona would come back stronger the following season but the night belonged to CSKA and Dmitri Karsakov.

The in-house newspaper of the Red Army, *Krasnaya Zvezda*, praised the collectivism of the CSKA players and lauded them for putting on a 'footballing tango'. The paper also put the victory into context: 'The daily reality unfortunately does not give us cause for joy. And yet there are still moments in our lives that bring a single gust of enthusiasm, excitement, and optimism.'

The Russian Bear could still roar. Only one eastern European team would be in the inaugural Champions League group stage and CSKA had earned their place by knocking out the holders.

Crème de la Crème

CSKA MOSCOW'S reward for knocking out Barcelona was a place in Group A of the inaugural UEFA Champions League. Joining Moscow in this four-team, double round-robin stage were Rangers, Marseille and Club Brugge.

Foeke Booy was a Dutchman playing for Brugge and one of two key reasons they won the 1991/92 Belgian Pro League. His 23 goals, backed up by 15 from teenage Nigerian striker Daniel Amokachi, fired the Blauw-Zwart (Blue-Black) ahead of their domestic rivals.

'Great memories,' sighs Amokachi when asked about the title campaign. 'That season made Daniel Amokachi. I was a 17/18-year-old who started the season as third choice but I got my chance and by the end of the season I won the league for Brugge. I couldn't stop scoring.' He chuckled as he added for emphasis, 'It was a damn good season.'

Brugge had some European pedigree too. They been European Cup finalists in 1978 when they lost to

Liverpool at Wembley via a solitary Kenny Dalglish goal. They also lost a UEFA Cup Final in 1976 to the same opposition and in 1991/92 they reached the semi-final of the Cup Winners' Cup.

'We played well in the Cup Winners' Cup the year previously beating Atlético Madrid and losing to Werder Bremen by one goal,' remembers Amokachi.

'We were having a good run in the league and had good players like Lorenzo Staelens, Dany Verlinden and Franky Van der Elst, who had been to a World Cup semi-final. We had a feeling that we would "give it a go", anything could happen but we knew Marseille would give us a headache.'

On Wednesday, 25 November 1992 at 8.30pm Central European Time all four group stage matches kicked off. Club Brugge vs CSKA Moscow and Glasgow Rangers vs Olympique Marseille were in Group A while AC Milan hosted IFK Gothenburg and Porto played PSV Eindhoven in Group B.

There was no staggered kick-off times nor split matchdays. UEFA organised four games simultaneously and terrestrial channels had to choose what match to show, if any. While showing Rangers vs Marseille was a no-brainer in the three Scottish ITV regions only, Central, Granada, Thames and Ulster opted to show the match in the rest of the UK. Football fans in Tyne Tees, Yorkshire, Anglia, Wales and the south of England had to wait until 10.40pm local time for highlights.

The first goal of the new competition was scored by Amokachi. Brugge sprang a poorly executed offside trap to put the Nigerian clear and he rounded the CSKA keeper before passing the ball into the net from the edge of the box.

'The goal is in my head but I didn't know it was the first goal in the Champions League when I scored it,' reminisced Amokachi. 'Only years later did people talk about the history of the goal.'

It was Amokachi's first game back that season, after he had sustained a muscle tear playing for Nigeria in an African Cup of Nations qualifier in Lagos against Uganda. 'Luckily for me the coach [Hugo Broos] believed in me and put me in the team,' he said.

It was the solitary goalmouth action of that game, giving Brugge the two points for the win.

By the autumn of 1992 Olympique Marseille were a Rorschach test – you saw what you wanted to see. There was the pedigree: Marseille had won the previous four French championships and had been to a European Cup Final plus another semi-final. But equally, there was the chaos, including a president who seemed more interested in his political career than the football club he once doted on, a revolving door of coaches and the regular suggestion of financial implosion.

In 1986 the mayor of Marseille, Gaston Deferre, practically begged Bernard Tapie to buy the club and revive their fortunes. Tapie had made his name as the boss of La Vie Claire, a chain of health shops, and showed his sporting inclinations by forming a road cycling team.

For his cycling team he signed the most sought-after free-agent rider, Bernard Hinault, a four-time Tour de France winner who had fallen out with his Renault team after injury dropped him below Laurent Fignon in the pecking order. In their first Tour, the La Vie Claire team finished second, behind only Fignon. In response, Tapie signed Greg LeMond, Fignon's top domestique, and the next year Hinault won a fifth Tour de France to equal Eddy Merckx's record.

The following year La Vie Claire placed four riders in the top ten of the general classification and the yellow jersey was fought out between the top two team-mates, Hinault and LeMond – with the American winning his first grand tour. With innovations like the use of heart rate monitors and carbon fibre, Tapie's operation was very much the Team Sky of its day.

Marseille, at the time, were living on their history. The club was one of the most successful in France in the 1920s and had a renaissance in the late 1960s and early 1970s, winning two leagues and two cups. Since then they had suffered some humiliating European results (including a 6-0 loss to FC Köln and a 4-0 defeat to Southampton), relegation and bankruptcy. Only in 1984 did they regain top-flight status.

Tapie immediately brought about an uptick in Marseille's fortunes. Bordeaux achieved the double but shrewd signings like Alain Giresse and Jean-Pierre Papin meant that Marseille were their closest challengers, finishing runners-up in both league and cup. This gave Marseille their first European football for over a decade, which led to a run to the semi-finals of the Cup Winners' Cup, before losing to Ajax.

In the 1988/89 season Marseille won their own double but it wasn't all plain sailing. Tapie sacked his coach just two games into the season and promoted Gérard Gili from the youth team. Gili blooded the younger players and many, such as Eric Di Meco, went on to be club stalwarts.

For the assault on the citadel that was the European Cup, Tapie figured he needed to overhaul his squad. His number one target was the best player in the world – Diego Maradona.

L'Équipe 's front page on 3 June 1989 splashed with 'Maradona in Marseille'. An article continued, 'The greatest footballer in the world will be in Marseille to meet Bernard Tapie. The talks between the two men – prepared yesterday in Naples by Michel Hidalgo – could lead to the transfer of the century.'

'I was at Napoli and the president Ferlaino had told me that if we won the UEFA Cup he would let me leave,' remembered Maradona. 'Marseille offered to double my salary.'

Maradona said he wanted to end his career somewhere calmer. That Tapie's Marseille was seen as a calmer port speaks more to the chaos of Naples than the tranquility of Provence.

Napoli did win the UEFA Cup in a thrilling two-legged final against Jürgen Klinsmann's Stuttgart but Ferlaino backtracked on his promise to let Maradona leave. 'I was Maradona's jailer,' he said some years later.

A pre-contract agreement had been signed but Napoli were refusing to sell. Maradona won one more Scudetto in Naples, further entangling himself with controversy, cocaine and the Camorra. Tapie's plan B was to sign one half of Britain's most famous synth pop duo.

Chris Waddle was at the All England Tennis Club watching Steffi Graf and Chris Evert battle it out for a place in the 1989 Wimbledon ladies singles final against Martina Navratilova when he was told to report to White Hart Lane. His club, Tottenham Hotspur, had accepted a £4.5m bid from Marseille.

The first half of Glenn & Chris – as named on their 1987 single, 'Diamond Lights' – had already been in France for two years at Marseille's rivals Monaco. In his first season, Glenn Hoddle won the league and in his second he scored 20 goals, second only to Papin.

Waddle joined two other foreign imports in the south of France. The Brazilian centre-back Carlos Mozer was lured from Benfica and Uruguayan playmaker Enzo Francescoli joined from Racing Paris.

And a 17-year-old Marseille native who had just made his professional debut for Cannes was enthralled by Francescoli, modelling his playing style after him. 'He was my favourite player and I used to hang around to watch him train,' recalled Zinedine Zidane.

The foreign legion was bolstered by several domestic signings as well. Didier Deschamps joined from Nantes, Alain Roche from Bordeaux and Les Bleus skipper Manuel Amoros from Monaco.

That season Marseille won the league but lost an agonising European Cup semi-final against Benfica. With less than ten minutes remaining in the tie, Angolan striker Vata scored from a corner to give Benfica the advantage on away goals. However, Vata had clearly punched the ball into the goal. The error was so egregious that UEFA hauled the Belgian referee Marcel van Langenhove in front of a tribunal to answer questions about whether he was bribed. They concluded not and Van Lagenhove was allowed to referee at the 1990 World Cup.

In 1990/91 a further influx of talent including goalkeeper Pascal Olmeta, Basile Boli, Abedi Pele,

Franck Sauzée and Red Star Belgrade playmaker Dragan Stojković prepared to take another tilt at European glory. Ghananian Pele was about to be voted African Footballer of the Year for the first of three consecutive seasons but owing to the amount of time he had spent in France he was no longer classed as a foreign player under UEFA rules and instead qualified as an assimilated player.

The high point was in March 1991 when Marseille beat the two-time defending European champions Milan in the quarter-finals. In the San Siro they matched the Rossoneri stride for stride and their goal came courtesy of their exceptional front three. Pele ran a literal ring around Carlo Ancelotti and drew Alessandro Costacurta; he found Waddle who in turn played Papin in with a gorgeous curved pass. Papin didn't miss when one on one.

Carrying an away-goal advantage in their back pocket, Marseille turned in a flawless performance. Waddle may have had his finest of many fine nights in a Marseille shirt, fully justifying his 'Magic Chris' moniker bestowed on him by the Velodrome faithful. He tormented Paolo Maldini all evening, something that rarely happened, and scored the Marseille winner. This time it was a Pele cross, a Papin flick-on and a right-footed Waddle volley, in off the post.

In that match Waddle nearly scored a contender for the greatest goal of all time. Picking up the ball halfway inside his own half he dribbled for 50 yards, glided past Maldini, Costacurta and Franco Baresi, only to trip himself up when rounding the keeper at top speed. When Waddle left Sebastiano Rossi for dead, Barry Davies on commentary blurted out 'that's a brilliant goal'. It would have been Barry, it would have been.

During that run, two of the four floodlight pylons at the crumbling pre-renovation Velodrome went out. The game was still perfectly playable especially with just two minutes remaining but sensing their goose was cooked, Milan director Adriano Galliani refused to let the team return to the field. Milan's hopes of a replay à la Red Star 1988 were quashed. UEFA saw through the ruse and not only awarded the game 3-0 to Marseille but banned Milan from its competitions for a season.

That campaign would end in tears from 12 yards for Marseille. Their attacking power scared Red Star so much that it became their own undoing, even though the side should have won France's first European Cup.

The following season, perhaps suffering a European hangover despite at one stage leading 3-0, Marseille were eliminated in the second round on away goals by an underrated Sparta Prague outfit. However, for many observers the bloom was off the rose.

Tapie had joined the government as City Minister and was told by François Mitterrand to clean up his business affairs if he wanted to ever seek higher office. Tapie wanted to sell sports equipment manufacturer Adidas, which he had bought in 1989, and needed Marseille to stop costing him quite so much money.

Papin, the 1991 Ballon d'Or winner and darling of the fans, left for Milan in exchange for £10m – a world record transfer fee. In an emotional speech on the pitch before a home game, Papin said, 'I don't want to linger or else I will start crying. For six years now we haven't told each other any lies, we have been truthful. So I think that if I'm going where I am going it's because I owe you all. Thank you from the bottom of my heart. I will never forget you.'

Trevor Steven, who had joined Marseille from Rangers in 1991 for £5.5m, was shipped back to Glasgow for less than half that. Mozer returned to Benfica and Magic Chris was off too as Sheffield Wednesday parted with £1m. Waddle was described by then Owls boss Trevor Francis as 'the best £1m Wednesday ever spent', and he would know about million-pound signings having been Britain's first when moving to Nottingham Forest from Birmingham City in 1979.

In their place came a mixture of younger and cheaper options such as Fabien Barthez, Marcel Desailly, Jean-Jacques Eydelie, Alen Bokšić and the veteran German striker Rudi Völler. ITV's Jim Rosental had said in the pre-match build up that Völler, a veteran of two

World Cup finals had been living on past glories. Were Marseille a side in decline or just transition?

Eight days before their opening Champions League group stage tie against Rangers, coach Jean Fernandez was told to take four weeks rest by club president Tapie. For the third season in a row the veteran Belgian Raymond Goethals was called to take command of the team mid-campaign.

Goethals was nearly 70 when he stepped into the Marseille cauldron for the first time. Nicknamed 'Raymond la Science' in the press for his tactical acumen, his players knew him as 'Grandpère' (Grandad). Even today you can hear the affection Goethals was held in when you talk to one of his former Marseille foot soldiers.

Like only old men could he had zero regard for the sensibilities of others. His opening remark at his first press conference as Marseille manager was 'silence in the barracks' as he demanded the assembled media quieten to hear from him. He would coach with a laconic cigarette dripping from his lips and once Eric Cantona told him that he wouldn't sit on the bench, so Goethals shrugged, 'Sit next to it then.'

Rangers were without their top scorer McCoist through injury. Mark Hateley would lead the line as a lone forward with support from Ian Durrant, wearing McCoist's number nine shirt from midfield, Steven on the right flank and Alexei Mikhailichenko on the left. Mikhailichenko was a Ukrainian who helped Sampdoria win their first (and to date only) Scudetto in 1991. He also came fourth in the 1988 Ballon d'Or voting, apparently making him the best player not playing at AC Milan in world football.

Marseille's first test was a high ball from Steven into a swirling Glasgow wind. This allowed his fellow Englishman Hateley to jostle Barthez's attempted punch but Mikhailichenko's finish with only Jocelyn Angloma guarding the net was not something that the Ballon d'Or voters would approve of.

But it was Rangers who succumbed to the most British of tactics, the long ball. Richard Gough completely missed a Barthez clearance that had the wind at its back and when both he and John Brown swarmed on Völler, who had taken up possession, they left Bokšić unmarked in the area. Völler found him and the Croat added another to go with his brace against Dinamo Bucharest.

Rangers's defence was shambolic for large parts of the first half, not aided by a groin injury to Gough. Völler in particular was a handful, rolling back the years. Boos could be heard when Sandor Puhl blew for half-time but Jean-Jacques Eydelie, who was among the visitors' substitutes, said after the booing the Ibrox crowd stood to applaud the Marseille team on their way back to the dressing room. A generous gesture that he remembers to this day.

Steven Pressley, a 19-year-old who Rangers had signed from Inverkeithing United Boys Club, came on at half-time to replace the Scotland captain. Unfortunately, it was Pressley's mistake that gifted Völler a second ten minutes into the half.

The driving rain made conditions difficult for defenders in the latter stages. Many players were slipping and the penalty boxes were arguably more mud than grass.

Hateley, a colossus in the aerial duel with Boli and Desailly all evening, was finally given a strike partner when Gary McSwegan was sent on for Steven with a quarter of an hour to play. Mikhailichenko pumped another high cross into the Marseille box and the heavy-legged defenders so used to sandwiching Hateley hadn't seemed to notice McSwegan had joined the fray. Unmarked, he steered a beautiful looping header back across goal which cushioned in off the post and the game was very much on.

As Marseille were preparing a match-killing substitution, Mikhailichenko dispossessed Pele with a firm but fair challenge. The Ukrainian fed Durrant, then a quick exchange of passes with McSwegan saw Durrant's low and dangerous cross from the byline met by Hateley's magnificent half-balding, half-mulleted head. He had run across a flat-footed Desailly and Barthez was furious with rage.

There would be one final chance for Marseille and had the Ibrox penalty area not resembled a ploughed field then the ball would have found an unmarked Pele ten yards out. Instead the ball stuck in the surface and the Ghananian slightly overran it.

It was an astonishing evening's football. My thoughts watching from my childhood bedroom were if this was the Champions League, sign me up.

When Brugge travelled to the south of France two weeks later they found their hosts smarting from throwing away a lead in Glasgow. The night started badly for Brugge when Vital Borkelmans, an international defender who should have known better, clattered Bokšić from behind to gift wrap Marseille a penalty after four minutes.

Future Hibernian cult hero Franck Sauzée addressed the kick with the sort of long run-up more usually associated with Dennis Lillee and Michael Holding. The result was just as devastating.

Jean-Christophe Thomas nearly scored an Olympic goal on ten minutes. His inswinging corner was inexplicably allowed to skim through the six-yard box curving on to the inside of the far post. Bokšić tapped in the rebound before scoring a third goal more fitting of his prodigious talent. Marseille were in irresistible form and Brugge had been blown away. Amokachi was full of praise for his opponents: 'Abedi Pele, my African big brother, was probably the best midfielder in the world at the time and they had great experience with the likes of Rudi Völler.

'Basile Boli was one of the most difficult defenders to play against and Marcel Desailly had so much quality that season. But don't forget Di Meco. I always say the left-back Eric Di Meco was one of my toughest opponents. He gave me a hard time and we never had it easy against Marseille.'

The official reason why CSKA Moscow had to play their Champions League home games outside of Russia was the inhospitable winter climate. Previously, a Moscovite team would take a game to the Black Sea or one of the Caucasus but the political situation made that impossible.

With inflation running at more than 2,500 per cent though, CSKA surely wouldn't have minded getting their hands on some foreign currency. Their preferred venue was Santander in Spain but UEFA nixed that idea and instead proffered Bochum in Germany's North Rhine-Westphalia.

The move was popular with Rangers, as not only was Bochum a relatively easy trip for their fans but they would be able to draw huge numbers of supporters from the large British army bases in that part of Germany.

CSKA goalkeeper Aleksandr Guteev, made an horrendous error on 13 minutes when he failed to claim a cross. After Ian Ferguson scored in the unguarded net there was no doubt that the 9,000-strong crowd was predominantly British. Guteev, normally a reserve, had been pressed into service because the club had sold their captain Dmitri Kharine to Chelsea. Rangers won 1-0.

As the Champions League entered its winter break Marseille and Rangers topped Group A on three points, with Brugge third on two and CSKA yet to score.

Marseille would have hoped that they could use their meetings with CSKA in rounds three and four to stretch their advantage over their principal rivals. The Russian season takes winter off so they were playing a rusty Moscow. Again their 'home' tie would be played in Germany but Berlin not Bochum this time.

If UEFA or CSKA were hoping for some of their former Warsaw Pact comrades to turn out to cheer on the football team of the Red Army at the Olympiastadion, deep in the heart of the former East Berlin, that was a misreading of both history and economics. What crowd there was in the unsuitably large stadium was heavily pro Marseille.

The teams drew 1-1 on a bitterly cold evening. Völler missed the contest thanks to an injury sustained against Monaco and most of the Marseille players wore what appeared to be ski gloves, as did even some of the

Russians. Barthez, who despite being a brilliant keeper always looked like he had a mistake in him, had to be bailed out by Desailly when his attempted clearance connected with nothing but air.

Goethals's men would make up for their lacklustre performance with a 6-0 victory that can only be described as a walloping. Völler was back and Sauzée claimed a hat-trick.

Brugge and Rangers then drew in Belgium with a goal from Polish forward Tomasz Dziubiński for the Belgians and Peter Huistra of the Netherlands for the Scots.

Amokachi says it was fantastic for him to be able to fly to Glasgow for the second match: 'Rangers, Celtic, Dundee United, Aberdeen – when we were growing up in Nigeria buying *Shoot!* and *Match* magazine these were the teams we learned about.'

Durrant opened the scoring on 39 minutes with a trademark burst from midfield, brilliantly picked out by Steven. Rangers sat down at half-time with the advantage but a numerical deficit as Hateley had been dismissed shortly after the goal for violent conduct. Brugge regained parity shortly after the break thanks to Staelens, assisted by the cultured left foot of Stéphane Van der Heyden

Right-back Scott Nisbet is referenced in Irvine Welsh's *Trainspotting* as an example of the type of local player that Rangers looked over in favour of more expensive foreign imports. Nisbet had been at the club since 1985 and recently established himself in the first team.

In the Brugge game Nisbet instinctively swung boot at ball during a scrappy passage of play in the final third. His strike ballooned skywards off Van der Heyden and the goalkeeper Verlinden began to come to deal with the danger. However, the topspin generated from the half-block meant that the ball was dropping faster than Verlinden could scramble forward and he aborted his pursuit. Upon landing, the ball spun and bounced viciously up and over Verlinden who could only have been three yards off his line. The freakiest of freak goals but Nisbet, Ibrox and half of Glasgow did not care. Rangers won 2-1, they were level on points with Marseille and were potentially two games away from the Champions League Final.

Luck is a fickle mistress though, and three days after it smiled on Nisbet against Brugge it deserted him. Playing against Celtic in the Old Firm derby, Nisbet suffered a career-ending pelvis injury and Rangers lost for the first time in 44 matches.

If either Rangers or Marseille won their match in the Velodrome that side would qualify for the final. It was in essence a semi-final and UEFA entrusted it to a 37-year-old school teacher from the Netherlands. Mario van der

Ende had a reputation for being a no-nonsense sort of referee who was comfortable with a physical contest.

Trevor Steven, who had spent a season on the French Riviera, claimed before the match: 'I know they respect us and are prepared for a long 90 minutes.' And he added, in typical footballer speak, 'I've a funny feeling it won't be settled until the last five minutes or so.'

Rangers would need to be at their best to win. Marseille had won their last 14 home ties in Europe and their visitors were without Hateley through suspension. The public address system blasted out Van Halen's 'Jump' as the white and blue shirts marched to the centre of the pitch. The crowd didn't need a second invitation.

Walter Smith and co. talked a good game before the contest. Outwardly they projected confidence and talked of attacking even if the 4-5-1 formation they used suggested more counter than outright attack. The fans too were optimistic, one banner predicting the final matchup – 'AC Milan versus AC Govan'.

Mike Tyson once said, 'Everybody has a plan until they get punched in the face.' Rangers could agree with that sentiment after going one down on 15 minutes. Völler was again the provider for Sauzée to fire home from the edge of the area.

At the interval Rangers trailed and headed to the catacomb-like belly of the Velodrome to regroup. En route to the away dressing room they passed the officials' changing area where McSwegan said Tapie was trying to talk to the Dutch group but was being vigorously waved away.

Van der Ende confirmed the account: 'It is true. In the break Tapie came to ask if he "could do anything for us". I immediately ordered him to leave the dressing room in a compelling tone. Fortunately I spoke French. In my opinion, this was very inappropriate for a club president.'

Tapie was powerless to influence the outcome; it would be decided by the 23 men on the pitch, and Sauzée started the second half with a 25-yard free kick that crashed on to the crossbar. Goram's feet were rooted like a great oak. The shot was so forceful that it carried straight back to Sauzée but he and Pele got in each other's way when trying to volley home the rebound.

Rangers then earned a corner and Steven delivered a right-footed inswinger from the left. Völler's famous perm readied to clear but at the last moment Angloma rose to meet it as well, and his glancing touch was enough to deflect the ball towards Durrant who met the flick on the half-volley. For once Boli wasn't a lion and he half pulled out of the charge-down, turning his back at a crucial moment to reduce the space he was occupying. Durrant's strike was the sweetest connection and rippled into Barthez's net.

Visiting fans exploded in what may have been the original inspiration for the 'limbs' meme. For Durrant the goal was a starter's pistol and he careered around the pitch with his arms outstretched messiah-like in search of an embrace. Ferguson, Gough and McCoist obliged him.

As the seconds ticked away the tackles grew in ferocity. Neil Murray kicked Pele up and down the flank, while Marseille's Di Meco left his studs in on McCoist without sanction. Even Deschamps, normally the very picture of calmness in the midfield, was flying in on his opponents.

Neither team really showed enough ambition to risk what they had in pursuit of a victory. They were two prizefighters in the 12th round content to let it go to the judges.

After 450 minutes of Champions League football the French and Scottish champions were locked together on seven points each. Marseille held the slenderest of advantages though, as if the teams matched each other's results on matchday six then they would go through by virtue of scoring two away goals at Ibrox to Rangers's one at the Velodrome.

Brugge had beaten CSKA in front of just 2,000 supporters in Berlin and sat on five points. Theoretically they were still alive but they would need a Moscovite victory in Glasgow and to beat Marseille by four goals at home. Their most realistic role now was as a spoiler.

Goethals spent the build-up to the match telling anyone who would listen that he was going to retire at the end of the season. The 71-year-old was upset that several of his squad were set to bolt for Serie A clubs. He was widely quoted as saying the players he would be left were 'too weak' to make it worthwhile his continuing. That's one way to motivate a team.

Come matchday six the bookies had Rangers as favourites to make the final, as they were odds-on to beat CSKA at home with Marseille just given an even money chance of getting the result they needed in Belgium.

As it happened Bokšić scored after two minutes for Marseille, and try as they might, Rangers couldn't find the net in their game. Gough put a free header in the Broomloan Stand, Steven hit the crossbar, while McCoist, who scored 49 goals in 1992/93 to win the European Golden Boot for the second straight season, missed three chances that he would normally devour. The respective final whistles in Glasgow and Bruges confirmed Marseille's return to the showpiece of the European club game.

Speaking some years later, Walter Smith offered a positive view: 'The boys gave everything on the night, as they did over that entire campaign. We fell short in the sense that we didn't go all the way, but there was still enormous pride and satisfaction in that we went as far as we did.'

Rangers thought they would be back the following season for another crack, adding a £4m striker from Dundee United in the shape of Duncan Ferguson. He was needed too. Ally McCoist broke his leg on international duty the week after Rangers crashed out to CSKA.

Big Dunc couldn't prevent a first-round exit to Levski Sofia on away goals in 1993/94 and the following season even the additions of Brian Laudrup and Basile Boli couldn't get Rangers past AEK in the qualifying round for the 16-team group stage.

Finally, signing Paul Gascoigne to their squad was enough to beat Cypriot champions Anorthosis Famagusta 1-0 on aggregate to make the group stage in 1995/96 but only once since then have they progressed out of the groups into the knockout rounds. That happened in 2005/06 when Rangers lost on away goals to surprise semi-finalists Villarreal of Spain.

Their greatest European adventure of recent times occurred when Walter Smith returned for a second spell as manager and led a 19-match odyssey that began in Podgorica, Montenegro and culminated in a defeat to Zenit St Petersburg in Manchester in the 2007/08 UEFA Cup Final.

Once more a Russian side got between Rangers and European glory.

The Group of Death

WE ARE assured that the 1992/93 Champions League group stage draw was random but had UEFA just announced to groups of 'haves' and 'have nots', the results would have been the same.

Group B contained sides that had won six European Cups, three UEFA Cups, two Cup Winners' Cups, three Super Cups and four Intercontinental Cups. Group A's only European trophy between them was Rangers's 1972 Cup Winners' Cup.

Even IFK Gothenburg of Sweden, the least celebrated team in Group B, had won two UEFA Cups in the past decade. Porto, the 1987 European Cup winners, 1988 champions PSV Eindhoven, AC Milan, winners in 1989 and 1990, were the other participants.

In the first round Porto barely broke sweat against Union of Luxembourg in a comfortable 9-1 aggregate victory. Their tour of European countries with the highest per capita GDP continued with a second-round visit to Switzerland to face Sion. The Portuguese found themselves 2-0 down with ten minutes to go in the first leg and could have been more adrift had Vítor Baía not been playing so well. Sion's goals were courtesy of Davide Orlando and Roberto Assis. The second from Assis was the type of free kick that we would come to associate with his younger brother – Ronaldinho.

José Semedo, a squad member in 1986/87, pulled one back before a powerful Fernando Couto header made it all square. Couto was so elated at scoring that it looked like he momentarily considered a somersault to celebrate. Had he done so his 110-cap international career could have been in jeopardy, not to mention his future continental success. Couto went on to win the 1995 UEFA Cup with Parma and two Cup Winners' Cups, one each with Barcelona and Lazio.

This Porto squad had three survivors from the team that beat Bayern Munich in the 1987 final – António André, Jaime Magalhães and the captain João Pinto. Rabah Madjer, the Algerian scorer of an outrageous back-heel in said final (seriously, YouTube it), had sadly retired but Porto didn't miss his firepower and ran out 6-2 winners on aggregate. Class of '87 alumni Magalhães completed the scoring.

Porto would play PSV in their first Champions League match. PSV had won the 1988 European Cup in Guus Hiddink's first full season as a coach. They had done it the hard way too – drawing all five of their last matches to produce away-goals victories over Bordeaux and Real Madrid, before relying on penalties to beat Benfica in the final. The curse of Béla Gutmann, who after leaving his coaching role with the two-time winners in 1962 following a fall-out said they would never be European champions again, struck once more.

The Dutch champions in six of the previous seven years, Eindhoven had firmly set their sights on European success. Former England manager Bobby Robson delivered two league championships in two seasons but disappointing continental results saw him sacked in favour of Hans Westerhof.

PSV had five of their European Cup winners on display when they lined up against Porto in November 1992 – Hans van Breukelen, Jan Heintze, Gerald Vanenburg, Edward Linskens and Wim Kieft. But the only name on anyone's lips was Romário.

Romário's attitude to coaching is best summed up by his own words: 'The coach should keep out of the way. He is an important figure, of course, but is more likely to lose a match than win it. Matches are won by players.'

Believe it or not, Romário liked training even less than he liked coaching. Robson, a man who had barely a cross word for anybody, labelled the Brazilian 'pathetically lazy' – but he still picked him. Not without coincidence, Romário scored 165 goals in 167 games in five seasons at PSV.

In the second round against AEK Athens, PSV trailed 1-0. It wasn't a problem for them and Romário netted a hat-trick to earn qualification for the Champions League. Two were fantastic centre-forward's goals, anticipating through balls and finishing with just one touch. His third delved into his bag of tricks and showed his game had more to it than poaching.

'He was my room-mate at PSV, when we were on the road. An amazing player. But he hated training!' confirmed Kalusha Bwayla, Zambia's greatest ever footballer. 'Over five metres there was no one faster than Romário.'

Against Porto, Romário scored a brace. One of those goals was after getting on the end of a driven cross and one was via an effortless-looking free kick. He could do it all, when he wanted to.

Unfortunately, for PSV they were reduced to ten men with Adri van Tiggelen becoming the answer to the quiz question that never gets asked. Who was the first player sent off the UEFA Champions League? The subsequent free kick took a wicked deflection to beat Van Breukelen and it finished Porto 2 PSV 2.

If the game in Porto was all about one striker, so was the one in Milan. Despite the arrival of more than £27m of attacking talent in the summer, in the shape of Gianluigi Lentini, Jean-Pierre Papin and Dejan Savićević, there was still only one Marco van Basten. Just so you didn't forget, Van Basten knocked four past IFK Gothenburg. The third goal, a bicycle kick, is still replayed as one of the best goals in Champions League history.

At the time there was a view that IFK might be the whipping boys of Group B – a wholly incorrect prediction as it turned out – making Van Basten's exploits all the more remarkable.

Van Basten was the first player to score a hat-trick and get four goals in a Champions League match. It would take another seven and a half years and 323 matches before anyone would equal him, when Simone Inzaghi scored four for Lazio vs Marseille in 1999/2000.

Since his early days, fans had called Van Basten the 'Swan of Utrecht' as a tribute both to his power and serenity. Berlusconi had another nickname for his Dutch master, addressing him as 'Milan's Nureyev' after the great Rudolf Nureyev, commonly held to be the finest ballet dancer of his generation.

Historically an important city for trade and shipping, Gothenburg was enjoying a rare moment in the cultural spotlight in 1992. Apart from being posterised by Marco van Basten, Gothenburg was in the cultural zeitgeist thanks to the Berggren siblings. Ace of Base temporarily had a whole continent going gaga for reggae-inspired

Euro-pop. *Happy Nation*, with its UK and US number one singles 'The Sign' and 'All That She Wants', became the biggest-selling debut album of all time and shifted more than 23 million copies.

On the football pitch Gothenburg hosted the final of Euro 92 but the Swedish national side had already lost in the semis to a newly unified Germany. However, it was ten years prior that IFK Gothenburg announced themselves to the footballing world. A young manager, playing a rigid 4-4-2 system with a direct passing style would lead IFK to the 1982 UEFA Cup Final.

Sven-Göran Eriksson led a team of cooks, plumbers and clerks to victory over German giants Hamburg 4-0 on aggregate, including winning the second leg in Germany 3-0. That Hamburg side were no mugs and the following season, with only the addition of Wolfgang Rolff, they would win the European Cup. Eriksson's success meant he wouldn't be long for IFK – taking the opportunity to join Benfica, the first step on a journey that saw him coach all over the globe.

Swedish club football was historically the strongest of the Nordic countries but that is more an indictment of their neighbours than anything else. Malmö FF, coached by former Maidstone United manager Bob Houghton, had improbably made the 1979 European Cup Final where they lost to Brian Clough's Nottingham Forest.

Prior to Malmö, Sweden's best European Cup performance was arguably Åtvidaberg's first-round loss to Bayern Munich in 1973/74. The Bavarians needed penalties to get past the Swedish champions who were not much more than a works team of the mechanical calculator manufacturers Facit.

The most remarkable thing about IFK's success in the 1980s was that they sustained it. In 1984/85 they reached the European Cup quarter-finals and went one better the following season. Gunder Bengtsson, an Eriksson assistant in 1982, took IFK to within a penalty shoot-out of a European Cup final.

The 1986 European Cup semi-final between IFK and Barcelona is one of the more remarkable in the competition's history. Barça were completely feeble in the first leg, unable to cope with the directness of IFK. Torbjörn Nilsson, who Eriksson said was the best striker he ever managed (take note messrs Baggio, Bokšić, Crespo, Owen, Rooney and Vieri), scored twice in the first half and the Swedes were value for the 3-0 lead they had before the hour.

Glenn Hysén, a commanding centre-half as well as a future Fiorentina and Liverpool defender, missed the game in the Camp Nou through injury. Through the striker Pichi, Barcelona scored first in the second encounter but there was still no doubt that IFK were the better side.

Twice Gothenburg had the ball in the back of the net only for an offside flag to cancel out their strikes, while Johnny Ekström was taken out when clean through on goal, the sort of 'professional foul' that UEFA would legislate against in the early 1990s.

Barcelona's frustration was evident and Lobo Carrasco shoulder-charged IFK goalkeeper Thomas Wernersson, leading to a melee. Ángel Pedraza dived to try to win a penalty and José Ramón Alexanko somehow avoided scoring an own goal when he turned the ball on to his own crossbar. IFK were battering Barcelona in front of their own fans. But somehow Pichi managed to find two more goals and took the game to the lottery of penalties.

To add to the amateur feel of the IFK team, Wernersson took and converted their second penalty in the shoot-out. Next he did what you wish all keepers would have the guts to do – he didn't move and Carrasco's tame left-footed shot went right at him. It was advantage IFK and right-back Roland Nilsson had a penalty to take IFK to the final, but his shot was also saved. Nilsson went for placement over power. Two kicks later, IFK were out.

Not to rest on their laurels, IFK made the UEFA Cup final the next season – beating Inter Milan and Ernst Happel's Swarovski Tirol on their journey. At the time Happel was the only coach to win the European Cup with two different clubs (Feyenoord and Hamburg) and Swarovski Tirol were playing in a UEFA Cup semi-final in their first season after formation. The Swarovski crystal company had bought FC Wacker Innsbruck's Austrian Bundesliga licence and established a new team. In the final, IFK defeated another feel-good story, Scottish side Dundee United. European football in the 1980s was wild.

By 1992 none of the IFK players who had won the UEFA Cup were still playing for the club. Their only link with their past was Johnny Ekström, a part of the 1986 side, who had returned to Gothenburg following a five-year rumspringa that took in Empoli in Italy, Bayern Munich and Cannes.

The other less obvious link was the manager Roger Gustafsson. He had been a youth team coach from 1983 to 89 before getting the senior gig in 1990. Gustafsson brought through a lot of his youth team protégés into the first team and IFK were able to win back-to-back Swedish championships in 1990 and 1991.

'Roger is a fantastically good coach, who invested a lot in the younger players,' insists Jonas Olsson, one of those younger players. 'We trained extremely hard and had a very clear idea of our game.'

After beating Beşiktaş and Poznań, the Swedes were playing with house money. They had already surpassed their pre-tournament goal of making the group phase, so everything from there on was a bonus.

'In the 90s, the other European teams were professional while we were amateurs,' Olsson explains. 'We worked or studied alongside football and had limited opportunities to train during the day, which our opponents could do.'

Olsson had only just come back from a two-year layoff and missed the whole group stage because of a broken leg, which was a particularly tough injury for a part-time footballer.

'No one expected anything from us as we had an inexperienced team and we did not have a good season in the Swedish league in 1992,' he remembers.

IFK's knockout matches were played at the Gamla Ullevi stadium (literally 'Old' Ullevi), which had been built during the First World War with a capacity of around 18,000. For the Champions League, IFK moved their fixtures to the Nya Ullevi (New Ullevi), a 43,000-seater with a rich history.

Built for the 1958 World Cup, the Nya Ullevi was where Wales nearly shocked Brazil in their only World Cup appearance to date; in 1983 and 1990 the stadium hosted the Cup Winners' Cup finals and its record attendance was set when Bruce Springsteen fans saw the Born in the USA tour stop in Gothenburg. Some 65,000 Boss fans dancing in the dark were so enthusiastic they actually damaged the stadium. Its foundations had to be reinforced and no concerts could be held at the bigger venue for six years.

When only 22,000 fans turned out for IFK's opening group contest against Portuguese champions Porto, the Gothenburg brass must have wondered whether playing at Nya Ullevi was worth the extra expense. The game was goalless and meandering towards a draw when midfielder Peter Eriksson thought he spotted a bit of space at Baía's near post. From an audaciously acute angle he let fly and scored. The future UEFA European Goalkeeper of the Year and winner of more than 20 major club honours in his career was left red-faced. He had a long plane trip home and three-month winter break to dwell on the error.

Matchday two's other clash was PSV vs Milan, or Romário vs Van Basten. Romário gave the edge to his opponent when he revealed who he thought the seven best players in the world were, in this order: Van Basten, Rijkaard, Bebeto, Baggio, Bergkamp, Matthäus, Romário.

In the first half it was Van Basten the provider as his left-footed cross found Rijkaard's head for an exquisite opener straight from the Ajax training ground. On 62 minutes Milan doubled their lead, Marco Simone meeting a Stefano Eranio cross.

To get back into the contest PSV looked to their Brazilian striker. Gerald Vanenburg, another member of the 1988 Dutch European Championship squad with Surinamese ancestry, found Romário with his back to goal. Flick. Chest. Knee. Swivel. Instep. Goal. The only man faster in a box than Romário in the early 1990s was Clark Kent.

In the dying stages PSV had a penalty claim for handball waved away. Had VAR been in operation, UEFA's refereeing unit in Nyon would be buzzing the referee asking him to review his decision. Rijkaard's arm position could only be considered natural if he was a marionette.

No one knew this at the time but we had just seen the last game Milan's three tulips would ever play together. Gullit, Van Basten and Rijkaard; the most iconic trio on football's most iconic team never saw the same field again.

Four days later Van Basten suffered a recurrence of his long-standing ankle problem and opted to have surgery – there was time to recover as the next meaningful Champions League game was months away. Domestically Italy was about to head into a winter break and Milan were already eight points clear, in the days of two for a win, of Fiorentina. While he was recovering from his surgery, Van Basten was announced as the winner of the Ballon d'Or for the third time. Only Johan Cruyff and Michel Platini could match that accomplishment.

March 1993 rolled around and Van Basten still wasn't fit, but Milan had a £10m former Ballon d'Or winner in Jean-Pierre Papin to lead the line. Berlusconi's largesse looked like shrewd insurance, especially given the Frenchman's form with six goals in his last four games. Papin's display against Sampdoria the weekend before Milan renewed acquaintances with Porto bordered on cruel and surely hastened Des Walker's return to England.

Of the Dutchmen, only Gullit was fit enough to appear but by now he was a role player, doing a job on the right of midfield. The responsibility for creativity had been ceded to the impressive young duo of Zvonomir Boban and Gianluigi Lentini, the world's most expensive player.

Papin delivered the 1-0 win away in Porto with a sumptuous volley recently nominated as one of the 50 greatest Champions League goals. The shock news from the Philips Stadion in Eindhoven was that IFK had won 3-1, the three goals coming in a 25-minute burst before half-time. The pick of the goals came from a Mikael Nilsson dribble from just outside his own penalty area before he played a one-two and smashed the ball home from 20 yards

In the return match-ups two weeks later, Milan once more beat Porto 1-0 with Eranio scoring. IFK took it upon themselves to hit another three past PSV. Once more Nilsson brought a gun to a knife fight.

IFK had been awarded a central free kick, just outside the box. Nilsson aimed to the right (as he looked) of the wall, which Van Breukelen had lined up centrally. The strike swerved round the wall and kept on swerving so prodigiously that it beat Van Breukelen on his right-hand side. Had it been scored by a Brazilian, it would feature on every goals and gaffes compilation. In 2020, Bleacher Report crowned Nilsson's goal as the best Champions League goal ever.

Improbably IFK had six points from four games and Milan sat pretty with the maximum eight points from their four. Porto and PSV, with a point each, were eliminated. If IFK could beat Milan at home they would draw level on points and take the group to the final matchday.

Now the word was out and 40,000 fans packed the Nya Ullevi. Gothenburg were boosted by the falling-out between Papin and Capello and the continued absence of Van Basten.

Olsson remembers it as an evenly matched game but added that Milan were 'virtually impossible to score against'. Lentini crafted the big chance and Daniele Massaro, playing in place of Papin, finished it.

The final group game presented Capello with a chance to rotate his squad. Roberto Donadoni saw his first Champions League action of the season and players like reserve goalkeeper Carlo Cudicini were blooded lest they be called upon in Munch.

In the six games they had played, Milan notched six wins and only conceded one goal. With the exception of their first match against IFK, the Milanese hadn't really got out of third gear.

For PSV the Champions League had been a chastening experience. They had lost five of the six matches, drawing the other. Even with one of the best strikers in the world they were far off the pace.

'In a large pool of good players, we had one tropical fish,' former PSV manager Guus Hiddink said. 'The Romários of this world don't realise how much they can undermine the fabric of a team.'

Romário didn't care. He was off to Barcelona, recruited to be the final piece in Cruyff's Dream Team jigsaw. Neither did Eindhoven at this point. The newspaper *Trouw* called the Brazilian 'a divisive fungus'.

While Romário would make the Champions League the following season, and indeed play in its final, it would take PSV five seasons to return to the competition and while they were a regular fixture in the group stages through the late 1990s and early 2000s they didn't reach the latter stages until the middle of the decade.

In 2004/05 against Milan, PSV were eliminated in the semi-finals thanks to a 91st-minute away goal. *The Guardian* offered: 'Liverpool can count their blessings that they're not playing PSV in the final.'

FC Porto had reason to celebrate the early 2000s as well. In 2004, under the watchful eye of José Mourinho, they became the last side outside of England, Germany, Italy and Spain to win the Champions League.

That Porto team included two veterans who first cut their teeth for the club in the 1992/93 Champions League in the shape of Vítor Baía and Jorge Costa, who would lift the trophy as captain.

However, IFK Gothenburg would make the most immediate impact on future Champions Leagues. After a one-year hiatus from the competition Gustafsson led his IFK charges back to the 1994/95 competition.

They negotiated a tricky qualifying round game against Sparta Prague. Sparta had been ordered to play the game more than 300km from Prague due to crowd trouble but somehow an explosive charge was smuggled into the stadium.

'In the middle of the second half, it exploded,' Olsson recalls. 'The whole stadium fell silent, it screamed in my ears and was really nasty.'

Crisis averted and the Swedes then received a difficult group stage draw as they were paired with Barcelona, Manchester United and Galatasaray. They were expected to struggle but seven of their squad had just placed third in the 1994 World Cup with Sweden.

After losing their opening match 4-2 away to United (IFK had led but were one of the first recipients of a Ferguson European comeback), Gothenburg rattled off a remarkable string of victories by beating Barcelona and Ferguson's side at home, and Galatasaray home and away. Neither of the big boys got a result in Istanbul.

However, they nearly didn't make it back from Manchester. About an hour into the flight home the IFK plane had to turn around to make an emergency landing due to a serious fault with the plane. It was the players' second brush with death and it was still only mid-September.

Magnus Erlingmark scored four goals in the next four group games but even he was eclipsed by Jesper Blomqvist, who had a hand in all three goals that beat United, scoring one and assisting two. Despite playing the same position as Ryan Giggs, United boss Ferguson wanted to sign Blomqvist.

'Left-footed players like Jesper have a special quality and are wonderful to watch,' praised Gustafsson. 'Jesper has the ability to attack defenders and dribble very fast with the ball at his feet, and he has an excellent technique.'

Milan beat United to the Swede's signature but four years later a persistent Ferguson eventually signed him at the fourth time of asking. Blomqvist would play a key role in United's treble-winning season including starting in the 1999 Champions League Final in Barcelona.

It might have been a second Champions League final for Blomqvist if only IFK hadn't squandered a great position in the 1995 quarter-finals. After a 0-0 draw away in Munich, the German champions found themselves a man down after 20 minutes in the second leg in Gothenburg. Goalkeeper Sven Scheuer was correctly dismissed for a professional foul on Mikael Martinsson, who was put clean through on goal by Blomqvist. Uwe Gospodarek, who had played five times for Bayern in four seasons, came off the bench to make his European debut.

An inexplicably poor ten-minute spell in the second half saw IFK concede twice and despite pulling two goals back they couldn't find the third they needed to qualify before the full-time whistle sounded.

IFK would hang around the group stages for a couple more years, scoring a famous victory against George Weah's Milan in 1996 and getting revenge on Bayern with a 1-0 win in 1997. Since the turn of the millennium IFK's European season has usually been over by August, typically with defeat in the qualifying rounds of the Europa League.

Helsingborgs IF made the group stage in 2000/01 as Malmö did in 2014/15 and 2015/16, but after scoring just once in six group matches and equalling the record group stage defeat, losing 8-0 to Real Madrid, no Swedish team has been in a hurry to return.

A Header for Eternity

FOR RUDI Völler the 1993 Champions League Final was a homecoming as Olympiastadion in Munich was a venue he knew well from his time at TSV 1860 Munich. Völler played two seasons for the white-and-blue lions between 1980 and 1982. He described himself as filling out only half a shirt when he arrived in Munich from Kickers Offenbach as a 20-year-old.

In his first season Völler scored nine goals but after working hard on his fitness and physical conditioning he added 37 in 1981/82 to earn a move to Werder Bremen and international recognition. The stadium continued to be kind to him after he left Germany for AS Roma, when Völler scored both West German goals as the Euro 88 hosts beat Spain to qualify for the semi-finals.

His Marseille team-mates appreciated Völler and what he had brought to the team that season. The German veteran filled a Jean-Pierre Papin-shaped void. Lesser players would have crumbled under the pressure.

'Rudi had a special character,' says Eric Di Meco fondly, 'but he was a bit crazy.'

The Munich venue was a fitting setting for a clash between Europe's two best teams. Originally constructed for the 1972 Olympics, the stadium's iconic roof design, described as 'a series of dancing spider's webs, hovering weightlessly above the arena', was created by Frei Otto and his pioneering of lightweight tensile and membrane structures. In a way you can thank Otto for the Millennium Dome.

The idea was to design a venue built with the principles of lightness and transparency as a counterpoint to the strength and dominance projected by Germany's other Olympic stadium – the one used for Hitler's 1936 Berlin Olympics.

After the Munich games, the stadium hosted the 1974 World Cup Final. It was also the scene of Brian Clough's greatest triumph when Trevor Francis scored the goal that made Nottingham Forest champions of Europe and in 1988 it had been kind to Völler's opposite number, Marco van Basten, who scored a career-defining volley to win the Netherlands their only major tournament.

The two presidents, Silvio Berlusconi and Bernard Tapie, met for a tête-à-tête on the turf before the contest. Two 'socialist', multimillionaire, media barons were comparing notes on how in a few short years they had turned around the fortunes of their respective clubs. It was all smiles and bonhomie before kick-off. Each flashing toothy grins and projected confidence and their jobs were done. Over the next 90 or possibly 120 minutes the cup would be won. Or would Marseille again be put through trial by penalty kick?

The two managers were at opposite ends of their careers. Fabio Capello was 42 and in just his second year in management whereas Goethals, 71, kept trying to retire only to be called back into service after newer, flashier models broke down under the weight of Tapie and Marseille's expectation.

Goethals had already been coaching for 15 years when he found himself leading Belgium against Italy in the 1972 European Championship quarter-final. In that game a young Capello made his debut for Italy, although Goethals won 2-1.

Looking at just their European form, Milan would have been favourites after ten wins from ten matches in the competition and they only conceded one goal in the Champions League group stage (a record that still stands). But domestically they were a team in crisis with only one win from their previous ten Serie A games, which also included seven draws and two losses.

Milan's great rivals Inter were unbeaten in 1993 and had closed the gap at the top of the table to four points. Van Basten was still out injured with his ankle problem but the desperate situation prompted Milan to take a risk with their star striker.

Van Basten got his first action in five months as a substitute against Udinese and then started the following week against already-relegated Ancona. He scored a header, helping Milan to their first league win in two months. It was clear though that the Dutchman was not fit.

To help Milan's Champions League prospects, their Serie A clash against Cagliari was moved forward by two days to Friday evening. There was no way that Van Basten could play two games in six days so he was omitted from the team and Milan drew a bad-tempered contest 1-1. Evani was sent off, and Dejan Savićević even managed to get into a fight later on with the 65-year-old concierge of his apartment block. It was fair to say that tensions were running high.

Sentiment alone can have been the only reason for Capello to include Van Basten for that final. It was not a decision without risk as it effectively reduced Milan to two foreign players. Papin was needed on the bench to cover any injury to the number nine, which meant Rijkaard starting and Gullit, Boban and Savićević watching from the stands. Roberto Donadoni was recalled to the starting line-up to provide the requisite number of Italians. In a 4-4-2 system they picked this side: Rossi; Tassotti, Costacurta, Baresi,

Maldini; Donadoni, Rijkaard, Albertini, Lentini; Van Basten, Massaro.

Marseille, in contrast had only lost once in three months, a French Cup quarter-final where they had heavily rotated their squad. The team was settled and relatively free from injury, and only Basile Boli had a question mark coming into the final. He had missed the league match against Valenciennes immediately prior.

Didier Deschamps might have been the captain but Boli was the team's leader. Eric Di Meco affectionately called him 'mad dog', a sentiment Stuart Pearce was familiar with. At Euro 92 Boli acquainted his forehead with Pearce's cheekbone. It takes a certain kind of bravado to lay one on someone nicknamed 'Psycho'.

Chris Waddle, Boli's team-mate for two seasons, called him a great defender, and added, 'You can't run on him, you can't beat him with skill. He's not the greatest footballer in the world and he'll be the first to admit that but he's got a big heart and if he's not playing they've [Marseille] got problems.'

It is possible Boli's recovery was aided by some form of injection. In his 2006 book Jean-Jacques Eydelie told of suspicious injections. 'The only time I agreed to take a doping product was the 1993 Champions League final,' he claimed.

'In all the clubs I played in, I saw some doping going on … but this was the only time I accepted. We all took a series of injections and I felt different during the game, as my physique responded differently under strain. The only player who refused to take part was Rudi Völler.'

Other players, including Völler and Deschamps, have disputed Eydelie's story but his experience was corroborated by Tony Cascarino, who joined Marseille in the summer of 1994.

'It was always before the match,' the Irishman admitted to *L'Équipe*. 'We received an injection in the lower back. I was not quite sure what it was but as everybody told me it was good and as I felt great after every injection, I accepted what was being done to me. I cling to the sliver of hope that it was legal, though in reality, I'm 99 per cent sure it wasn't.'

So Marseille's players may or may not have taken performance-enhancing injections before the final and they may or may not have contained banned substances.

In the 1990s the line between sports science and doping was a very blurry one. The World Anti-Doping Agency, which is responsible for much of the medical and ethical framework around doping, hadn't been created yet, meaning each sport policed doping differently. Many obvious performance-enhancers would have been perfectly lawful, if not necessarily ethical.

Even long before the Lance Armstrong saga the undisputed champion sport of doping was cycling. Riders in the early Tour de France events powered round the French countryside aided by stimulants and in 1930 the official race guide reminded teams that they were responsible for bringing their own drugs. The US track cycling team pioneered blood doping to deliver success at the 1984 Summer Olympics.

Kim Andersen, a cyclist with Bernard Tapie's La Vie Claire team, failed five doping tests between 1985 and 1986. Is it possible that something that Tapie learned from the world of cycling was brought into football?

What we know for sure is that when UEFA acted on this information and re-examined the doping test samples they didn't find anything.

For the final, Marseille went for a 3-2-2-3 system and lined up with: Barthez; Angloma, Boli, Desailly; Eydelie, Di Meco; Sauzee, Deschamps; Pele, Völler, Bokšić.

In most stadiums an athletics track detracts from the atmosphere. At the Munich Olympiastadion, because of the innovative design, supporters resorted to covering the track with their flags, which produced a pleasing visual.

UEFA's initial idea was that the Champions League moniker would only apply to the group phase. That decision was reversed in 1994 and subsequently this game was reclassified as the first Champions League final but it did mean that there was no blast of the Champions League anthem nor a starball logo covering the centre circle. Instead there was a banner promoting fair play.

Kurt Rothlisberger was the Swiss referee in charge of ensuring that the game was fair. He had overseen three games at the 1990 World Cup including the quarter-final between Argentina and Yugoslavia.

When the game got under way, the Marseille fans outsang their Italian rivals but both sides had lots to shout about in a frenetic opening 15 minutes.

Milan took a page from the Dinamo Bucharest playbook and sought to put balls into the channels behind the wing-backs Eydelie and Di Meco in the hope of drawing Angloma and Desailly wider to create space in the middle. Daniele Massaro had the game's first good chance – but he headed over.

Völler, meanwhile, drew inspiration from his national team colleague Jürgen Klinsmann, diving to win a free kick. Mauro Tassotti was none too pleased and nothing came from it.

Marseille did get two chances in quick succession though. First Völler was put through but couldn't beat Rossi in the Milan goal. Then Sauzée looked set to hammer home the rebound, which would have been his seventh European goal on the season, before Maldini arrived from out of frame to save the day with a last-ditch tackle.

Later in his career Maldini would say of his approach to defending, 'If I have to make a tackle then I have already made a mistake.' It's probably fairer to say that if Maldini had to make a tackle then somebody had made a mistake.

Massaro drew a sharp near-post save from Barthez, Bokšić beat the vaunted Milan offside trap but the ball bounced awkwardly for him, and Maldini headed just over from a corner.

The game couldn't continue at that speed and Milan came into it more and more. Marseille's offside trap was their best defence, the Swiss linesman getting quite the aerobic workout. Albertini had another good position but Eydelie nipped the ball away from him as he shaped to shoot. On the half-hour mark there was a moment of sportsmanship when the two captains clashed. Baresi required treatment but afterwards Deschamps helped him up and the two shared a friendly half hug. But Marseille's talismanic defender was someone who Deschamps needed to worry about – Boli was struggling and told the bench to ready a substitute. 'From the stand, I told Raymond Goethals via a walkie-talkie not to replace him,' insisted Tapie.

Soon afterwards, Boli made a meal of a routine clearance. He was not moving well and he sent another player to the bench to get an ETA on a replacement. Goethals said he was happy to replace Boli but, gesturing to the stands, added that it was 'the other prick up there who doesn't want to'. Goethals kept the walkie-talkie channel open to be sure Tapie heard.

*Mark Hateley
about to be sent off
vs Club Brugge,
March 1993.*

Berlusconi and Tapie shake hands on the pitch before the 1993 Champions League Final, in Munich.

The Marseille team before the 1993 final (L-R: Back: Barthez, Sauzée, Desailly, Völler, Boli; Front: Angloma, Pelé, Deschamps, Bokšić, Eydelie, Di Meco).

Boli's goal in the 1993 final.

Van Basten being substituted by Fabio Capello in the final.

Marseille players and fans celebrate Boli's goal.

Boli and Tapie celebrating becoming the first French team to win the European Cup together.

Boli leading the celebrations in Munich.

Sauzée & Eydelie celebrate on the plane journey back to Marseille.

Marseille fans finding out they've been banned from defending their Champions League title.

Tapie arriving at court for the OM/Valenciennes trial, March 1995.

Tapie and Eydelie in the dock together, October 1995.

Marseille players returning to the Stade Velodrome for the 25th anniversary of their Champions League victory. (L-R: Back: Olmeta, Durand, Amoros, Angloma, Boli, Di Meco, Front: Bokšić, Ferreri, Thomas, Eydelie)

Just before half-time Abedi Pele won a corner. Rossi was insistent that Maldini's clearance had touched the Ghananian last but Rothlisberger was equally insistent that it didn't. Before he trudged to the flag Pele told Boli, 'I had forgotten how tall these guys are, please don't go to the far post.'

Boli listened, he darted to the front post and holding off Rijkaard's challenge he glanced the ball into the far corner of the net. Milan had a defender on the near post but the far post stood in splendid isolation. Marseille took a one-goal lead into the break.

'Without the offside trap Milan will kill you,' was Goethals's assessment. 'The secret of surviving the Milan cyclone is not allowing them near your goal. Van Basten, Lentini, Papin, Maldini, Massaro will destroy you if you let them overcome you in your area. We took a risk, defending 50 metres from our goalkeeper and counter-attacking.'

At the start of the second half that risk should have backfired when Rijkaard sprung the offside trap and was erroneously flagged. He was a good two to three yards onside but the linesman's flag shot up, voiding the chance.

The other way Marseille were keeping Milan far from their goal was with violence, and one notable incident involved Boli and Van Basten. The striker was doubled over in pain from the blindside poleaxing he received.

The normally composed Van Basten jumped up in Rothlisberger's face, showing him five fingers to show the number of similar fouls he had had endured. The protestations induced a yellow card but nothing sterner.

After ten minutes of the second half Capello readied Papin for action, but he was not yet prepared to admit his mistake in starting Van Basten. Papin then came on for Donadoni and the Marseille team who were happy to find out Papin was a substitute were now wary. The history of French teams in the European Cup tilted towards tragedy, and they were fearful of losing thanks to one of their own.

'It must not be Jean-Pierre who takes this dream away from us,' Di Meco remembers feeling.

Papin immediately found acres of space but Massaro, Milan's best attacker on the evening, couldn't locate him. Waddle would have done so, as would Donadoni. Anyone with a working left foot and the vision to look up at the right moment would have found him but Massaro's head was down and his pass went elsewhere.

Papin was fired up, motivated both by Capello's snub and playing against his former team. Looking for his first contribution he offered a high foot when challenging for a bouncing ball that Barthez was favourite to claim. The keeper took exception but not as much as his left-back Di Meco. The long-time team-mate was incensed with Papin and got into a shoving match. Even after the two were separated, Di Meco could be seen screaming invective at the striker.

'I don't remember exactly what I said to him, but it was certainly not nice,' a sheepish Di Meco admitted. 'I know that Jean-Pierre resented me for a long time, because we were good friends when we played together, but hey, it's the game.'

The Marseille fans were whistling for full time from around the hour mark. Every free kick and clearance was greeted with the sincerity of a goal, but it wasn't a backs-to-the-wall effort. Milan didn't look threatening. Lentini was dealt with competently all evening, Rijkaard offered nothing like his scene-stealing performance in the 1990 final and any threat that Papin and Massaro hinted at was counterbalanced by Van Basten's ineffectiveness.

With five minutes remaining Capello bowed to the inevitable and withdrew Van Basten, Stefano Eranio being judged to be a more likely scorer or provider.

When the camera panned up to VIP seats separated by UEFA and FIFA presidents Lennart Johansson and João Havelange, they captured the taciturn head-shake of Berlusconi contrasting with Tapie's trying-not-to-look-too-pleased-with-himself poker face.

Deschamps and Sauzée had been superb in midfield, putting in a very disciplined performance. Likewise Di Meco and Eydelie worked tirelessly on the flanks and Pele was their best attacking outlet. But this was Boli's final – he underlined his importance by clearing the last Milan aerial ball with the same ferocity he had dealt with everything else thrown at them all evening.

Two years prior Boli had laid on the turf in Bari heartbroken, wondering if he would ever get a better chance at being a European champion. Now, with tears streaming down his face he had won the Champions League for Marseille. 'It was a header for eternity,' he claimed after the game.

For the second time in three years Papin was experiencing the gut-wrenching emotions of defeat, covering his face to hide his pain and protect himself from the joy that might have been his had he stayed in France. At this moment an unlikely figure offered some comfort – Bernard Tapie, who paused in his moment of vindication to commiserate with his former striker.

'I'm delighted for Mr Tapie. There's been a lot of misunderstanding about the way he works,' said Goethals in the aftermath of victory. 'Tapie has great ambitions, he believes [as president] he has a role to play in everything.'

While distributing praise for his boss, the Belgian septuagenarian was also quick to take a chunk of the credit for himself. 'It was a victory for our tactics,' Goethals claimed. 'After the problems we had in the opening stages we were better organised and had a clearer idea of our tactics.'

As many victors do, Tapie claimed a post-event certitude that is impossible to prove. 'We were absolutely sure of winning, none of us had any doubt,' he boasted. 'Two years ago, on paper, we had maybe a better team, but in 1993 I had 11 players who were ready to die for each other.'

Di Meco agrees with both coach and president: 'This final is a bit of the story of my life. That evening, we hurt AC Milan. For the beauty of the game, I preferred the team of 1990/91, but if I had to go to war I chose the '93 team, not particularly beautiful but very tactical, very physical.'

The defeated boss from Milan saw the cup as half-empty. 'We gifted them the final in the first half,' lamented Capello. 'We missed too many good chances: that's the reality, ugly and sad. We had most of the play.'

Sadder still was that this would be the last game of professional football that Marco van Basten, aged 28 years old, ever played. The three-time Ballon d'Or winner tried in vain to rehabilitate his ankle but in 1995 he would be forced to admit defeat.

The abridged version of football history says that Van Basten was kicked out of the game and had FIFA's crackdown on the tackle from behind happened sooner we might have seen more years of him at his peak. The man himself disagreed, laying the blame for his early retirement on a series of botched surgeries and bad medical advice.

THE FIX

'If you are a defender and you are playing on the edge, that's good,' reflected Van Basten. 'Football is a contact sport. Being tough is part of the game.'

After more than two years trying to rehab, Van Basten called time on his career. The last goals he scored with his feet were the four he put past IFK Gothenburg in November 1992. What a statement to end with.

Before Milan played a pre-season friendly against Juventus, Van Basten was paraded before a grateful San Siro. Wearing stonewash jeans, a pink button-down and a suede jacket he lapped up the adulation. It was all too much for his manager, though, and the usually stoney-faced Capello wept like a baby.

'Marco was the greatest striker I ever coached. His early retirement was a mortal misfortune for him, for football, and for Milan,' said Capello in 2010.

The now former striker wanted to cry too, but somehow held it together. He would later say that it felt like attending his own funeral.

Van Basten was the last of Milan's tulips. Rijkaard left after the Marseille defeat, Gullit likewise departed, came back and went again. Milan fans hung a banner reading 'Grazie Marco per sempre Rossoneri'. Thank you Marco forever Milan. Van Basten never left – he was taken.

There is, however, one positive that Van Basten took from his early retirement: 'You never saw me get old.'

Liberté, Égalité, Conspiracy

MARSEILLE'S CELEBRATIONS went late into the Munich night. Bernard Tapie sat down for a meal with his players to toast their triumph as the first French team to win a European trophy. The big-eared cup started the meal between the president and the captain Didier Deschamps before making its way around the various tables for photographs with the players and their families.

Basile Boli, the beating heart of the team and the scorer of the goal that won the final, was at the heart the celebrations. As the wine flowed, Boli also led the team in celebratory song. Somewhere along the way he lost his club blazer and tie but found a giant cigar to accompany the suitably giant grin he deservedly sported for delivering Marseille their greatest triumph.

The next morning there were some deservedly bleary faces on the tarmac of Marseille's Provence airport when the team disembarked, brandishing the European Cup to the waiting press scrum. However, far more significant events were unfolding 750km away in Paris.

At the Ligue 1 headquarters a stone's throw away from the Arc de Triomphe, its president Noël Le Graët had received disturbing news from Valenciennes. The team from northern France were an unfashionable and unremarkable yo-yo team; just as likely to be found at the upper reaches of the second division as the bottom rungs of the first, although with somewhat of a reputation for good youth development Valenciennes was where Jean-Pierre Papin and Didier Six got their first tastes of professional football.

In 1992/93, Valenciennes, who had been promoted the season prior, were in one of their relegation battles and just so happened to be playing Marseille six days before the Champions League final against Milan.

Marseille were four points clear of Paris Saint-Germain with three games remaining (the French league still awarded two for a win at the time). Three days after the final, which had the potential to go to extra time and penalties as Marseille knew well to their cost, the leaders were scheduled to play PSG in the Velodrome.

For their part Valenciennes were in a relegation dogfight. They were one point behind both Lille and Le Havre but with a better goal difference – everything was to play for in their final three fixtures: Marseille at home, Saint-Étienne away and Sochaux at home.

If Marseille had rested too many key players and slipped up against Valenciennes then the league title could have been in jeopardy. If they played their best 11 in a full-throttle match against a Valenciennes side battling to stave off relegation then they risked injuries before the biggest game in their history.

At half-time, Valenciennes were trailing to an Alen Bokšić goal and their manager Boro Primorac reported to the referee Jean-Marie Véniel that some of the Valenciennes players had been offered bribes to throw the match.

Nothing was made public initially but Marseille's European Cup celebrations were placed on hold anyway. They needed a result against PSG on 29 May to stop the title going to a final-day decider. For some of the players this game was even more special than the Champions League Final win.

'In the warm-up, I saw a rage to win in the eyes of my team-mates,' Rudi Völler explains. 'Before kick-off, when we ran from the tunnel to the central circle, it was sensational. I had chills. The public carried us.'

Despite George Weah and David Ginola's best efforts, and PSG taking a deserved lead, nothing could stop the Marseille juggernaut. Another Boli header proved decisive as Marseille won 3-1 and claimed a fifth consecutive league championship, eclipsing the previous record set by Saint-Étienne.

The next day, Marseille held a huge celebration on the pitch for their fans, parading the European Cup and saluting the terraces. For good measure the players hoisted the president Tapie on to their shoulders so he could receive the adulation his millions of francs of investment merited.

'You know Marseille is a special place, it's a crazy place for football,' says Marcel Desailly. 'I was at Nantes as a youngster, but I was a Marseille supporter. And it was a great moment – first Champions League for the country, for the club, for the fans.'

Simultaneously another slightly more subdued party in Milan was just getting going. After days of mourning, Capello's team were back in domestic action and secured the point they needed to win their second successive Serie A title. Milan could now look forward to a 1993/94 rematch with Marseille in the Champions League.

Four days later Marseille were being hosted at the Élysée Palace by the president of the republic, François Mitterrand. Tapie and Mitterrand were well acquainted. Tapie won a parliamentary seat in 1989 on the back of his support for Mitterrand and three years later he was rewarded by being made a cabinet minister.

It must have been nice for the men to be able to celebrate something as both Mitterrand and Tapie had endured a tough year in politics. Mitterrand's socialist coalition had lost over 200 seats in the legislative elections whereas Tapie was forced to leave the government – twice. One occurrence was under a French constitutional law concerning a legal indictment and the other came when Prime Minister Pierre Bérégovoy's ministry fell. Tapie and Mitterand had been together just a month previously at a much more sombre event, the funeral of Bérégovoy after his suicide.

The day after Marseille's celebrations at the Élysée, the French football league handed over its case file to the public prosecutor. The league alleged that Marseille tried to bribe three Valenciennes players to fix the outcome of the Ligue 1 match.

Jean-Jacques Eydelie was the least celebrated player on the pitch for Marseille against Milan in Munich and he had marked Gianluigi Lentini, the world's most expensive player, out of the game. He had joined the summer previously from Nantes, making the same southward journey as Marcel Desailly. Eydelie's role as a wing-back or defensive midfielder grew over the course of the season as Manuel Amoros and Bernard Casoni fell out of favour with coach Goethals. His starring role, however, would be as the fixer in the swindle Marseille were intent on perpetrating.

Marseille general manager Jean-Pierre Bernès approached Eydelie and asked him to sound out Jorge Burruchaga, the 1986 World Cup winner with Argentina, and Christophe Robert, two of Eydelie's former team-mates at Nantes who were both with Valenciennes. Eydelie also got in touch with Jacques Glassman, who he had spent a season on loan with at Tours.

'It is imperative that you get in contact with your former Nantes team-mates at Valenciennes,' Bernès told Eydelie at the team hotel the day before the game. 'We don't want them acting like idiots and breaking us before the final with Milan.'

The offer was 250,000 francs (about £30,000) to go easy on Marseille and in doing so help condemn their own side to probable relegation.

Robert had already been prepped by Bernès to expect a call and was happy to accept. He sent his wife Marie to meet Eydelie at the Marseille team hotel to collect the bribe. Burruchaga also accepted but claimed he changed his mind once he considered the consequences and played 'normally'. That account was disputed at the time by referee Véniel, who believed the home team were unusually passive against Marseille.

The biggest problem for Bernès, Eydelie and Marseille was that Jacques Glassman had no intention of taking part in the corruption.

'Do you realise what you're saying, Jean-Jacques?' asked Glassman. After Eydelie realised an appeal to Glassman's patriotism to consider the benefits of Marseille beating Milan was falling on deaf ears he passed over the phone to Bernès. 'Do you prefer to lose the game for nothing?' enquired the Marseille general manager.

Glassman blew the whistle. He reported the approach to Primorac who in turn flagged it to Véniel when he believed his side wasn't trying against Marseille.

Encouraged by Primorac, Robert, who faked a muscle injury in the first half to get substituted, turned himself in for questioning by Éric De Montgolfier, the public prosecutor. On 24 June, Robert admitted his part in the affair and led prosecutors to a relative's garden where they dug up the dirty money he had buried. 'That cash stunk so much I had to bury it,' Robert would later protest.

The Valenciennes captain fingered Eydelie as the culprit who provided the funds. Eydelie was arrested but initially denied the accusations, as did Burrachaga and Bernès.

The investigating judge, Bernard Beffy, ordered a raid on Marseille's headquarters which lasted for seven hours. Items recovered include a distinctive brand of envelope that matched the cash recovered from Robert's aunt's garden. Twelve members of the playing staff were interviewed by prosecutors when they arrived in the Pyrenees for pre-season training.

Publicly, Tapie declared the allegation was 'unproven innuendo', suggesting the actors were motivated by envy and jealousy. In private, sensing things spiralling out of control, Tapie made the huge error of phoning Primorac, the Valenciennes coach, offering him a deal to recant and take the blame for the whole fiasco. An incandescent Primorac reported this further approach to prosecutors who now had cause to raid Tapie's Paris offices.

Former government minister Jacques Mellick contradicted Primorac's version of events, claiming to be in the room when Tapie made that call. Unfortunately for Mellick and Tapie, there was photographic evidence of Mellick at a reception in Béthune, 200km north of Paris, where Mellick was the mayor, when Tapie placed the call.

Prior to this faux pas, Tapie did enjoy parliamentary privilege which protected him from prosecution under French law but after this attempt at witness tampering there would be successful moves to revoke that status from the Marseille president.

Gennadi Kostylev, the CSKA Moscow coach, came forward claiming that he had 'received a telephone call at our team hotel in Marseille from a person claiming to be a Marseille director, offering money to lose the match'. CSKA did lose that one, 6-0.

A po-faced UEFA spokesperson said the organisation would investigate the claims but added that it was 'surprising that the Russians should have waited so long to come forward'.

Kostylev would later withdraw the allegations, as Tapie had hoped Primorac would. Meanwhile, Eydelie's wife Christine contradicted his denials to prosecutors, saying her husband was acting on Bernès's orders. After this, M. Eydelie changed tack and cooperated with the investigators.

France had moved their 1993/94 season forward in the calendar by two weeks, the idea being that starting on 24 July would give the French national team the best chance of success in the 1994 World Cup held in the United States. If only there was a French word for hubris.

Le Graët, the French league president, vowed 'to deal with this gangrene', but said that punitive action should wait until the criminal investigation was completed.

'Marseille will start the new season in the First Division,' La Graët affirmed. 'If it is proved they committed an offence, they will be punished later. Let the inquiry follow its course.'

Around 30,000 defiant Marseille fans packed the Velodrome on Saturday, 24 July to watch their team in theory begin a quest for a sixth consecutive domestic crown. RC Lens were the opposition and Boli was the difference once more in a 1-0 win. Further morale-boosting victories against PSG, Saint-Étienne and Bordeaux were played out in front of large, vociferous crowds.

This laissez-faire approach of the French Football Federation wasn't universally welcomed. On 31 August FIFA threatened to suspend France from international football for taking no action in the Marseille affair. It gave the FFF a deadline of 23 September to act, threatening to strip France of the right to host the 1998 World Cup in the process.

Just nine days before Marseille were to begin their Champions League defence against AEK Athens, UEFA opened Pandora's box and banned the title holders from the 1993/94 competition. Tapie immediately lodged complaints in both the French and Swiss courts.

The FFF offered Marseille's Champions League berth to their great rivals and runners-up from the previous season, PSG – but the Parisians declined under pressure from their main sponsors Canal+. The pay TV service didn't want to alienate and anger hordes of Marseille fans. Third-placed AS Monaco, managed by Arsène Wenger, were happy to accept.

Tapie successfully sued UEFA in Bern, winning an injunction that forced UEFA to reinstate Marseille at the expense of Monaco. Just a week before the Champions League started, AEK didn't know who they'd be playing or if the match would go ahead at all. Then, uncharacteristically, Tapie backed down under behind-the-scenes pressure from the FFF and withdrew the lawsuit and conceded defeat.

On 22 September, just one day inside the FIFA deadline the FFF announced sweeping provisional punishments in what became known as 'L'affaire VA-

OM'. Burruchaga, Eydelie, Robert and Bernès were banned from football indefinitely. Marseille were stripped of their 1992/93 domestic title and the championship would remain vacant rather than being awarded to the runners-up.

The following day, tensions boiled over at the Velodrome when Boli and Barthez were sent off in a bad-tempered home loss against Metz. Marseille fans invaded the pitch after 87 minutes with their side trailing 3-0 to showcase their displeasure.

Milan were deputised to represent Europe in the Intercontinental Cup in Japan where they would face Copa Libertadores winners São Paulo. They were also be asked to play in the UEFA Super Cup against Parma.

What's never mentioned is how the Milanese sealed their 1992/93 Scudetto with a shameful performance against Brescia. Much of the game just four days after they lost in Munich to Marseille was played at walking pace and neither side looked to attack. This gamesmanship was designed to help Brescia relegate Milan's historic rivals Fiorentina.

With eight minutes remaining, Demetrio Albertini scored, either forgetting the script or refusing to go along with deception. Perhaps Albertini was trying to shoot wide but his muscle memory had other ideas? No one but Albertini knows.

Regardless, after barely crossing the halfway line in the second half the Brescians suddenly poured forwards. Maldini tamely passed to a player in blue while Baresi, the apparent best defender in the world, was more matador than man-marker, guiding defender Luca Brunetti through on goal. Barely a minute later Brescia were level.

Peter Brackley, commentating for *Football Italia* on Channel 4, called it 'amazing'. Joe Jordan, the former Leeds and AC Milan player on co-commentary, immediately smelled a rat and had the guts to give voice to it: 'I don't think it's amazing at all. Milan have let them score there. Baresi didn't seem bothered.'

After that burst of action, the game re-settled down and petered out to its synthetic conclusion. Jordan added knowingly, 'Our viewers are certainly getting an insight into the Italian way of playing football.'

Milan's approach may be less offensive as the fix resulted from a mutually beneficial circumstance rather than a naked bribe, but it was still a fix. It still harmed the sporting integrity of the league.

Fiorentina were relegated because of Brescia's ill-gotten point. The Florence club had to sell players like Brian Laudrup and Stefan Effenberg to fill the hole in their finances. To add insult to injury, the next season Laudrup was running out at the San Siro in Rossoneri red and black. The gods didn't smile on Brescia either – they lost their relegation play-off against Udinese.

A week either side of the Champions League final both its participants had been involved in fixing matches. One was punished, one wasn't.

To add a further layer of irony to the sordid affair, in 1996 Kurt Rothlisberger, the final's referee, was caught offering to fix a Champions League game for Swiss club Grasshoppers. He was banned from football for life.

All told, Marseille's punishments amounted to an expected loss of revenue somewhere up to £20m. However, if Tapie had designs on following Sevilla's Maradona playbook and recouping some of that lost money through high-profile international friendlies then FIFA had other ideas.

From conspicuously far up on the moral high ground, FIFA general secretary Sepp Blatter proclaimed that Marseille could be barred from playing any opposition from beyond France.

It took until April 1994 for the FFF to complete its investigation and hand out definitive punishments.

Eydelie, Robert and Burruchaga were banned from French football until July 1996 (later reduced to 1995) with the players free to appeal to FIFA for international clearance to play after the 1994 World Cup. Burruchaga headed back to his native Argentina for a career swansong with Independiente. Robert followed his former team-mate to Buenos Aires, turning out for Ferro.

Marseille would be relegated to the second division as punishment, and their fans reacted with predictable ire. Michel Tonini, president of the ultras supporters' club, threatened the FFF administrators with mob justice: 'They've hit us hard, we're going to do the same. We're going to go to Paris to fix this lamentable affair. We hate these old men who think they can play with Marseille with impunity.'

Tapie had his licence as a football director revoked, meaning his nine-year spell in charge of Marseille would come to an end. The federation also vowed never to give him another licence in the future, while former general manager Bernès would also be barred for life.

A defiant Marseille took to the pitch at the Velodrome the day after the verdict was handed down to pummel Lyon 3-0. Two Sonny Anderson goals and one from Dragan Stojković made PSG wait another week to claim the title.

Bizarrely, Marseille would be allowed to compete in Europe the following season because they had earned a UEFA Cup spot by finishing second. In 1993/94 they had been banned from Europe but competed in Ligue 1; in 1994/95 they were banned from Ligue 1 but competed in Europe.

Spring 1995 was supposed to be the moment that Tapie ran for the presidency of France. Instead of battling Jacques Chirac and Jean-Marie Le Pen in television studios and hustings around the country he was holed up in a courtroom decrying the trial as part of a political plot against him.

The idea of Tapie as 'Président de la République' is not as fanciful as it might seem. You only have to look across the Alps to see a powerful media mogul/football chairman taking political power. France has a presidential system that allows multiple candidates to stand in the first round of voting with the top two vote-getters progressing to a run-off election.

Tapie would have been trying to out-poll Jospin, the socialist party candidate, in the first round as a moderate left option and then looked to defeat Chirac in the final ballot. It was essentially the electoral coalition that Emmanuel Macron would pull together two decades later.

Mitterrand had served for 14 years in the post and wasn't going to stand for another seven-year term. Tapie had been fast-tracked into the cabinet by Mitterrand and had the business credibility that left-of-centre candidates dream of. Additionally, he had found political fame as one of the few prominent voices prepared to directly take on the National Front.

In 1989, French TV channel TF1 was looking to stage a debate on immigration with the party leaders. However, when TF1 invited Le Pen, the other leaders refused. Tapie put himself forward to debate Le Pen and performed admirably.

Later he would doorstep an FN meeting and ask to speak.

When given the microphone Tapie suggested, 'We take all the immigrants, men, women, children, put them on boats, and send them very far from here and when they're far enough away, to make sure they don't come back, we sink the boats.'

The audience cheered and Tapie's demeanour changed. 'I was not wrong about you. I spoke of a massacre, of a genocide, of killing men, women and children, and you applauded. Tomorrow, when it's time to shave or put on make-up, when you see yourself in the mirror, stick yourself on it.'

Tapie broke ranks with mainstream politicians who said they despised Le Pen but 'understood' the concerns of his voters. 'I call that man a bastard, and I will continue to call him a bastard until the end of my life. If we judge that Le Pen is a bastard, then those who vote for him are also bastards.'

The adjective Tapie would have used to describe Judge Bernard Langlade is lost to history but we can be sure it would be adjacent to his feelings for Le Pen.

In May 1995, Judge Langlade presided over the criminal trial stemming from L'affaire VA-OM.

Bernès had consistently denied involvement in the alleged plot. But, he told the court, 'It is time to tell the truth.'

'There was an attempt at bribery on my part, on Bernard Tapie's orders, with Jean-Jacques Eydelie as the intermediary,' he alleged.

Eydelie corroborated this version of events but did admit that he had been offered lighter footballing punishments for implicating Tapie. He told the court an investigating judge told him that 'if I went further in my allegations against Mr Tapie, I would be able to play again much quicker'.

Tapie at one point shouted at the judge, saying that the search for truth demands that 'you should not say any old thing'. The judge warned Tapie, 'I will not allow myself to be abused by anyone.' 'Nor will I!' Tapie shot back.

As the trial wore on and the evidence mounted against Tapie he became less resistant and more resigned to his fate. At one point he told the court that he had 'lied in good faith'.

'If I have to go to prison, I will. I'm not going to kill myself over it,' Tapie told reporters as the evidence concluded and the deliberations began.

The court decided that jail was appropriate and gave him one year, with a further year suspended. Bernès got two years suspended while Mellick received a one-year suspended sentence for providing the false alibi. Tapie and Mellick were also banned from holding political office.

While fighting the bribery allegations, Tapie's business empire had crumbled. He had lost millions in the Crédit Lyonnais scandal but he eventually recouped it years later from the French government. His super yacht, which held the record for fastest single-hulled sailing across the Atlantic, was repossessed, and worst of all Marseille were denied immediate promotion back to Ligue 1 on account of Tapie's debts.

Tapie was the only defendant to go to jail for this saga, spending approximately six months incarcerated, and he remains the only person to ever receive a custodial sentence for a footballing crime in France. The original prosecutor, Éric de Montgolfier, declared in 2009, 'If he hadn't been Bernard Tapie, he wouldn't have gone to jail for this case. The facts didn't deserve it. He paid for other reasons.'

After the conclusion of the legal case against Tapie, FIFA bestowed its annual Fair Play Award on Jacques Glassman for blowing the whistle on the attempted match fixing. It was one of relatively few rewards Glassman would receive for his noble part in a sordid affair.

Glassman was often jeered by French fans as a traitor when he travelled with Valenciennes the next season. He was unable to find another French team to take him at the end of his contract and had to travel halfway around the world to the Indian Ocean territory of Réunion to find his next club.

'People look at me as a traitor without stopping to demand an explanation from the people who really did betray the game,' Glassman laments. 'Sometimes I wonder why denouncing a scandal is considered worse than the scandal itself?'

Valenciennes were also losers in this equation. They found player recruitment harder because of the taint of scandal and were relegated to the third division for the first time, so had to become an amateur team. They did bounce back and returned to Ligue 1 in 2006/07.

Three years later Marseille won their only French title since the scandal. Club legend Didier Deschamps returned to guide them to their first silverware since he lifted the European Cup aloft in Munich.

The club has reached three UEFA Cup/Europa League finals since their European ban expired, losing each time. In the Champions League their best result was in 2011/12 when they reached the quarter-finals thanks to some heroics from André Ayew, the son of class of 1993 legend Abedi Pele.

The main danger of a second Champions League winner from France now comes from their Le Classique rivals, PSG. Qatar Sports Investment are following a Tapie playbook by massively outspending their challengers, treating Ligue 1 as a formality and putting all their efforts into winning in Europe. In 2020, PSG became just the second team from France to get to a

Champions League Final (the fourth for the whole European Cup era) but Tapie predicted that they would fall short in their first final like Marseille did.

He said, 'In 1991, for the first OM final we had no experience. We had no player who played in a final, and we made the mistake of locking ourselves up. As a result, we put ridiculous pressure on ourselves and what should have been a wonderful time almost turned into pain. In 1993, we did the opposite. PSG, I'm sure, will do the same.'

If taken as an isolated incident, L'affaire VA-OM is understandable. Of course Marseille would have wanted to avoid injuries before the Champions League final. The punishment meted out might even seem a quaint over-reaction from overly zealous, patrician authorities.

The problem was that L'affaire VA-OM was far from an isolated incident. That Al Capone went to jail for tax fraud didn't mean he wasn't also bootlegger and a gangster. Tapie had instituted a win-at-all-costs mentality at Marseille that crossed a number of sporting and ethical lines, not merely what was proven in the Valenciennes case.

'Cheating had become second nature,' Eydelie admitted in his autobiography. 'We were all solicited at one time or another to make a call to a former team-mate or a friend.'

Tapie's former parliamentary aide Marc Fratani said, 'Tapie is a person who knows no limits. He would do anything to get to the top.'

In 1995, while Tapie was appealing his conviction, further allegations emerged that Marseille fixed European Cup and Champions League matches. The examining magistrate, Pierre Phillipon, said three fixtures were under suspicion: a 1989 tie versus AEK Athens, the 1991 semi-final against Spartak and the 1993 Champions League match against Club Brugge.

Fratani worked with Tapie for almost 30 years but admits his decision to go public was motivated by a personal falling out between the two men around 2016. He says he was particularly aware of all the activities of Jean-Pierre Bernès, the club's sports director, but that Bernès acted with authorisation and the full knowledge of Tapie. 'The corruption was not intensive, it was not a question of buying all the matches,' said Fratani. 'They targeted the main opponents.'

That targeting included doping. Fratani claimed that Marseille doped opposition players with Haldol, an antipsychotic medicine that commonly causes involuntary muscle reactions such as spasms, muscle rigidity and akathisia.

'Using syringes with ultra-fine needles, the product was injected inside plastic bottles,' alleged Fratani.

'Anything that could be consumed by the adversary was treated.'

Former Milan organisational director Paolo Taveggia certainly didn't take any chances when visiting Marseille for the now-infamous quarter-final.

'A few days before the game, Uli Hoeneß of Bayern Munich called me and said [Marseille director Franz] Beckenbauer had told him they were planning something nasty for Milan in France, including the potential to tamper with the food given to the players at the hotel.'

Whether Hoeneß had been tipped off or was merely gossiping, conscious of what the Poznań players had alleged in the round previously, Taveggia, who was in charge of logistics, decided to act. 'Without telling anyone I changed the hotel where we were staying at the last minute,' he recalled

On 2 July 1996, Philipon, the investigating judge looking into allegations of false accounting confronted Tapie with Bernès as a key witness.

Bernès swore, 'I confirm my previous statements: a sum of five to six million francs per year came out of OM's coffers through fictitious invoices to buy matches.

'I have been dishonest for four years. There have been several matches bought. There are 45 French players who may be involved. I don't want to say their names. With Bernard Tapie, we knew how much money to get out for a match.'

entry.

'What Bernès says is false,' fired back Tapie.

Bernès indicated that the system of payments started in the 1989/90 season. 'According to Bernès, you wanted to win the European Cup, you learned that buying matches was practised and you wanted to do the same. What are your explanations?' Judge Philipon enquired of Tapie.

'If I won matches, it's because I had the best team in the world,' professed Tapie. 'I remind you that I put my money in OM and I do not see why I would have used a system of false invoices to put money abroad.'

At the end of Philipon's investigation, Tapie was convicted of false accountancy and sentenced to a further 18 months' imprisonment (reduced to a suspended sentence on appeal).

Fratani also claimed that Bernès bragged about stealing two titles from Monaco and that to finance the corruption, false invoices were established.

The match-fixing allegations themselves were not explicitly proven, but with Tapie banned from football and politics at this point the imperative to get another criminal conviction was diminished.

That does not explain UEFA's continued refusal to seriously re-examine its initial judgement in September 1993. Despite all the revelations that followed, the club being stripped of the French title and their president being jailed, UEFA never decided to strip Marseille of the 1993 Champions League.

Cornel Dinu was one of Romania's star players at the 1970 World Cup, a Dinamo Bucharest legend and in 1992/93 was the national team coach of Romania. In his 2019 autobiography *Misterle Lui Mister* (Mysteries of the Manager) Dinu claims himself to have acted as intermediary to bribe the referee of the Marseille vs Club Brugge match, Ion Crăciunescu, a fellow Romanian.

The referee's instructions were to not yellow card Basile Boli as another booking would see him miss the final. Dinu alleges $20,000 changed hands with Crăciunescu receiving the payment weeks after the match.

For what it's worth both Crăciunescu and Tapie deny the allegation, with the referee challenging Dinu to take a lie detector test.

A sarcastic Tapie welcomed the revelation: 'Thirty years have passed, it has taken him a long time to reconcile his conscience.'

Tapie is also supposed to have told Dinu on the day prior to the Brugge match, at the Marseille team hotel, 'Thanks to him [Goethals], I took all the necessary measures to prevent the Belgians from causing us trouble.'

Dinu took this to mean that Goethals, a Belgian, had used his connections to ensure the result wouldn't be in doubt. It was certainly plausible. Not only did Goethals and the Brugge coach Hugo Broos have a relationship (Goethals managed Broos for three seasons at Anderlecht where they won the 1978 Cup Winners' Cup together) but match fixing was an area the elder Belgian had some form in.

After leaving Anderlecht, Goethals had won the Belgian league in each of his first two seasons in charge of Standard Liège. Investigating judge Guy Bellemans, who was carrying out an inquiry into corruption in Belgian football, came across evidence that indicated a bribery scandal involving Goethals and Standard.

Standard were also preparing to play in a European final – the 1982 Cup Winners' Cup Final versus Barcelona. If only their league match against Thor Waterschei could be made easier?

The Standard squad offered up their match bonuses in return for an easy afternoon. The subsequent scandal rocked Belgian football, especially Goethals's role in initiating the bribing of the Waterschei players.

Standard were fined but were allowed to keep their title whereas Goethals became persona non grata in his homeland, being banned for managing in Belgium for two years. Was he up to his old tricks versus Brugge?

Daniel Amokachi, who played in the 1993 game in question, says he would be 'embarrassed' if it were true that the Brugge players didn't try to win against Marseille. He says he is still good friends with many players from his time at Brugge and contends that 'three decades later someone would have said something by now' had it been true.

The week before the Brugge match, Bernard Tapie flew Amokachi via his private jet from Ostend to Paris to discuss a potential summer transfer to Marseille for the 1993/94 campaign.

Amokachi believes 'if Tapie wanted to fix the game he would have approached me then'. However, Tapie's modus operandi was to work at arms length with plausible deniability.

In the media, responding to Dinu's 2019 allegations, Tapie claimed, 'In front of a court, it will not be complicated to prove that these things are delusional. Marseille won their matches because, at the time, they were the best team in Europe, along with Milan.'

While that narrative of defiance works well in a media context, the allegations are notable for their striking similarity to other attempts at match fixing that we know about from the period in question.

The games tended to be European matches or at least big domestic ones. The targets of the bribes were often eastern European – be that a referee or a player. Eastern Europeans were generally poorer and seen as more susceptible to financial inducement. They were also more used to the practice of bribes as part of how business was conducted as a legacy from the communist era.

A key player in all this was the Croatian fixer Ljubomir Barin. Barin was a charming, well-spoken Yugoslav, fluent in seven languages and had got his start in French football working as an agent or transfer broker. Barin notably helped PSG's 1982 signing of Safet Sušić, who would become one of the club's most beloved players of all time.

Barin began to work closely with Claude Bez, the charismatic owner of Girondins de Bordeaux, France's most successful team of the 1980s. He brokered the transfer of the Vujović brothers, Zlatko and Zoran, from Hajduk Split and began to be entrusted with more sensitive matters.

Ahead of the 1987/88 European Cup quarter-final between Bordeaux and PSV Eindhoven, UEFA rules stipulated that match officials had to be in the city at least 24 hours before kick-off and the home club would provide a liaison. Barin was entrusted to act as the liaison officer for the tie and supposedly took his duties to include the procurement of prostitutes for the German officiating crew. All this hospitality could only help facilitate a 1-1 draw.

Initially, Tapie and Bez were pantomime rivals – both enjoyed tweaking the other one's nose through the media – but behind the scenes they were united in their drive to monetise football. Competition for players was expected – Alain Giresse and Jean Tigana swapped Bordeaux for

Marseille in this period but Tapie also wanted Barin to put his skills to use for OM.

In the 1989/90 European Cup second round Marseille took a modest 2-0 lead to Athens for their return leg against AEK. Barin was enlisted as an intermediary to bribe Helmut Kohl, the Austrian referee. Kohl apparently had financial troubles at the time so the 100,000 Deutschmarks that Barin wired him nine days after he presided over a 1-1 second leg would have come in handy.

Kohl would get the appointment for that year's final between Milan and Benfica, who beat Marseille in a controversial semi-final. The prospect of a referee in the pocket of one of the teams in the European Cup final doesn't bear thinking about.

Not even a 1991 FFF investigation into corruption and attempted match fixing in games against Caen, Brest, Saint-Étienne and Bordeaux could dissuade the Marseille hierarchy from their illicit path. That investigation resulted in Bez receiving a three-year ban from football and Bordeaux being administratively relegated to the second division.

The FFF threatened to suspend Tapie for 12 months for 'damaging sporting morale and insulting referees'. In response, the Marseille players threatened to strike and Jean-Pierre Papin said he would quit the national team if Tapie was punished.

Less than three months later Marseille were still trying to corrupt matches. After being drawn against Spartak Moscow in the European Cup semi-finals they paid 2.2 million francs for 'television rights' to Spartak Moscow via a Swiss bank to a Panamanian company to another Swiss bank account belonging to Jean-Louis Hagueneuer. A French businessman with links to both Russia and Marseille via his friendship with Manuel Amoros, Hagueneuer would later admit that the money was used to bribe Spartak players.

Before kick-off in Moscow Tapie was alleged to have visited the press box and given a journalist a note with instructions to open it after the game, which the journalist complied with. The note read '3-1', the scoreline that the reporter had just witnessed play out.

As the consequences never arrived, the flouting of norms became more brazen. Goalkeeper Pascal Olmeta claimed that Tapie bragged about fixing their 1991/92 European Cup tie against Sparta Prague.

'He came into the locker room with the ball under his arm, and he said, "Okay guys it's good, tonight we win, I just saw the referees,"' Olmeta said. 'We looked at each other and wondered what that meant.'

If Tapie did try to bribe the referee in the stadium that evening it spectacularly backfired. Two penalties were awarded against Marseille which would prove their undoing on away goals.

The following season in the Champions League, several suspicious incidents occurred which left Rangers fans in particular wondering whether they were cheated out of a place in the final.

In addition to the Brugge game on matchday six, Rangers point to three incidents in particular: Marseille's 6-0 win over CSKA Moscow, the CSKA players' reaction to their dead-rubber 0-0 draw with Rangers and an allegation from Mark Hateley that he was offered money to miss a Champions League game against Marseille.

'He was not an agent I knew, but another agent had given him the number,' recalled Hateley in 2011. 'It was a French-speaking person, offering me large sums of money not to play against Marseille.'

Hateley said he refused the advances but he did miss the match anyway through suspension. The former Monaco and Milan forward was sent off by Polish referee Ryszard Wójcik for an incident that the Englishman described as handbags. 'I couldn't work out why Hateley was sent off,' his Scottish manager, Walter Smith agreed. 'I still can't.'

This narrative of injustice has taken root among many of the Ibrox faithful in the intervening years. The truth about this incident was that it was a rather forceful elbow to the face and the match report of *The Herald*, a Scottish newspaper, criticised Hateley for his 'foolish' dismissal.

Not all elbows went punished in 1993 – just ask Gary Mabbutt and Paul Gascoigne each on the receiving end of fractured skulls following aerial challenges with John Fashanu and Jan Wouters respectively. However, judged by modern standards, Hateley would probably be public enemy number one on Twitter until the next outrage came along.

Whether the Polish referee had been 'got at' to deprive Rangers of their star players ahead of the Marseille game, Hateley only had himself to blame for presenting him with such an open-and-shut opportunity.

The 6-0 victory is suspicious for its scale but in one sense that should also make us question it. Goal difference wasn't a factor in separating teams who finished level on points, and instead head-to-head record was decisive. Why engineer a suspicious result? Also, if Marseille were going to bribe the CSKA players on 17 March to lose 6-0, shouldn't they have bribed them on 3 March in their 1-1 draw as well?

When Gennadi Kostylev, the Moscow coach, came forward with the allegations he later recanted he was in effect only reporting an approach and didn't provide any evidence that the game was fixed.

It is equally plausible that CSKA weren't all that good. They had qualified for the Champions League by winning the last Soviet Top League in 1991 but by 1993 they were a bottom-half side in a league of diminished quality.

Between beating Barcelona and playing Marseille, the club had sold their captain Dmitri Kharine to Chelsea and central defender Sergei Fokin had left for Germany. The remaining players had just not played competitive football for more than three months owing to the Russian winter break.

Rangers's final accusation was that the CSKA players celebrated excessively when they drew 0-0 at Ibrox, a result that gave Marseille a place in the Munich final.

Setting aside the moment of the possibility of a false memory or a collective exaggeration aided by time, Rangers's complaint boils down to the fact that CSKA tried. They were supposed to try. By all rules of football and natural justice they were supposed to try to win. Your complaint can't be 'we wished they had not bothered against us'.

Incentivising sides who otherwise have nothing meaningful to play for has long been an accepted practice in places like Spain.

'In Spain where there's one or two matches left in a season we always talked about the suitcases [of money],' said former Real Madrid and Barcelona star Michael Laudrup, speaking as Swansea manager in 2012. 'It's just a bonus. I don't see anything bad about that.'

'For me, match-fixing is [when] somebody pays someone to lose a game,' Laudrup added.

The practice of *maletínes* (which literally translates as briefcases) is said to have been invented by none other than Santiago Bernabéu himself. He wanted to make sure that city rivals Atlético were sufficiently incentivised to play fulsomely against Sporting Gijon. Atlético won 7-2, giving their neighbours Real the opportunity to climb out of the relegation zone by beating Oviedo.

The most famous *maletíne* occurred at the end of the 1993/94 season, when Deportivo La Coruña had the opportunity to win their first championship. They led Barcelona by one point going into the final match and only had to beat Valencia to bring the title to Galicia. Valencia had nothing to play for and Barcelona offered three million pesetas per player (about £15,000) for a positive result.

With the game tied at 0-0 in the 89th minute, the referee awarded Deportivo a penalty. Regular taker Donato had been substituted and Bebeto, their top scorer with 16 league goals that season, refused the responsibility. The spot kick fell to Serbian sweeper Miroslav Đukić and was saved. José González in the Valencia goal punched the air as if he had just won the lottery, because he had.

The Spanish federation officially outlawed the practice in 1994 but it is commonly accepted to still occur. Davor Suker, for one, admitted to receiving money after the ban while at Sevilla from Atlético for an end-of-season draw against Barcelona that helped Atlético win the 1995/96 La Liga.

So, while Rangers fans might feel aggrieved at the events of nearly 30 years ago, substantively there's not a lot of concrete evidence to support that lingering doubt. Did Marseille fix the Brugge result? The Brugge players say no, as does the referee, and the footage of the game certainly shows Brugge appearing to try to score right until the final whistle is blown.

Even if Brugge had scored, Rangers hadn't held up their end of bargain by beating CSKA. All the money in the world couldn't make McCoist miss. The more probable truth is that Rangers lost it on the pitch to a side that was marginally better than them. Drawing four of your six Champions League matches was a ratio never likely to produce success.

Any bad luck that Rangers players or fans can point to could equally be offset by the good fortune they had against Marseille at Ibrox, when they were played off the park for the majority of the game and Dany Verlinden only needs to say the words 'Scott Nisbet' to recall a key reason behind that draw.

It would be fair to argue definitively that Marseille shouldn't have been allowed to be in the 1992/93 Champions League to represent France because of the litany of previous abuses of trust both domestically and in Europe, but in that scenario Rangers would likely have played Monaco.

Arsène Wenger's side would become semi-finalists in 1993/94 after replacing Marseille and it's by no means certain that their team, which featured Lilian Thuram, Emmanuel Petit, future Rangers manager Claude Puel, Jürgen Klinsmann and Youri Djorkaeff, would have fared any worse than Marseille in the group stages.

Arguably no one suffered more than Wenger at the hands of Tapie's schemes. Speaking to *L'Équipe* in 2006, Wenger referred to the scandal as 'the worst period French football has been through' and claimed that French football 'was gangrenous from the inside because of the influence and the methods of Tapie at Marseille'.

His Monaco side were often the runners-up to Tapie's Marseille in league and cup competitions and he could have spent the turn of the decade competing against Barcelona, Milan and Red Star instead of being perennial Cup Winners' Cup entrants.

'You hear rumours and after that you cannot come out in the press and say, "This game was not regular,"' Wenger said. 'You must prove what you say. To come out is difficult. It is very difficult to prove it. From knowing something, feeling that it is true and after coming out publicly and saying "look, I can prove it" is the most difficult.'

Disgusted with French football, Wenger took an opportunity to go to Japan and the newly formed J-League. The assistant coach he took with him was Boro Primorac.

Primorac and Wenger bonded through a shared loathing of Tapie and stayed together as a coaching team for the next 24 years, 22 of them at Arsenal. Together they won the double, built the Invincibles and nearly, honourably, won the 2006 Champions League Final in the Stade de France. Sadly for the duo, Arsenal lost 2-1 to Frank Riijkard's Barcelona despite playing most of the match with ten men after Jens Lehmann's red card.

While Tapie might have scattered whole families, cities and leagues like flotsam and jetsam in his wake, the man himself has remained serenely bobbing along like his prized *Phocea* yacht. Outwardly he has been untroubled by years and years of legal and political battles.

Bankrupt and barred from business and politics he dedicated time to the arts. He was cast as the lead in the romantic comedy *Hommes, Femmes, Mode d'Emploi (Men, Women, Instructions for Use)* as an unscrupulous businessman. He wrote a novel, *Des Yeux Trop Grands (Eyes Too Big)*, set behind the scenes at a football club and in the corridors of the courthouse. Art imitating life.

Tapie found time to tread the boards reprising Jack Nicholson's role of Randle McMurphy in a theatre production of *One Flew Over the Cuckoo's Nest* and even tried his hand as an analyst co-commentating on the Porto-Monaco 2004 Champions League Final.

In 2007, his business fortunes improved too. After Tapie backed Nicolas Sarkozy in the presidential elections against his former cabinet colleague Ségolène Royal, Sarkozy announced an independent investigation into the Crèdit Lyonnais scandal when the state-owned bank sold Adidas on behalf of Tapie – allegedly at a huge loss. The panel ordered Finance Minister Christine Lagarde to pay Tapie €403m in compensation.

Lagarde tried to defuse the uproar by claiming that Tapie would only get around ten per cent of the award after taxes and debts were factored in. It was a claim that turned out to be false.

When François Hollande became French president, he ordered an investigation into the pay-out. Hollande and Tapie's enmity stretched back to the early 1990s when as a socialist deputy Hollande called Tapie's reappointment to the government 'offensive'.

Now head of the International Monetary Fund, Largarde was hauled back to France and found guilty of negligence and France's highest court ordered Tapie to repay the €403m.

Don't feel too badly for him though, as by one estimate even without that sum Tapie was still the 400th-richest man in France with a fortune of €150m.

The person most deserving of sympathy from the entire saga might be Jean-Jacques Eydelie. As a player he paid his dues at Nantes and in his mid-20s he fought his way into a talented Marseille side just as they realised their enormous potential.

When approached for an interview for this book, Eydelie was understandably wary. After all, there's only ever one subject anyone wants to talk to him about.

For more than an hour we spoke – about his career, every game in the Champions League campaign and even his brief loan spell in Walsall. His continued reverence for the fans at Ibrox that he called 'special' and his love of the supporters at the Velodrome was evident all these years later.

Offering the money to Valenciennes wasn't his idea, nor was it his money. He was put up to it by a powerful executive at a powerful club with a powerful president. This was the pre-Bosman era where clubs could vindictively hold on to player registrations and refuse to transfer them even after their contracts expired.

His career in France never really recovered from his arrest and ban, yet he was only one of the supposed 45 players that Bernès would later claim were involved in match fixing at Marseille.

Eydelie was almost entirely a victim of circumstance. Had Marseille's game been against Toulouse, Cannes or Metz, someone else would have been tapped to make that fateful call. He was a small cog in an organised crime machine and often it is easier for authorities to treat the symptom rather than the disease.

After his footballing ban expired Eydelie transferred to Benfica but never played for the Portuguese side. He returned to France but not the mainland and instead played for two seasons with Bastia from Corsica, home of another famous exile, Napoleon.

In January 1997 Eydelie returned to the Velodrome to face Marseille for the first time since the affair. He was one of only two players on the field that day who had played in the Champions League final – the other being Jean-Phillipe Durand, who came on for Angloma. But there was no fairytale ending and Eydelie lost – again.

Eydelie then moved to Switzerland. He got to play in the Champions League qualifying rounds for Sion (losing to a Gheorghe Hagi-inspired Galatasaray) and the UEFA Cup proper for Zürich, for whom he scored a rare goal to help secure progress past Lierse. From there, in his mid-30s his career began circling the professional drain.

For a time he was ostracised and kept at arm's length by the club he had simultaneously helped to elevate and sink. An explosive tell-all book in 2006 did not endear him to some team-mates but nowadays he says he has a good relationship with Marseille and was invited back for celebrations of the 25th anniversary of the European Cup victory.

When conversation switched from what happened on the pitch to his more famous off-field indiscretion, the atmosphere of the interview palpably changed. But Eydelie is not angry or defiant; he is sorrowful, ashamed even. The burden of one mistake has hung with him for more than a quarter of a century and likely will forever. His greatest sporting triumph is forever entwined with his gravest personal mistake.

Desperately, I tried to elicit a newsworthy soundbite with a line of questioning around the severity of the punishments that he and others were handed. Almost mournfully he tells me, 'When you break the rules in sport or in life, you have to accept whatever punishment is given to you.'

Tapie has spent the best part of 30 years denying the wrongdoing of his Marseille tenure and Eydelie has seemingly spent the same trying to come to terms with it.

The Real Fix

BETWEEN 1983 and 1993, eight different countries won the European Cup or Champions League: Germany, England, Italy, Romania, Portugal, Netherlands, Yugoslavia, Spain and France.

A further seven had countries close to reaching the final: Poland, Scotland. Greece, Sweden, Belgium, Soviet Union and Czechoslovakia.

Since Porto won the Champions League in 2004 the final has been the exclusive domain of clubs from the big five European leagues – England, France, Germany, Italy and Spain.

Frankly, it's a novelty when France or Italy break the hegemony of the big three.

The big shock of the past 15 years in the Champions League was Ajax getting to the 2018/19 semi-finals. Ajax, with their four previous European Cup titles, were a Cinderella story against the might of Tottenham Hotspur's Premier League spending power. Going further back, the last semi-finalist from eastern Europe was Dynamo Kiev over 20 years ago.

Fans are left to cheer for clubs like Atlético Madrid and Juventus if they want to back an underdog. Juventus, the Old Lady of Italian football, with nine consecutive Serie A titles and Cristiano Ronaldo in their team are the underdogs. Think about that.

Football has been heavily sanitised since the heyday of the European Cup. While the safe stadia, reduction in football violence and efforts to tackle racism are to be welcomed, the watering down of the on-field 'product' is not.

Fans liked the risk and the jeopardy because they provided stakes to matches. When there wasn't an 'oh well, we'll get them next year attitude' because your team had no guarantee of qualifying for Europe again next season the game was better.

The Champions League has become a de facto European Super League and UEFA has connived with the largest most powerful clubs to make it happen.

In the 1992/93 season the last 32 teams in the competition came from 32 different national associations. Almost all of UEFA was represented. From 2018/19 the Champions League was, by design, limited to just 15 nations. Eleven countries automatically qualified at least their champion and the remaining 44 associations competed for just four places.

In 1994/95 the Champions League group stages were expanded and moved to the beginning of the tournament (the original Rangers proposal). Eight berths were guaranteed and the other eight were decided by two-legged ties between champions.

Three years later UEFA abandoned the principle that only champions could participate in the Champions League. Runners-up from the eight best-ranked leagues were allowed to enter an expanded qualifying round. All eight qualified for the 24-team group stage but only Bayer Leverkusen advanced further, losing to Real Madrid in the quarter-finals.

The following season, two important milestones occurred. Metz became the first non-champions not to successfully negotiate the qualifying rounds when losing to HJK of Finland. Manchester United became the first non-champions to win the Champions League, beating fellow domestic runners-up Bayern Munich in that rather famous final.

The 1999/2000 season was really the watershed year in the Champions League's metamorphosis as UEFA went from dipping its toe in the water with a few non-champions from the best leagues to revamping the entire competition in search of TV money.

A second group stage was introduced, adding 48 matches to the calendar. It was staggered across Tuesday and Wednesday to provide for two TV windows and the number of non-champions increased by 200 per cent from eight the previous season to 24.

Six non-champions were even given an automatic berth in the group stage for the first time, alongside the ten top-ranked champions. This arrangement benefited Lazio, Real Madrid, Arsenal, Bayer Leverkusen and Willem II, a tiny team from Tilburg who had finished ahead of PSV and Ajax.

For the first time, third- and fourth-placed clubs were allowed in as well as runners-up. Germany, Spain and Italy were given the right to enter four teams. England, France and the Netherlands were permitted three each, while Austria, Croatia, Czech Republic, Denmark, Greece, Norway, Portugal, Russia, Turkey were now allowed their league runners-up as well as their champions.

Of the 16 teams who qualified for the group stage only seven were domestic champions, including Maribor of Slovenia, who beat Lyon, and Rangers, who defeated Parma.

Fourth-placed Valencia lost to second-placed Real Madrid in the 2000 Champions League Final. Three Spanish teams qualified for the semi-finals that season. Molde, the Norweigan runners-up, were the only non-Spanish team to knock out a La Liga side that season when they dumped Mallorca out in the qualifying round.

Since the definition of Champions League was expanded, Real Madrid have played in every season of the competition, never failing to make it to the knockout stages. Barcelona and Bayern have only missed one, while Manchester United have been absent twice.

The majority of big clubs successfully navigated the qualifying rounds when they found themselves placed in them but there were a few notable scalps and scares. Swedish side Helsingborg knocked out an Inter Milan team featuring Laurent Blanc, Andrea Pirlo and Clarence Seedorf in the 2000/01 third qualifying round. Two years later, AC Milan, on their route to winning the title and also featuring Pirlo and Seedorf, nearly lost to Czech side Slovan Liberec. Milan won on away goals.

Less well-established sides from the big European leagues occasionally struggled – Newcastle lost to Partizan Belgrade, Chievo couldn't get past Levski Sofia and Everton similarly fell flat on their face in their only Champions League campaign to date.

This system lasted for a decade. On average 8.4 different countries were represented in the last 16 and teams from 16 different nations managed to progress to the latter stages (Austria, Belgium, Czech Republic, England, France, Germany, Greece, Italy, Netherlands, Norway, Portugal, Russia, Scotland, Switzerland, Turkey and Ukraine). For comparison, in 2019/20 the number of countries represented in the last 16 was just five – England, France, Germany, Italy and Spain – the big five.

In 2009/10 Michel Platini piloted through reforms that increased the number of guaranteed places in the group stage from 16 to 22. This mainly benefited third-placed teams from leagues such as England, Spain and Italy. Platini's reforms split the qualifying process into two pathways; one for champions of domestic leagues and one for non-champions delicately named the 'league path'.

The results were initially promising. CSKA Moscow and Shakhtar Donetsk became the first two eastern European quarter-finalists for a decade. Copenhagen made the last 16, while APOEL of Cyprus also made a quarter-final. But since then the bigger leagues have consolidated their power.

Now 26 of the 32 group stage places are automatically awarded. The fourth-placed teams from Europe's biggest leagues don't have to bother with qualification. There are only four places available for champions each season in the Champions League outside the top 11 leagues.

In the 1994/95 season, if you were the champion of the 20th-ranked league in Europe you had to win one two-legged match to be in the Champions League. In 2021, Celtic who as Scottish champions represented the 20th-ranked league, began in the first qualifying round and had to win four two-legged matches to reach the group stage. They could not. The odds are so stacked against teams that start in the first qualifying round that only three out of the 95 entrants at this stage between 2018 and 2020 advanced to the group stages – and twice that was Red Star Belgrade. Most of the continent is now shut out of what was once called the European Cup.

The lack of access to the Champions League exacerbates and perpetuates the financial inequalities within football. A group stage place is worth €15m in prize money alone, plus teams get nearly €1m per point. A Europa League group stage berth is worth less than €3m in prize money and €190,000 per point. If a team doesn't even qualify for the Europa League they get a relatively mere €480,000.

The money available in the Champions League doesn't just distort itself, it also distorts national leagues. Since Tavriya Simferopol won the first Ukrainian championship in 1992 only two other sides have won the league: Dynamo Kiev and Shakhtar Donetsk. Only twice since 1996 have Dynamo and Shakhtar not finished first and second. Domestic success brings European prestige which brings financial rewards which brings more domestic success. It's a closed loop.

Similarly, Skonto Riga won 14 successive Latvian titles while BATE Borisov and Rosenborg won 13 consecutive Belarussian and Norweigan leagues respectively.

The longest active streaks are currently Ludogorets Razgrad of Bulgaria (nine), APOEL, Qarabağ of Azerbaijan and Red Bull Salzburg of Austria (seven each).

The old European Cup wasn't a perfect competition. At the business end it was the best versus the best but the clashes weren't regular enough to sate the appetite.

When it first began the Champions League was appointment viewing because it melded the best elements of the European Cup with a desire fans had to see the top European sides play each other more regularly.

The group stage was meaningful and exclusive, and there was genuine danger to navigate to reach that point. It also gave a chance to the smaller sides – the IFK Gothenburgs, Galatasarays and Rangers of this world.

The sad truth now is that the larger teams only tolerate the few smaller countries they permit into the Champions League so they have somebody to beat. This is why the threat of a European Super League is vastly overplayed.

Across five seasons from 2016/17 to 2020/21, teams from leagues outside the big five played against big-five teams 276 times in the Champions League. The smaller league teams won just 13 per cent of the time.

The status quo gives the big clubs what they want, virtually guaranteeing participation with limited risk.

Anyone trying to challenge their pre-eminence has to play with their stacked deck. Not content with direct qualification for the group stage and having a coefficient seeding system that favours established clubs, UEFA bowed to pressure to introduce Financial Fair Play – an anti-competitive set of rules that sought to entrench the financial advantage of those already fortunate.

The high rollers own the casino now and UEFA has diminished itself to acting as their pit boss.

1992/93 Results

Preliminary Round
KÍ (Faroe Islands) vs **Skonto Riga** (Latvia) 1-3; 0-3; **1-6**
Shelbourne (Ireland) vs **Tavriya Simferopol** (Ukraine) 0-0; 1-2; **1-2**
Valletta (Malta) vs **Maccabi Tel Aviv** (Israel) 1-2; 0-1; **1-3**
Olimpija Ljubljana (Slovenia) vs Norma Tallinn (Estonia) 3-0; 2-0; **5-0**

First Round
AC Milan (Italy) vs Olimpija Ljubljana (Slovenia) 4-0; 3-0; **7-0**
Lech Poznań (Poland) vs Skonto Riga (Latvia) 2-0; 0-0; **2-0**
PSV Eindhoven (Netherlands) vs FK Žalgiris (Lithuania) 6-0; 2-0; **8-0**
FC Barcelona (Spain, holders) vs Viking (Norway) 1-0; 0-0; **1-0**
Rangers (Scotland) vs Lyngby (Denmark) 2-0; 1-0; **3-0**
Slovan Bratislava (Czechoslovakia) vs Ferencváros (Hungary) 4-1; 0-0; **4-1**

Kuusysi (Finland) vs **Dinamo Bucharest** (Romania)
1-0; 0-2; **1-2**

Maccabi Tel Aviv (Israel) vs **Club Brugge** (Belgium)
0-1; 0-3; **0-4**

Austria Vienna (Austria) vs CSKA Sofia (Bulgaria)
3-1; 2-3; **5-4**

Sion (Switzerland) vs Tavriya Simferopol (Ukraine)
4-1; 3-1; **7-2**

Union Luxembourg (Luxembourg) vs **Porto** (Portugal)
1-4; 0-5; **1-9**

AEK Athens (Greece) vs APOEL (Cyprus) 1-1; 2-2; **3-3**
(AEK win on away goals)

Víkingur (Iceland) vs **CSKA Moscow** (Russia)
0-1; 2-4; **2-5**

IFK Gothenburg (Sweden) vs Beşiktaş (Turkey)
2-0; 1-2; **3-2**

Glentoran (Northern Ireland) vs **Olympique Marseille**
(France) 0-5; 0-3; **0-8**

VfB Stuttgart (Germany) vs **Leeds United** (England)
3-0; 1-4*; **3-3**

* UEFA awarded Leeds the second leg 3-0 due to
  Stuttgart playing an ineligible player. Leeds won the
  play-off 2-1 on a neutral ground.

Second Round
IFK Gothenburg (Sweden) vs Lech Poznań (Poland)
1-0; 3-0; **4-0**

Rangers (Scotland) vs Leeds United (England)
2-1; 2-1; **4-2**

Slovan Bratislava (Czechoslovakia) vs **AC Milan** (Italy) 0-1; 0-4; **0-5**

Dinamo Bucharest (Romania) vs **Olympique Marseille** (France) 0-0; 0-2; **0-2**

Club Brugge (Belgium) vs Austria Vienna (Austria) 2-0; 1-3; **3-3 (Club Brugge win on away goals)**

Sion (Switzerland) vs **Porto** (Portugal) 2-2; 0-4; **2-6**

AEK Athens (Greece) vs **PSV Eindhoven** (Netherlands) 1-0; 0-3; **1-3**

CSKA Moscow (Russia) vs FC Barcelona (Spain, holders) 1-1; 3-2; **4-3**

Champions League Group A

Matchday 1

Club Brugge 1 CSKA Moscow 0

Rangers 2 Olympique Marseille 2

Matchday 2

CSKA Moscow 0 **Rangers** 1

Olympique Marseille 3 Club Brugge 0

Matchday 3

CSKA Moscow 1 Olympique Marseille 1

Club Brugge 1 Rangers 1

Matchday 4

Olympique Marseille 6 CSKA Moscow 0

Rangers 2 Club Brugge 1

Matchday 5
CSKA Moscow 1 **Club Brugge** 2
Olympique Marseille 1 Rangers 1

Matchday 6
Club Brugge 0 **Olympique Marseille** 1
Rangers 0 CSKA Moscow 0

	P	W	D	L	F	A	Pts
Olympique Marseille	**6**	**3**	**3**	**0**	**14**	**4**	**9**
Rangers	6	2	4	0	7	5	8
Club Brugge	6	2	1	3	5	8	5
CSKA Moscow	6	0	2	4	2	11	2

Champions League Group B
Matchday 1
AC Milan 4 IFK Gothenburg 0
Porto 2 PSV Eindhoven 2

Matchday 2
IFK Gothenburg 1 Porto 0
PSV Eindhoven 1 **AC Milan** 2

Matchday 3
Porto 0 **AC Milan** 1
PSV Eindhoven 1 **IFK Gothenburg** 3

Matchday 4
AC Milan 1 Porto 0
IFK Gothenburg 3 PSV Eindhoven 0

Matchday 5
IFK Gothenburg 0 **AC Milan** 1
PSV Eindhoven 0 **Porto** 1

Matchday 6
AC Milan 2 PSV Eindhoven 0
Porto 2 IFK Gothenburg 0

	P	W	D	L	F	A	Pts
AC Milan	**6**	**6**	**0**	**0**	**11**	**1**	**12**
IFK Gothenburg	6	3	0	3	7	8	6
Porto	6	2	1	3	5	5	5
PSV Eindhoven	6	0	1	5	4	13	1

Final
Olympique Marseille 1 (Basile Boli 43) AC Milan 0
Venue: Olympiastadion, Munich
Attendance: 64,400

Acknowledgements

THERE ARE many people I need to thank and acknowledge for helping bring this book to life. Firstly, my wife Jennie and daughter Aubrey for their love and support. My second most important vote of thanks goes to the players of Leeds United, VfB Stuttgart, Glasgow Rangers, Olympique Marseille, Club Brugge and AC Milan alongside the broadcasters and producers for ITV for bringing me this classic Champions League story as an eight-year-old boy.

David Cameron Walker of The Athletic has been a huge help in sourcing interviews, putting me in touch with people and as someone to bounce ideas off. John Kirby helped me get through a crisis of confidence. Paul 'RB' Murphy has been nagging me to finish since he found out about it. John Parker, who helped with some of the translation elements, and Chris Voss gave me the misplaced confidence to think that it couldn't be that hard.

THE FIX

I would like to thank all the people who gave me their time in interviews. I can't name everyone but I would particularly like to thank people like Garry Haylock and Barney Bowers who helped capture the uncelebrated parts of the 1992/93 Champions League season.

Thanks should also go to players like Andreas Buck, Jonas Olsson, Daniel Amokachi and others who were fantastically generous with their time. Special thanks to Jean-Jacques Eydelie for trusting me and allowing me to hear about his whole story, not just the Valenciennes affair.

To the press officers, publicists, agents, social media channel managers and secretaries that I bombarded with requests – thank you, for your good grace and (mostly) polite replies.

I also need to thank a number of people I've never met, including Axel Springer who founded the amazing website Transfermarkt, which is hands down the most complete database of European football results on the internet. Also, Shahan Petrossian – the man behind the YouTube channel SP1873, where so much archival footage of old European Cup and Champions League seasons has been lovingly curated; and Ross Howard for doing the same with *Football Italia* content.

One final acknowledgement should go to Gérard Houllier. The former Liverpool manager was one of the first to say yes to be interviewed for this book. Gérard was on UEFA's technical committee that analysed the group stage in 1991/92 experimentation and recommended its adoption going forward. He was very supportive of the idea of a history being written of this first Champions League season and wanted to meet me in person when travel rules would allow it.

Unfortunately, we didn't get to meet. Gérard passed away in December 2020; a loss to this book but more importantly his family and friends. You'll never walk alone.

Also available at all good book stores

9781785316548

9781785316869

9781785316463

9781785316531

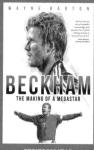

9781785316760

9781785316708

9781785316487

9781785317194

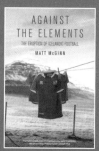

9781785317200